REGIONALISM IN THE POST-COLD WAR WORLD

Regionalism in the Post-Cold War World

Edited by
STEPHEN C. CALLEYA
Mediterranean Academy of Diplomatic Studies
Malta

Ashgate

Aldershot • Burlington USA • Singapore • Sydney

Published by
Ashgate Publishing Ltd
Gower House
Croft Road
Aldershot
Hants GU11 3HR
England

Ashgate Publishing Company
131 Main Street
Burlington
Vermont 05401
USA

Ashgate website: http://www.ashgate.com

British Library Cataloguing in Publication Data
Calleya, Stephen C.
    Regionalism in the post-Cold War world
    1. Regionalism
    I. Title
    337

Library of Congress Catalog Card Number: 99-76647

ISBN 1 84014 417 3

Printed and bound by Athenaeum Press, Ltd.,
Gateshead, Tyne & Wear.

Table of Contents

Section Three:

About the Editor

I am Deputy Director and international relations senior lecturer at the Mediterranean Academy of Diplomatic Studies at the University of Malta. I am also International Representative of the International Office at the University of Warwick, England and Mediterranean Editor of the journal Mediterranean Politics published by Frank Cass, London.

I have compiled several analytical articles in refereed journals and the international syndicated press. My most recent publications in the refereed journals Mediterranean Politics and Mediterranean Quarterly have focused on the evolution of the Euro-Mediterranean process that was launched in Barcelona in November 1995 and the impact this multilateral initiative is having on relations in the area. My most recent edited book is Economic Diplomacy in the Mediterranean which has just been published.

Other publications include a book entitled Navigating Regional Dynamics in the Post-Cold War, Patterns of Relations in the Mediterranean Area, (Dartmouth, Aldershot, 1997) which provides a reality check of relations in the Mediterranean in contemporary international relations.

I am also a member of several International Relations organisations including the International Institute of International Studies (IISS) in London and the International Studies Association (ISA) in the United States.

I am also a Euro-Mediterranean analyst with the Euromoney publication Euro-Mediterranean Journal which is published quarterly in London and an External Associate of the Centre for European Policy Studies (CEPS) in Brussels. In February 1999 I was appointed adviser to the Malta/EU Steering and Action Committee (MEUSAC) which is responsible for monitoring Malta's EU application to join the European Union. As a guest analyst I have participated in numerous interviews including regular contributions to the BBC World Service.

Notes on Contributors

Stephen C. Calleya is Deputy Director and Senior Lecturer in International Relations at the Mediterranean Academy of Diplomatic Studies, University of Malta, and international representative of the International Office, University of Warwick. He is the author of *Navigating Regional Dynamics in the Post Cold War World: Patterns of Relations in the Mediterranean,* (1997) and *Economic Diplomacy in the Mediterranean* (1999).

Sophia Clément is Special advisor for crisis management in the Balkans with the Delegation for Strategic Affairs at the French Ministry of Defence. She is author of *Conflict Prevention in the Balkans: Case Studies of Kosovo and the FYR of Macedonia* (1997).

Richard Falk is the Albert B. Milbank Professor of International Law and Practice at Princeton University. He is author of numerous books and articles on globalisation, international relations, international law, conflict, and human rights. He is author of *Predatory Globalisation: A Critique,* (1999).

James Mittelman is Professor of International Relations in the School of International Service at American University, Washington, D.C. He is the author of *The Globalization Syndrome: Transformation and Resistance* (2000); editor, *Globalization: Critical Reflections* (1996); co-author, *Out From Underdevelopment Revisited: Changing Global Structures and the Remaking of the Third World* (1997); and co-editor, *Innovation and Transformation in International Studies* (1997).

Bjørn Møller is Senior Research Fellow, Project Director and Board Member at the Copenhagen Peace Research Institute (COPRI) and Associate Professor of International Relations, Institute of Political Science, University of Copenhagen. He is author of *Dictionary of Alternative Defense* (1995).

Vilma E. Petrash is Professor of International Relations, Universidad Central de Venezuela. She is the author of several articles on free trade in the Americas.

Eberhard Rhein is Senior Analyst at the European Policy Centre in Brussels and former Director for the Mediterranean, Near and Middle East at the Commission of the European Communities. He is the author of numerous articles including *Euro-Med Free Trade Area for 2010: Whom Will It Benefit?*, in Perspectives on *Development, The Euro-Mediterranean Partnership*, (1999).

François Taglioni is Lecturer, University of Reunion Island. PO.Box 7151. 97715 Saint-Denis Messag Cedex 9. Reunion Island and also Laboratoire Espace et Culture. University of Paris-Sorbonne. 191, rue Saint Jacques. 75005 Paris. He is author of several publications *Les Départements Français d'Amérique et la République d'Haïti : poussières d'empires isolées dans la non-francophonie Caraibe*, (2000), (proceedings of the conference on : "The Pan-American French-speaking World"). Winnipeg, Canada; Les méditerranées eurafricaine et américaine : essai de comparaison, *in* A. L. Sanguin (dir) *Mare Nostrum, dynamiques et mutations géopolitiques de la Méditerranée.* L'Harmattan. Collection "Géographie et Cultures". Paris, (2000).

Monika Wohlfeld is Diplomatic Advisor at the Organisation for Security and Co-operation in Europe (OSCE) Secretariat. She is author of *The OSCE and subregional co-operation in Europe, OSCE Yearbook* (1998).

Preface

This book deals with the issue of regionalism in the aftermath of the Cold War. The study of the international politics of regions has often been described as being underdeveloped (Buzan, 1991a: 198; Neumann, 1994: 53). This book seeks to clarify the ambiguity often associated with the theories, models, paradigms, and analytical frameworks already existing in this field. The aim of this introductory chapter is to provide a summary of the main theoretical and empirical issues that are discussed. The comparative analysis that follows demonstrates that although the 'regionalism' theme has re-emerged as a dominant topic in contemporary international relations literature, there is no standard type of regionalism in world politics. Post-Cold War international relations rather consist of different patterns of regionalism simultaneously taking place.

Main Trends and Approaches in the Study of Regionalism

Although the parameters of the post-Cold War world are still in a state of flux, it is clear that the bipolar international system that existed between 1949 and 1989 has been replaced by a more multipolar configuration. The demise of the Soviet Union has left the United States as the lone superpower at the centre stage of international affairs. During the past decade the United States has had to come to terms with the demands that this new position entails while at the same time cope with a backdrop of international power relations that are more erratic. The equilibrium that the bipolar Cold War provided, through its configuration of blocs, alliances, stalemates and sustained crisis, has been superseded by a much more fluid system. A distinct feature of the present transformation is that regional politics have gradually gained in prominence.

As the post-Cold War label suggests, the post 1989 period is not completely different from that of the Cold War days. It is characterised by a level of continuity and discontinuity with the previous bipolar international system. Contemporary international relations tend to be neither moving in the optimistic direction of a new world order nor in the pessimistic one of "chaos" and "turbulence" as has been suggested (Rosenau, 1992). Instead, the dynamics of international relations appear to be going through a transitory phase, which one author describes as "disorder restored" (Mearsheimer, 1992: 213-237). Cantori recently described the post-Cold War pattern of relations as a dynamic multipolar international system based on regions and regional subordinate systems within which the struggles of nationalist identities and hegemonic leadership rivalries are taking place (Cantori, 1994: 22). From a regional perspective, this is illustrated by the fact that the principal change in the geopolitics of the world-system in the 1970s and 1980s has been the decline in the relative power of the United States. The 1990s has seen a resurgence of American power particularly in the economic and military sectors. This trend is a key feature of the post-Cold War international system and is a normal cyclical occurrence (Wallerstein, 1993: 4).

The economic strengths of the European Union (EU) and Japan have been steadily increasing since the mid-1960s, and the United States had not been able to keep pace. As a result, U.S. foreign policy in the past two decades has been centred around ways to slow the pace of this loss of hegemony by exerting pressure on its allies to share the burden of global security. The American led coalition of forces under the auspices of the United Nations during the Gulf War to liberate Kuwait and the American orchestrated military action in Yugoslavia under the NATO umbrella are indicative of this tendency.

The emergence of a more polycentric power structure at the system level is therefore certain to have a profound impact on regional relations. The superpower grip on international relations in some instances resulted in overlay. This occurs when the direct pressure of outside powers in a region is strong enough to suppress the normal operation of security dynamics among the local states (Buzan, 1991a: 198).

In some instances overlay stifled interaction among regional actors by limiting the parameters within which they could operate. The United States' foreign policy in Central America and the Soviet's policy in Eastern Europe are examples of this development. Bipolar intervention quelled regional hostilities when it took the form of overlay, as in Europe. But when it took the form of direct intervention, as was the case throughout the Third World, it often amplified crises across a larger geographic area rather than subdued them (ibid: 208).

The collapse of superpower overlay has led some international relations scholars to forecast that regional international politics will again become a dominant characteristic of the international system (Rostow, 1990: 3-7). In 1992 the World Bank stated that economically, "regionalism is back and here to stay" (Melo and Panagariya, 1992: 1). The increase in regional agreements that have been reported to the GATT in recent years tends to verify this trend (see Graph 1.1). In his economic analysis of the world's future, Paul Kennedy proceeds by regional analysis and comparisons and by identifying likely regional winners (Kennedy, 1993). These analysts base their assumptions on the premise that a multipolar system of states, where power is more evenly distributed among a number of regional powers, is in itself conducive to the rise of regional politics (Buzan, 1991a: 207). Buzan illustrates this development by identifying that regional dynamics are evolving against a background in which the higher-level complex is also entering a period of transformation. In other words, the intrusive patterns from higher to lower levels which were characteristic of the bipolar rivalry between the superpowers (the creation of alliances, sustained crises and military conflicts) have shifted as a result of the Cold War's breakdown.

A plethora of paradigms have been conjured up by international relations scholars, to help explain the implications of the sea-change in international affairs since 1989. Huntington predicts that the end of the Cold War does not mark the end of history, or a return of traditional rivalries between nation-states, but a new phase in world politics where conflicts of global politics will occur between nations and groups of different civilisations (Huntington, 1993: 22). Joseph Nye, Jr. describes world order after the Cold War as *sui generis* which cannot be understood by "trying to force it into the procrustean bed of traditional metaphors with their mechanical polarities" (Nye, Jr. 1991: 88). Power is constantly becoming more multidimensional. Nye, Jr. states that the distribution of power in world politics has become like a layer cake. The top military layer is mainly unipolar, with the U.S. dominant in military power. The economic middle layer is tripolar and has been for two decades, with the United States, the European Union, and Japan governing. The bottom layer of transnational interdependence shows a diffusion of power to the peripheral sector of the international system (ibid., and Nye, 1991: 191-192).

Buzan agrees that the diffusion of power in the contemporary system raises the importance of actors at the bottom of the power hierarchy for the functioning of the system as a whole. A reduction in the intensity of global political concerns and a decrease in the resources available for sustained intervention is conducive to the rise of regional politics (Buzan, 1991b: 435). Buzan adopts a structural realist approach and a centre-periphery model of the international system to depict the changes taking place. In his model of concentric circles, the "centre" implies a globally dominant core of capitalist states; the "semi-periphery" consists of the more robust and industrialised states in the periphery; while the "periphery" is a set of politically and economically weaker states operating within a network system mainly created by the centre (ibid.: 432).

A review of the various models noted above, reveals that there is no consensus about the fact that diffusion of power from the centre to the periphery is taking place. Although the pattern outlined above strongly suggests that a different pattern of geopolitics is evolving in the world, there is not enough consensus among international relations scholars on whether the advent of a multipolar system will increase or decrease the likelihood of regional conflicts.

Cantori and Spiegal suggest that a multipolar structure is the system most conducive to amplification of local conflicts. In areas where the superpowers had a strong degree of influence over the foreign policy agenda of client states, like U.S. dominance over South Korea, or the Soviet Union over Cuba, a high degree of cooperation took place. When either the United States or the Soviet Union lost power in international regions, hostilities increased and even led to outright conflict in places such as the Middle East, North Africa, South-East Asia, and the Gulf (Cantori & Spiegal, 1970: 33-37).

Buzan counters that although a multipolar architecture permits for a more uncertain chain of events, it is also less intense than a bipolar zero-sum competition. In addition, a multipolar matrix grants regional powers more room to manoeuvre when conducting their external political relations. Hence, the disappearance of superpower rivalry and the decentralisation of power throughout the international system are two tendencies that forebode an era where great power intervention in regional affairs is likely to diminish (Buzan, 1991a: 208).

Another factor that supports the regional resurgence school of thought is that for the first time the seeds sown during the period of decolonisation are in a position to develop now that the superpower strait-jacket has been removed. In his study on regional conflict formations, Vayrynen cites the 1950s as the starting point of the rise of regionalism time-line (Vayrynen, 1984: 339 and 345). At the time, integration efforts in the industrialised world were mainly sponsored by the great powers.

Decolonisation, the second main phase, paved the way for early efforts at regional economic integration and regional security arrangements in the Third World. Economic integration was mainly a response to the economic predominance by industrial powers. Security groupings tried to cope with the departure of colonial powers and the multiplicity of newly independent nation-states and their military establishments. The most recent phase of regionalism is a manifestation of the effective spread of power from the core of the international system to its peripheries. It has given rise to new regional power centres, integration schemes, and regional conflict formations. The European Union integration process and the process of fragmentation across the Balkans perhaps best illustrate the fluid nature of co-operative and conflictual regional dynamics that are simultaneously taking place.

Whether the absence of the superpower constraint will mute or exacerbate regional conflicts will very much depend on the circumstances of each particular regional grouping. In some areas it may increase the intensity of conflict as rivals attempt to settle long subdued scores, as is the case in the former Yugoslavia. In others, as the example of the Middle East demonstrates, it may encourage external assistance for regional endeavours at conflict resolution. In any case, post-Cold War developments support the theory that the intrinsic dynamics of subordinate systems are becoming more significant features of the international system, a trend that is likely to continue as technological advancements are more widely dispersed (Buzan, 1991a: 208). The recent increase in references to the regionalism by scholars of international relations is reflective of the multiplicity of regional agreements that have been signed since the end of the Cold War (see Graph 1.1).

Another example of the importance governments attach to regionalism is evident from the 1998 gathering of 34 presidents and prime ministers of the Americas in Chile. At the summit leaders agreed to launch talks toward a hemispheric free trade zone by 2005. If successful this effort will usher in a Free Trade Area of the Americas by the year 2005, encompassing 800 million people with a gross output of well over $13 trillion.

The two major trading blocs now in place are the North American Free Trade Agreement, established in 1994, which includes Canada, the United States and Mexico, and Mercosur, in effect since 1991, which comprises Argentina, Brazil, Paraguay and Uruguay. NAFTA countries have now 392 million people with an annual gross

Graph 1.1

Number of Regional Integration Agreements Notified to GATT 1948-1994

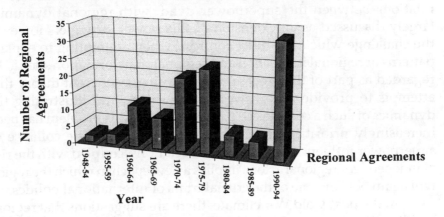

Source: The Financial Times, 27 April 1995: p.7

domestic product of $8.6 trillion and an intra-group trade worth more than $44 billion. Mercosur, with 204 million inhabitants, has a GDP of $1.2 trillion and trade among its four members was worth $19 billion last year.

The main issues that will continue to dominate relations in the coming months and years ahead of the next summit of the Americas scheduled to take place in Canada in 2002, are the implementation stages of a Free Trade Area of the Americas (FTAA) by the year 2005. The FTAA must also comply with World Trade Organization rules.

In Asia, China has already established itself as an independent great power, with India and perhaps South Africa poised to become dominant actors in their areas of the world. The gradual retrenchment of the United States and Russia in Europe and Northeast Asia, presents both the European Union and Japan with the opportunity to play roles in the international system commensurate with their power (ibid. 207-208). Despite this development, can we talk about the resurgence of regionalism in international relations? Or are we perhaps confronted rather by derivations and extensions of constellations and potential conflict, the nuclei of which lie elsewhere? What do the empirical indicators of regional transformation portray?

The complexities involved in formulating such a basis of analysis is one of the reasons that has discouraged research into this area over the last two decades. In particular, power theorists have tended to underplay the significance of the regional level in international relations (Buzan, 1991a: 186). During the 1970s and 1980s attention focused on relations between the superpower dyad, with regional dynamics largely discussed as an extension of this power struggle. However, the challenge which one must confront when attempting to explain patterns of regional interaction and regional transformation should be regarded as part of the process of developing a coherent theory that attempts to provide a framework categorising and illustrating the dynamics of such a complex research question. This problem has been increasingly prioritised in the post-Cold War era. The collapse of superpower influence in international relations, coupled with the rise of independent regional actors, implies a new epoch in which the region will again become one of the crucial traits of international politics.

In the post-Cold War climate, there are suggestions that region-building theories are re-emerging (Neumann, 1994: 53). After fifty years of stability under superpower constellations, secondary and more minor powers have been forced to re-assess their strategies on the basis of the changes in the world power structure. In the seventies, interest in the field declined, mainly because difficulties arose in locating empirical proof of the theoretical hypotheses concerning both the dependent variable (region transformation) and the various independent variables (geographical size, political system, and the degree of development) in the equation. This book therefore attempts to go some way towards filling the research gap that has existed for the last twenty years in this field of study and put the issue of regionalism back in centre-stage. For this purpose, this book is structured as follows.

The first chapter is conceptual in nature. James Mittelman and Richard Falk provide an analysis of the relationship between hegemony and regionalism. Chapters Two through Five consist of an empirical study of regional dynamics in different parts of Europe. Chapter Two examines the process of regional integration within the European Union. Eberhard Rhein also discusses the prospects of further integration and the implications of such an outcome. In Chapter Three Bjørn Møller provides a detailed perspective of the Nordic model of regionalism. The aim of this chapter is to outline the way in which the Nordic area of Europe has evolved as a region which will assist in evaluating contemporary regional tendencies. Chapter Four provides a review of regional trends in Europe's south east subregion. Sophia Clément assesses regional tendencies in what has become Europe's most conflictual territorial zone since the end of the Cold War.

In Chapter Five Monika Wohlfeld looks at the contribution that a leading international organisation, the Organisation for Security and Cooperation in Europe (OSCE), has being contributing in contemporary international relations.

Chapter Six to Chapter Eight are concerned with current trends in the international politics of three different geographical locations, the Mediterranean, the Americas and the Caribbean. Chapter Six examines the regional patterns of relations of the international regional subgroupings bordering the Mediterranean area, namely, Southern Europe, the Maghreb and the Levant. It also assesses future prospects for regional development in the Mediterranean.

In Chapter Seven Vilma E. Petrash assesses the challenges, limits and possibilities of inter-American regionalism by focusing on steps taken to create a Free Trade Area of the Americas. In the penultimate chapter François Taglioni elaborates on progress registered in regional integration in the Caribbean.

The final chapter provides a synopsis of the different regional trends discussed in the previous chapters and discusses the possibility of alternative patterns of interaction in the new millennium.

Dr. Stephen C. Calleya
December 1999

Acknowledgements

I am grateful to the Mediterranean Academy of Diplomatic Studies, University of Malta, especially the Director of the Academy, Professor Felix Meier for the support given in this research project. I also thank the staff of the IT Unit of the Mediterranean Academy, particularly Chris Borg Cutajar without whose assistance this book would not have been compiled in its final form. Thanks also goes to Dalibor Milenkovic and Ives De Barro for their continuous advice and support.

A special thanks to all the contributors of this book. The final product is the result of their expert analysis in the field of regionalism. Thanks to the American Centre at the American Embassy in Malta and the United States Information Agency that awarded me a scholarship which enabled me to follow an intensive research programme on U.S. Foreign Policy Making at the Centre for Political Studies, Institute for Social Research, University of Michigan in Summer 1996 under the direction of Professor Bill Zimmerman. Several preliminary contacts established at the time facilitated the task of putting together this book on regionalism.

I also thank Professor Guido de Marco, President of Malta, Dr. Joe Borg, Foreign Minister of Malta, and Dr. George Vella, shadow Foreign Minister of Malta, for their encouragement throughout the years.

I also appreciate the continuous support of the University of Warwick in general and the Director of the International Office in particular, Antony Gribbon, his staff, and the staff at the Department of Politics and International Studies, especially Barbara Allen Robertson. Thanks also to Sean Nicklin and Sharon Rathbone at the Euro-Med Journal in London.

Most of all, however, a special thanks to my brother, Peter Calleya, for bringing his corrective editorial expertise to bear on much scribbled drafts. The book has been improved a great deal as a result of his assistance.

List of Abbreviations

ACF - French Assistance and Cooperation Fund

ACS – Association of Caribbean States

AFTA – Asian Free Trade Area

AFTA – Arab Free Trade Agreement

AMU – Arab Maghreb Union

ANZUS – Australia-New Zealand-USA Pact

APEC – Asia-Pacific Economic Co-operation Forum

ASEAN – Association of South-East Asian Nations

BSEC – Black Sea Economic Co-operation

CACM – Central American Common Market

CARIBCAN - Canadian Economic and Trade Development Assistance Programme ainmed at the Commonwealth Caribbean

CARICOM – Caribbean Community and Common Market

CBI - Caribbean Basin Initiative

CBSS – Council of Baltic Sea States

CDB – Caribbean Development Bank

CEFTA – Central European Free Trade Area

CEI – Central European Initiative

CENTO – Central Treaty Organisation

CET - Common External Tariff

CFTA – Caribbean Free Trade Association

CFE – Conventional Armed Forces in Europe (Treaty)

CFSP – Common Foreign and Security Policy

CSBMs – Confidence and Security Building Measures

CUSFTA – Canada and United States Free Trade Agreement

EAI – Enterprise for the Americas Institute

EAEG - East Asian Economic Group

EAPC – Euro-Atlantic Partnership Council

EDF – European Development Fund

EEC – European Economic Community

EFTA – European Free Trade Association

EIB – European Investment Bank

EMMA - Euro-Mediterranean Maritime Agency

EMDC – Euro-Mediterranean Development Centre

EMP – Euro-Mediterranean Process

EMS – European Monetary System

EMU – European Monetary Union

EU – European Union

FDA – French Departments of America

FDI – Foreign Direct Investment

FSC – Forum for Security Co-operation

FTAA – Free Trade Area of the Americas

FTM – Free Trade of the Americas

FYROM – Former Yugoslav Republic of Macedonia

G7 – Group of 7

GATT – General Agreement on Tariffs and Trade

GCC – Gulf Co-operation Council

GDP – Gross Domestic Product

GNP - Gross National Product

GSP – Generalised System of Preferences

GUAM group – Georgia, Ukraine, Azerbaijan, Moldova)

IFC - French Interministerial Fund of Cooperation

IMF – International Monetary Fund

ISI – Import Substitution Industrialisation

LAC - Latin American Countries

LAFTA – Latin American Free Trade Area

LAIA – Latin American Integration Association

MENA - Middle East/North Africa Economic forum

MEPP – Middle East Peace Process

MERCOSUR – Common Market of the South (Mercado Común del Sur)

NACC – North Atlantic Co-operation Council

NAFTA – North American Free Trade Area

NATO – North Atlantic Treaty Organisation

NGO – Non-Governmental Organisations

NIC - Newly Industrialized Country

OAS – Organisation of American States

ODA - Official Development Assistance

OECS – Organisation of East Caribbean States

OSCE – Organisation for Security and Co-operation in Europe

PfP – Partnership for Peace

PICP – Economic Integration and Co-operation Programme

POSEIDOM - Programme of Options Specific to the Remote and Insular Nature of the French Overseas Departments

SEATO – South-East Asia Treaty Organisation

SECI – South East European Co-operative Initiative

SELA – Latin American Economic System

SLOC - Sea Lines of Communication

UN – United Nations

USAID - US Agency for International Development

WEU – Western European Union

WHFTA – Western Hemisphere Free Trade Area

WTO – World Trade Organisation

Section One

Regionalism and Contemporary World Politics

1. Global Hegemony and Regionalism

James Mittelman and Richard Falk

Hegemony is a recurrent feature of regionalism, contributing to polarisation and resource imbalances. Not to be confused with its non-Gramscian meaning of a preponderance of power, the concept of hegemony is used here in the Gramscian sense of a mix of coercion and consent in which consent is the dominant element. In this usage, neoliberal hegemony is instituted under global leadership to mediate between an oligopolistic market and domestic sociopolitical forces. After the Cold War, the United States plays this central role – as the phrase "the Washington consensus" suggests – in conjunction with its partners in different regions. When ideological hegemony proves fragile or is challenged, a hegemon may utilize a variety of instruments, including diplomatic means of maintaining harmony and military methods of coercion.

This chapter, then, turns to the politics. It explores the geopolitics of globalisation, and examines links between economic and military security in the context of globalising processes. Specifically, this chapter considers: Can the new regionalism be used to promote U.S. hegemony in a globalising world order? And what are the dilemmas associated with forging regional approaches to managing the globalising pressures of a post-Cold War era?

Our core argument is that the overall U.S. approach to sustaining hegemony – i.e., engraining the idea and practice of neoliberalism – incorporates a loose composite of regional policies that forms a patchwork. The conclusion holds that for U.S. policy makers, regionalism has nonetheless emerged as a critical, yet still tentative, and even inconsistent feature of a neoliberal multilateral order – an adhesive often used to join the political and economic dimensions of global restructuring.

We begin by delimiting the context and, then, exploring challenges to U.S. interests associated with the new regionalism. Since the United States, in effect, belongs to various regions, it is necessary to examine the three pillars on which U.S. policy rests: NAFTA; APEC; and the Atlantic Community. Other regional projects in far-flung, and in some cases marginalised, parts of the world, while of concern to Washington, are not central to this analysis, because, by the late 1980's they had by and large followed suit in a competitive liberalisation drive to attract foreign investment and expand international trade.

After the Cold War

In a manifest sense the collapse of the Soviet Union ended, at least temporarily, the debate about U.S. decline that had been so prominent during the 1980s. Indeed, the triumphalist mood emphasised the role of the United States as the sole surviving superpower. U.S. hegemonic diplomacy and military prowess were confirmed by the way in which the 1990-91 Gulf Crisis, initiated by Iraq's invasion of Kuwait, was resolved. The new era, what President George Bush christened as "the new world order", would seem to allow the United States to make use of the United Nations as a legitimising support in relation to hegemonic security concerns.

But such developments associated with the end of the Cold War obscured the weaknesses of the United States as a global hegemon. Even in the Gulf War the United States insisted upon shifting the financial burden of the military action to others, prompting Japan to complain about taxation without representation. Beyond this, the weakness of the dollar, which reflected huge trade and budget deficits in the early 1990s, meant that sustaining the U.S. hegemonic position required new methods that would not create a domestic backlash within America. The firestorm of criticism directed at the United States in 1993 after some 18 Americans died in an incident in Somalia disclosed that the multilateral frame of the Gulf War was an anomaly rather than an emergent pattern of geopolitics, and that the American public concurred with hegemony, but with few burdens on wealth and lives. The 1995 Bosnian peace agreement, forged in the heartland of the United States—Dayton, Ohio—represented a new phase of the trial-and-error dynamics with respect to shaping a hegemonic role in the overall setting of the 1990s. The diplomatic leadership of the United States seems firm and unchallenged, but the will and wherewithal are not at all assured, giving the hegemonic stature of the United States an ambiguous and tenuous quality.

Against this background regionalism in various formats is an important feature of *hegemonic geopolitics*. Unlike the globalist response to the Gulf Crisis, increasingly the effective locus of diplomatic and military initiative was a U.S.-led reliance on NATO, and to a lesser extent, the Eurocentric contact group. Whether this regionalisation of response can provide a pivotal moment for the *geopolitics of globalisation* is not currently evident. Also, the search for a hegemonic role for the United States in various economic settings also remains open-ended, as does the balance between reliance on unilateralist and regionalist approaches.

We argue that the relationship between regionalism and U.S. foreign policy is eclectic and uneven at the turn of the millennium. Regionalism associated with military-strategic goals is temporarily of questionable significance, despite Bosnia, as an instrument in the hands of U.S. foreign policy makers, while economic regionalism is of generally increasing importance. In part, this dual pattern expresses the basic shift from an era of geopolitics to one of *geoeconomics* shaped by the logic of globalisation. Regionalism for military-strategic security depends on common external or internal enemies, and in their absence is unlikely to take precedence over the tendency of states to rely on their own capabilities to uphold security, or in cases of particular threats, to seek support on a bilateral basis, as in the 1998 U.S. air strikes against support with British participation.

In contrast, regionalism for economic purposes depends on the logic of global capital that gives states an incentive to band together to achieve market shares and augment trading and investment opportunities. Furthermore, expanding economies pose threats to weaker state systems, giving regions and subregions incentives to integrate economically to offset the threat being posed.

Since 1989 U.S. foreign policy has been casting about for a mixture of political instruments to sustain its hegemonic role in the world in a manner that minimises fiscal and political strains. Although the overall relevance of regionalism to the U.S. global role is yet to be clearly defined, this chapter argues that for the present, U.S. foreign policy is diminishing its reliance on regional military-strategic arrangements while increasingly relying upon economic regionalism.

Indeed, regionalism has become a major theme in American foreign policy. The scholarly writing and public discourse on this issue focus on questions of regional security arrangements and trading blocs. Often these two sets of concerns are kept in distinct compartments, although there are large degrees of overlap, especially in relation to Europe.

With respect to military-strategic security in the current global setting, U.S. foreign policy is generally moving away from regionalism, with the partial exception of Europe. The NATO role in the latter stages of the war in Bosnia creates a misimpression of regional activism. Even in Europe the United States is losing its capacity to dominate European security policy by means of reliance on a common external enemy. What applies to Europe is even more decisively applicable to other regions where regional alliances of the Cold War such as CENTO, SEATO, and ANZUS survive merely as relics of a superseded past. During the Cold War, U.S. foreign policy, especially in the 1950s under the influence of John Foster Dulles, promoted and relied upon regional security arrangements as an integral element in its overall global policy of containment directed at the expansion of Soviet bloc influence. However, in the contemporary phase of globalisation, the United States has little need for such regional security arrangements. Besides, many countries seek to exercise their sovereign rights as independent states, and do not perceive themselves to be threatened by "expanding world Communism," or another systemic "menace". But there are other social forces and values that must be taken into account.

Foreign Policy Challenges and U.S. Interests

Domestic factors figure prominently in the orientation of policy makers toward regionalism. In the United States during the 1990s, the politics of discontent has taken different forms — calls for a third party candidate as an alternative in presidential elections, low voter turnout (37 per cent) to enable the Republican Party to form a majority in Congress in 1994 (for the first time in 40 years), and polls showing that even those who cast ballots for these Republicans did not expect meaningful change. There appears to be a sense — more than an undercurrent but rather a sophisticated understanding among the citizenry — that electoral politics does not produce leaders with credible solutions for the country's problems. Indeed, from the perspective of some critics of the type of "process-oriented" liberal democracy in the United States, leadership choice confined to a small, managed group alongside formal freedoms cannot deal with the fundamental issues of economic power and inequality (Robinson 1996). This dissatisfaction can, to a significant degree, be associated with pressures generated by economic globalisation, especially polarisation of incomes and benefits. Notwithstanding substantial stock market rises during the mid- and late 1990s, the economic circumstances for many — reductions in welfare provisions, the need to work more than one job, diminished employment security, etc. — grew harsh and mean-spirited.

While scholars explicate the particular set of structural changes that comprise the realignment known as globalisation, the state itself is seeking adaptive strategies to manage this trend. Additionally, politicians — members of Congress, for example — are responding to these new realities in a variety of ways, including a package of benefits for business and burdens for the laboring portions of the citizenry, especially its most disadvantaged segments. One expression of this adaptive dynamic has been to shrink the resources and roles of government, especially in relation to social spending, and in some instances, the environment.

This trend is reinforced by the weakening of organised labour, the public ascendancy of business and finance, and the mainstream ideological consensus of a neoliberal character. President Bill Clinton, a Democrat in the White House from 1992 to 2000 — despite being elected on the mandate of giving priority to the domestic economy — tilted foreign economic policy in the direction of global market forces, overriding the objections of the traditional constituencies of the Democratic Party, a process evident in the fight over the ratification of NAFTA and in the promotion of the World Trade Organisation (WTO). This pattern of adjustment by nominally liberal (and to some extent, social) democratic leadership has been repeated throughout the world, suggesting the structural impact of globalisation. For various reasons, especially associated with welfare and employment traditions, the specific character of adjustment has been much more painful in some countries than in others. The adjustment in the United States, with its turn toward a stark form of market-driven policy, has been particularly extreme.

This cluster of circumstances arising out of globalisation has generated a series of foreign policy problems that take their distinctive shape as a result of the interactions between a high degree of unipolarity with respect to global diplomacy and military capability and a general character of tripolarity or multipolarity (G-7) when it comes to economics.

First, U.S. foreign policy makers are struggling with the issue of how to cope with transnational economic forces for which there are no effective regulatory mechanisms. As evident in the 1995 collapse of Barings Bank as a result of fraudulent trading practices of a single employee in its Singapore branch office, international finance's highly leveraged market for derivatives is global in reach, but effective regulation depends on domestic frameworks. Similarly, the growing mobility of capital, its capacity to move, makes it increasingly difficult for any state to use its policy instruments to control polluting and environmentally destructive behaviour by corporations. Going one more step, to the extent that globalisation — and regionalism as one of its components — extends the boundaries of unregulated or deregulated capital accumulation, it shrinks governments' capacity to be responsive to democratic pressure, and thereby constrains citizen power to control their own economic lives. Subject to the constraining impacts of conditionality and structural adjustment, some developing countries experience this loss of control to a larger degree and in more blatant ways than do developed countries, but even a country as rich and powerful as the United States is increasingly a casualty of globalisation, at least as far as governmental policy on public goods is concerned.

Next, in practice, foreign policy makers in Washington, like their counterparts elsewhere, encounter a matrix of zones highly integrated into globalisation and others increasingly marginalised from it. A fundamental feature of a globalising world, this sharp polarisation threatens instability and recurrent eruptions of regional conflict.

The third challenge is the contradiction between the globalisation of markets and assertions of a community of values not premised on neoliberalism. Put differently, the issue is really one of moral order: Beyond gauging human worth in terms of market criteria and the amount of consumer goods one possesses, what is the moral component of globalisation? At bottom, this is the challenge of an alternative globalisation project — resurgent Islam, whose image is tarnished in Western media, but one dimension of which challenges powerfully the absence of an ethical dimension in neoliberal globalisation, as well as condemns the cultural consequences of the consumerist ethos (Pasha and Samatar 1996).

Finally, in the face of globalising forces that it cannot harness, the state surrenders a slice of sovereignty partly as a defensive measure and partly to reflect the globalised outlook of the governing stratum. Taking the most institutionalised form of regionalism, the EU is not the "United States of Europe" envisaged by its founders, but a new externalised authority structure that determines how much farmers can grow, specifies conditions for equity in pensions, allocates funds for economic development in poor regions, stops some national subsidies deemed anti-competitive, and requires countries to admit products they do not want. The EU is empowered to enforce rules on the environment, on mergers and acquisitions, and on standards in the workplace. In fact, EU decisions can supersede national law on a scale reflected by the 18,000 bureaucrats now employed in Brussels. Hence, the state is not so much a casualty of regionalism as it is a willing, even enthusiastic, partner in this process. While the state is pushing outward to adapt and because of its outlook, it is also coping with the disruptive pulls of subnationalism both at home and abroad, a second, countervailing process that can be partially understood as a backlash against globalisation.

In formulating a response to these challenges, Washington can draw on its military superiority, its great diplomatic leverage, its magnetic political culture so attractive to the youth of the world, its status as the world's largest national economy, and its vast resources in technological innovation and the knowledge industry. The United States is the world's leading trader, and its GNP is almost 1.5 times as large as the one in second place—Japan's—according to the most recent figures available (World Bank 1997b, 214-15). As is well known, however, the United States shifted from being the world's major creditor nation to being the chief debtor, and its share of world output dropped from one-third in the 1950s and 1960s to one-fifth in the early 1990s (Bach 1993, 11-12; Nye 1990). Yet, since hegemony cannot be fully measured in the appurtenances of overt power and wealth, there is also the matter of shared values, intersubjective meanings, a leadership role with considerable diplomatic assets. Hegemony is about the way that consent is produced. Machiavelli's sage advice that the ruler cannot rule by brute force alone is germane to a post-Cold War world. And the insight of his compatriot, Antonio Gramsci, that hegemonic structures embrace not only interests but also rationality in the form of consent may be extended by noting that the amalgam of coercion and consent is always changing, it is uneven and continually needs to be adjusted in response to challenges.

To refurbish hegemony after the Cold War, and to overcome the challenges of globalisation, the United States, above all, seeks to institutionalize the neoliberal idea that the basic building blocks of order are individuals rather than economic or social structures. And related to the tenet that left to their own devices, markets will lead to an efficient allocation of resources is the notion of flexibility such that both producers and consumers can readily respond to price signals. Of course, neoliberalism is not merely an economic model that trumpets the primacy of markets, but it is a means of action that translates into policies for opening markets. The impact is not neutral to different groups but favours certain forces: large firms; big investors; and the major capitalist countries. The ideology of neoliberalism is also associated with the decline of the economic sovereignty of states, reductions in social welfare, and a transformation of state capitalism into free-market capitalism.

Adopting neoliberalism as a cornerstone of foreign policy, Washington has enshrined flexibility as a hallmark of its post-Cold War strategy. In "reinventing government", the rubric of Vice President Al Gore's proposals for reducing the size of government and making it more efficient, policy makers utilised a principle, flexibility, drawn right from the market economy — "flexible production" a system of organisation designed for competitive strength in the globalised world economy. As an approach to regionalism, flexibility means a series of hub-spoke relations between the United States and its partners, sometimes reflecting a shallow form of interstate association and in other cases deeper interactions involving the protection of worker rights and civil society, but in all instances determined by trial-and-error in different zones of the global political economy ranging from Europe and the Americas to the Pacific. As the United States is not a member of the EU, even though it maintains diplomatic and cultural ties, as well as a huge economic presence, it has sought to rely on regionalism in North America and the Pacific Rim, with NAFTA providing the boldest move in the search for a template that would integrate regional arrangements with an overall response to globalisation.

Reconstituting Hemispheric Hegemony

Historically, the United States has experimented with various initiatives to build hegemony in Latin America dating to the Monroe Doctrine in the nineteenth century, while establishing strong historical, military, trading, and cultural ties. Although it is beyond the compass of this chapter to detail the provisions of the precursors to NAFTA, it would be remiss not to note the importance of previous bilateral and multilateral hemispheric arrangements spearheaded by Washington. In many respects, NAFTA and plans for future liberalisation in the Western Hemisphere flow from historical patterns that crystallised in the 1980s and 1990s.

President Ronald Reagan's 1982 Caribbean Basin Initiative was motivated in good part by his administration's desire to bolster rightist regimes in Central America, isolate and undermine the Sandinista government in Nicaragua, and exert further pressure on Fidel Castro's Cuba. Far from a narrow security or geopolitical concern, backing for the contras was in fact tendered in a sustained move to eradicate the Sandinistas' attempt to offer a second regional alternative to the neoliberal project. At the same time, the Reagan team offered expanded aid, investment incentives, and duty-free access to the American market in return for the political consent of the Central American countries and the Caribbean nations. Although there were many compromises in this legislation and its implementation, the link between U.S. expectations and rewards was patent even though Cold War considerations were intertwined with the attempted regionalisation of economic activity.

The carrot-and-stick model of consent formation was applied in other instances as well, though perhaps not as brazenly, and continued by Reagan's successors. Although Canada differs in most ways from developing countries in the Western Hemisphere, Canada is similarly highly dependent on the U.S. market and its investors. Here too U.S. power—and hence the provisions of the U.S.-Canada Free Trade Agreement of 1988—was used to push liberalisation for foreign investors. From the point of view of business interests, the objective was to facilitate capital mobility. In Canada, regionalism was presented as a necessary means to protect and expand access to the U.S. market (Fishlow and Haggard 1992, 21). Turning south, the United States sought to maintain political stability, to slow illegal immigration, and to cement a neoliberal economy. Hence, the United States-Mexico

Free Trade Agreement, which President George Bush presented to Congress in 1990, guaranteed Mexico access to the North American market, locked in neoliberal domestic reforms, and reassured private investors that new flows of foreign capital would be forthcoming. Finally, Bush's 1991 Enterprise for the Americas Initiative opened channels for a hemispheric free trade arrangement. Liberalisation included investment promotion, privatisation, debt reduction, and the removal of trade barriers (Fishlow and Haggard 1992, 22-25).

With these spokes radiating from the hub, the pattern for NAFTA was set in motion. All that remained was to systematize a set of bilateral and multilateral policies that had been put in place over the past decade. For U.S. business, represented by Democratic President Bill Clinton, who championed a Republican stance on economic regionalism even though it was opposed by his party's labour constituency, hegemonic regionalism meant instilling confidence in the neoliberal model. More than a set of trade provisions, NAFTA became an emblem of neoliberalism, a means of action, a method for forging transnational consent, and establishing investor confidence in the irreversibility of the arrangements. Along with U.S. capital, business and the state in both Canada and Mexico came to recognize that NAFTA was an instrument to pry open the U.S. economy, but with worrisome effects on labor and environmental conditions.

For all practical purposes, the North American triangle is a misnomer. Since the U.S. economy dwarfs those of its neighbours, the legs are of vastly unequal lengths. In fact, the third leg between Canada and Mexico does not really exist. Internalising the North-South problem, NAFTA incorporates wide discrepancies in income distribution and policy congruence. The asymmetry is so pronounced that NAFTA is not only a free trade zone but also inevitably functions as a sphere of ideological and political influence for the United States (Poitras 1995, 9). Less clearly perceived by most policy makers, but anticipated by some commentators, was the degree to which NAFTA created a danger zone for the United States, an embrace that imposed responsibility to rescue the weak member (Castaneda 1995). Pre-NAFTA it would have been inconceivable for the United States to put together a rescue package to restore investor confidence in the Mexican economy. Post-NAFTA it was inconceivable not to try.

While business and finance on both sides of the two borders supported the agreement, opposition came especially from U.S.

labourers who feared "runaway shops" and environmentalists aware of weaker standards in Mexico, but also from ultranationalists on the right such as Ross Perot and Pat Buchanan. Human rights groups pointed to widespread abuses in Mexico and accused the Clinton Administration of delinking the moral component of foreign policy from economic gain. When it was agreed in 1994 to admit Chile soon as a member of NAFTA, the Caribbean countries complained that their minuscule economies could be hurt by rapid market liberalisations. Also, there is a move in Latin America to find alternatives to NAFTA, some of them southern-based versions of neoliberalism — a Southern Cone Common Market among Argentina, Brazil, Uruguay and Paraguay, signed in 1991, as well as a revival of the Andean Common Market.

In order to prepare Mexico for NAFTA, the government of Carlos Salinas de Gortari embraced neoliberal reforms to allow the division of *ejidos*, land communally owned by peasants, making it easier for individuals to sell their property to more efficient large holders better equipped to compete with American and Canadian producers. This process dislodged many poor peasants and helped fuel the Zapatista uprising in the state of Chiapas that symbolically was timed to coincide with the day of the inauguration of NAFTA on January 1, 1994. The actual impact of NAFTA policies includes the loss of 41,201 manufacturing jobs in the United States, documented by the U.S. Labour Department, which is far below the number of Mexicans put out of work. This labour-shedding is variously attributed to trade liberalisation and a continuing trend of a drop in manufacturing employment in the Mexican economy since September 1990 (DePalma 1995; Cornelius 1995). Liberalisation, deregulation, and the integration of capital markets mean increasing economic insecurity for low-income earners and people of colour. Just as there is growing income inequality between Mexico and the United States, economic polarisation within Mexico is also on the rise, a notable development in light of the already vast disparities in income and wealth. The displacement of workers and farmers in all three countries has accelerated migration. Yet the escape valve of emigration to the United States is a less effective outlet, given the increasing resistance to newcomers in California and other states.

Fifteen months after the adoption of NAFTA, Washington stepped in to respond to Mexico's chaotic financial markets, providing a $52 billion guarantee programme. While cutting back on welfare at home, the U.S. government came to the rescue of private investors, both Americans and Mexicans who had knowingly taken a risk on an "emerging market" — Mexican equities — but were rescued from suffering the consequences of placing a bad bet. For all practical purposes, the U.S. government and the IMF became the central bank in Mexico, suggesting the burden-side of regionalism as an hegemonic instrument for the United States. Also, expediency, as might be expected, superseded neoliberal ideology, in the crunch. In a classic Polanyian move, the utopia of the self-regulating free market was silently sacrificed on the altar of massive state intervention.

In spite of this debacle, the long-term goal is to liberalize and integrate capital markets from Arctic Canada to near-Antarctic Chile. The aim is to enlarge and replace NAFTA by a Western Hemisphere Free Trade Area, with the United States paramount in its hegemonic role. In Asia, by comparison, the United States encounters a highly diverse region with much stronger states, ones with their own agendas for regionalism. Asian regionalism relies less on formal agreements and intergovernmental institutions and more on a web of bilateral economic relationships, but with a regional overlay.

Rethinking Hegemonic Regionalism in the Asia-Pacific

Important to reconfiguring hegemony in accordance with post-Cold War conditions and neoliberal globalisation are the competing ideas propounded by American policy intellectuals. Their proposals and explanations are influential, providing a key contribution in setting the policy agenda. One thesis that temporarily attracted widespread attention was put forward by Francis Fukuyama (1989), a former State Department official, who held that with the end of communism, the dialectic of history had come to a conclusion marked by the permanent triumph of capitalism, pluralist politics, and constitutionalism. Having reached the ultimate synthesis, the focus for political leaders should be on expanding prosperity and helping some laggard societies to integrate into the liberal economic system. Another and perhaps more durable facet of the hegemonic discourse is represented by Samuel Huntington (1993), whose article "The Clash of Civilisations?" argues that Cold War rivalries have been supplanted by the "fault lines of civilisations", including the identities of religion and culture, especially pitting Islam and Confucian elements against the West. For Huntington, post-Cold War conflicts and competition come down to two poles, namely, "the West and the rest". Not only do these representations disclose the thinking of major organic intellectuals apropos of American hegemony, but also they presume that there is only one neoliberal project. Not so in the Asia-Pacific region.

There is a dominant neoliberal scenario, which is an inclusive version, as well as an alternative neoliberal option, a more exclusive mode. APEC, the inclusive grouping, envelops all of the subregional bodies (e.g., ASEAN) and microregional experiments (e.g., EPZs) in the Pacific Basin. Its Asian flank subsumes two of the world's three largest economies — China and Japan; four countries heralded as NICs; two near-NICs, Malaysia and Thailand, with the Philippines and Indonesia trailing behind; and countries as different as Canada, Chile, and Papua New Guinea. Just as APEC must deal with ASEAN's fear of domination by Japan and the United States, so too it must try to encapsulate China and Taiwan in a single organisational structure. This structure is, of course, only a consultative forum without any rule making organ, though in 1994 it was decided to create a free trade area (AFTA) for the ASEAN six by 2003, but whether such a horizon is to be understood as a literal commitment is as yet unclear.

The rationale for regional deepening flows from a series of circumstances compressed into a short-time span — the dynamism of some Asian economies until 1997, the powerful thrust of globalisation, and the end of the Cold War. In many respects, the economic crisis of the late 1990s added to this rationale. In the wake of an attack by currency speculators and herd-like behaviour among foreign investors, there was contagion affecting Thailand, Korea, Indonesia, Malaysia, and to a lesser degree other Asian countries. When the policy agenda turned to economic recovery, it became increasingly evident that at present, most of Asian capitalism, while variegated, and irrespective of whether an IMF programme is adopted de jure or de facto, is dependent on broad conformity to the U.S.-guided model of development. There followed many proposals and modest initiatives for new forms of subregional unity.

For both the American and Asian wings of APEC, one incentive to deepen the regional structure is the potential gains from expanding trade and investment. Asia is now North America's primary market, and trans-Pacific trade exceeds trans-Atlantic trade. The 18 members of APEC account for a growing share of worldwide production and trade — almost 60 per cent of global GDP and 46 per cent of all exports in 1993, up from 38 per cent in 1983 (Higgott and Stubbs 1995; "APEC: The Opening of Asia" 1994). But which deepening agenda will prevail? What are the deep integration issues?

The Asian wing of APEC is wary that deepening will be a means for the United States to impose its notion of fair trade. The smaller, developing countries fear that the United States will seek to reshape tried and proven domestic economic policies that rely on large-scale state intervention, and insist on social issues — human rights as well as labor and environmental standards (though not of the sort demanded by some NGOs). Also, the effort to imagine or construct an Asian identity poses broad and nettlesome questions about conflicts between different value systems, not in Huntington's sense of intercivilisational tensions, but in terms of the moral content of a neoliberal regional project. In this vein, two observers strike a chord that resonates in some quarters in Asia: "APEC . . . is clearly the child of western-educated, international trade economists steeped in the methodology of positivism and utility maximising rationalism" (Higgott and Stubbs 1995, 531). Implicitly, the point is that if neoliberalism is a facsimile of neoclassical economics, does it respond to the deeper yearnings of ancient Asian civilisations caught in the vortex of rapid globalisation? Also, is it compatible with a range of coercive political styles and structures?

An alternative alluded to in Chapter Six is the Asianisation of APEC. Proposed by Malaysia's prime minister in 1990, an EAEG would consist of Japan, China, the East Asian NICs, and the rest of ASEAN as a strong counterweight to the EU and a U.S.-centered regionalism: Australia, New Zealand, Canada, and the United States would be omitted. In other words, in comparison to the Pacific scenario, the Asian scenario calls for a more exclusive membership, and emphasises the cultural dimension — identity — of regionalism as a central feature of deepening. Although the modalities of this arrangement were never set forth in detail, the United States from the very outset, not surprisingly, opposed it. The United States wanted to maintain its leadership role in the region, and could play its trump cards — guarantor of military security, container of China, and sheer market size — to deflect the Malaysian expression of frustration with the dominant neoliberal agenda. Outright U.S. opposition to Mahathir's idea resulted in its dilution, becoming only a weak Asian caucus within the larger Pacific formation, at least for now. There is but one other tripartite system to consider, with Europe as the third sphere of influence.

Revitalising Hegemonic Regionalism in the Atlantic Community

Heretofore, North Atlantic relations have been based on substantial historical and cultural ties, a high degree of market interpenetration, a central military alliance (NATO), and a series of bilateral relationships. Yet, after the Cold War, all parties needed to take account of changed conditions. Also, the United States is confronted by a strong regional organisation to which it does not belong, although some sort of participation cannot be entirely ruled out.

While Europeans with myriad visions debate a deeper integration agenda, it is necessary to invent more flexible strategies to cope with the needs of a community of thirty to thirty-five members early in the new millennium and the social implications of a single market, including the absorption of immigrants, high levels of unemployment, deep ethnic cleavages, and polarisation between rich and poor. Within Europe, there is a difference of opinion over whether there should be: (1) an advance guard of member states moving ahead to deepen regionalism, with the provision that other countries could follow later; (2) a prerequisite of all willing countries first subscribing to common goals; (3) a two-track system between those preferring and capable of adapting to tight integration and those favouring a looser framework, all within an umbrella of cooperation; or (4) an *á la carte* menu of integration options (Barber 1995). To change the metaphor, certain choices might have a bootstrap effect on regionalism in general. Additionally, there could of course be transitional arrangements from one tier of regional deepening to another.

Responding to this drive to further regionalism in Europe, U.S. officials have emphasised that insofar as it has proven itself the guarantor of European freedom and stability, America is a European power (Holbrooke 1995). The U.S. effort to refashion hegemonic regionalism in this sphere thus rests on the premises that Europe still does not have the capacity to meet its security needs, that the American connection rests upon a strong foundation of common interests and values that survived the long test of the Cold War, that without America a more objectionable German hegemony would result, and that Russia might soon again pose a challenge that could not be confidently met unless America remains enmeshed in Europe. Here is the rub. Since Europe failed in its response to aggression and genocide in Bosnia, the United States, which itself for a long time refused to dispatch its own troops during the ordeal of "ethnic cleansing," nevertheless questions whether Europeans have the *bona fide* capacity to bring peoples closer together. Beyond rhetorical flourishes, is there a genuine willingness to make the sacrifices necessary to sustain a community when its most basic values are under attack? The diplomatic end-game in Bosnia, as well as the Kosovo sequel, emphasised the reassertion of an American hegemonic role in relation to European security. Also, the shift from the UN to NATO as the arena responsible for peacekeeping in Bosnia, both reinforced the remarginalisation of the UN in relation to global security and the perception of a reassertion of U.S. leadership *in* Europe. Although NATO is European in its locus of operations, it remains a regional arrangement dominated by the United States, a point reinforced by the way in which Washington insisted on having the final word with respect to the selection of the new NATO Secretary-General after the discrediting of Willy Claes in 1995. Yet it remains highly questionable as to whether the U.S. military-strategic role in Europe can be parlayed into a comparable role in relation to European economic affairs. It would seem definitely not, at least within the present conjuncture of forces.

Just as there are limits to protecting professed ideals, so too there are palpable bounds to formal regionalism. Not only counterhegemonic forces but also hegemonic actors will avail themselves of informal or unofficial regionalism. Paradoxically, informal regionalism is often exercised through extraregional Fora — the G-7, the Paris and London clubs for international financial issues, the Davos World Economic Forum, the Trilateral Commission, etc. — which can be more effective in fastening down hegemonic nuts and bolts. Clearly, these fora may be public or private associations adept in their flexible management of both consent and structural forms of coercion. Both regional and extraregional vehicles are compatible with reconstructing U.S. hegemony so long as they are attuned to a multilateral world order, though they are encountering substantial barriers on the road to neoliberalising ends.

Toward a Global Strategy of Regionalism

In sum, in an effort to sustain hegemony, the United States, as the hub power, has attempted to radiate a series of regional spokes, all within the wheel of neoliberalism. Does it turn smoothly in the sense of successfully managing the foreign policy challenges noted above? We think not. Although regionalism can be a potent selective instrument in controlling agendas, cornering markets, and policing certain areas and activities, the United States has often not used it prudently or wisely, partly because there are sharp contrasts and tensions between different spheres. Cooperation is deepest between the United States and its NAFTA partners, but even here far more problematic than expected, due to economic distress that has resulted for Mexico and Canada; shallower, weaker, and less institutionalised across the Pacific; and more uncertain in the North Atlantic because of the growing salience of the other two zones (Haggard 1994).

Hence, the United States has used a differentiated approach to regionalism, abandoning its adherence to neoliberalism when decisions makers have deemed interventionary actions to be more efficient. The U.S. bailout of the Mexican economy serves as a spectacular reminder of such an expedient willingness to rescue market forces, as does U.S. support for comparable bailouts in such countries as Indonesia and Brazil.

Quite clearly, the speed at which global markets have evolved over the last thirty years has been much faster than the capacity of states and regional organisations to manage the effects or even directions of change. The structural impact of globalisation has narrowed the range of policy choice at the level of the state. This overarching reality has made it imperative for policy makers to reconcile globalisation and regionalism to the extent possible.

Regionalism is far from being monolithic, calling attention to political forces within formal groupings or transnational movements that consider it possible to convert regionalism into a shield against hegemony. Just as regionalism functions as a hegemonic strategy for the United States, it may also provide space for a variety of counter-hegemonic projects. Regionalism is thus not only a component and reflection of globalisation but also acts as a modifying response to it.

Whatever the American approach to regionalism in a given time and place, powerful forces — nationalism, religion, ethnicity, language, etc. — not only bind communities, but also continue to pull peoples apart and even set loose a destructive chain-reaction. Counteracting U.S. strategy has generated global strife, much of it violent. Expanding regionalism may not be powerful enough to neutralize other differences, many of them stymied and disguised by repressive states and bloc politics during the Cold War, but since 1989 substantially liberated from the geopolitical discipline of bipolarity.

Given these problems in developing a coherent and effective policy on regionalism, why does the United States persist? Why not discard this approach and stick to state-centered, power-oriented tactics? Why not link directly to the global economy and skip the intermediate layer of regionalism? For one thing, the United States is of course pursuing both statist and regional strategies, though finite resources constrain the capability to invest in two projects for the same ends. Moreover, with a changed power configuration and the reorganisation of the global economy along regional lines, new modes of competition impel states, firms, and banks to use regionalism as one essential means to reposition themselves vis-à-vis their competitors. If globalisation entails a reduction in control at the national level, then the best option for many states, including the United States may be regional fallbacks (Crone 1993). But, as argued, the current picture is clouded, especially since the European and Pacific regional arenas remain fluid and contradictory with respect to the United States' role as insider or outsider. It is likely that U.S. hegemonic ambitions will be realised to the extent that Washington's security contributions to these regions remain salient and are perceived by important member states as indispensable. If the European and Asia-Pacific macroregions can reduce, or eliminate, their military-strategic dependence on the United States, then it is likely that its economic participation will be more scrutinised, and likely constrained, thereby eroding hegemonic capacity. At present, there are two overriding and unresolved considerations that bear upon the reliance on regionalism as a means to sustain hegemony: Can traditional security factors be converted into influence in economic domains?; Will regional tendencies be neutralised by globalising pressures and by intraregional disruptions and unevenness?

References

"APEC: The Opening of Asia." 1994. *The Economist* (London) 333, 7889. 12 November.

Bach, Robert L. 1993. *Changing Relations: Newcomers and Established Residents in U.S. Communities: A Report to the Ford Foundation by the National Board of the Changing Relations Panel.* New York: Ford Foundation.

Barber, Lionel. 1995. "Delors Speaks Up for an EU Integration Led by Core." *Financial Times* (London), 24 February.

Castaneda, Jorge. 1995. *The Mexican Shock: Its Meaning for the United States.* New York: W.W. Norton.

Cornelius, Wayne A. 1995. "Nafta Costs Mexico More Job Losses Than U.S." *New York Times*, 17 October.

Crone, Donald. 1993. "Does Hegemony Matter? The Reorganisation of the Pacific Political Economy." *World Politics* 45, no. 4 (July): 501-25.

DePalma, Anthony. 1995. "For Mexico, Nafta's Promise of Jobs Is Still Just a Promise." *New York Times*, 10 October.

Fishlow, Albert and Stephan Haggard. 1992. *The United States and the Regionalisation of the World Economy.* Paris: Organisation for Economic Cooperation and Development.

Fukuyama, Francis. 1989. "The End of History?" *The National Interest* 16 (Summer): 3-18.

Haggard, Stephan. 1994. "Thinking about Regionalism: The Politics of Minilateralism in Asia and the Americas." Paper presented at the annual meeting of the American Political Science Association. New York, NY, September.

Higgott, Richard and Richard Stubbs. 1995. "Competing Conceptions of Economic Regionalism: APEC vs. EAEC in the Asia Pacific." *Review of International Political Economy* 2, no. 3 (Summer): 516-35.

Holbrooke, Richard. 1995. "America, a European Power." *Foreign Affairs* 74, no. 2 (March/April): 38-51.

Huntington, Samuel P. 1993. "The Clash of Civilisations?" *Foreign Affairs* 72, no. 3 (Summer): 22-49.

Nye, Joseph S. 1990. *Bound to Lead: The Changing Nature of American Power.* New York: Basic Books.

Pasha, Mustapha Kamal and Ahmed I. Samatar. 1996. "The Resurgence of Islam." In *Globalisation: Critical Reflections*, ed. James H. Mittelman, 187-201. Boulder: Lynne Rienner.

Poitras, Guy. 1995. "Regional Trade Strategies: U.S. Policy in North America and toward the Asian Pacific." Paper presented at the annual meeting of the International Studies Association. Chicago, February.

Robinson, William I. 1996. *Promoting Polyarchy: Globalisation, US Intervention, and Hegemony*. Cambridge: Cambridge University Press.

World Bank. 1997. *World Development Report*. New York: Oxford University Press.

Section Two

European Regionalism

2. European Regionalism - Where is the European Union Heading?

Eberhard Rhein

Regionalism had its origins in Western Europe at the beginning of the 1950s. It is from here that the basic concept has been transposed into different parts of the world, Africa, the Middle East, East Asia, South Asia, North and South America. But none of the 'copies', almost a dozen by now, that have been put in place, with various success, elsewhere has ever attained the complexities and the relative perfection of the European original.

In Europe, regionalism has profoundly altered the relationship of states among themselves and with the rest of the world. It has had two major consequences, both of which very much wanted by the 'Fathers' of European integration, i.e. to rule out the possibility of military conflict within Europe and, in parallel, to restore European influence in world affairs.

Regionalism in Europe has been largely identical throughout the last 40 years with the European Economic Community (EEC) and its successive constitutional offsprings, in particular the European Union since the Maastricht Treaty (1993). Without these, regionalism would have taken a very different, certainly much less ambitious course.

The change of name from EEC to EU symbolises the extension of the system from trade and economic matters to more and more central state activities. Its sustained success in solving problems and establishing an efficient, but very balanced inter-state relationship has led to an impressive geographic expansion, from six member states with some 180 million people in 1958 to 15 states with 370 people in 1996, so that the EU has become increasingly identified with Europe at large.

The present paper does not intend to analyse the steps through which these truly revolutionary changes within the European state system have become possible. Rather it wishes to focus on six future-related issues:

· What is the nature of the European regional system which distinguishes it from others?

· In what direction will the EU system move in the next two decades?

· Will the EU system continue to guarantee the absence of military conflict?

· How far will the system expand? Where are the limits to EU membership?

· Will a bigger EU still be manageable?

· How will the relationship with the EU's neighbours, east and south, evolve?

These are difficult questions to which no single set of answers can be given. No one is able today to read the future of the coming 20 years. Still, it is worth while to speculate on Europe's future, if only to provoke further thinking and alternative answers and thereby to better understand what goes on in the present.

The Essence of the European Regional System

The European regional system is unique. It differs from any other regional system because of the following five characteristics:

First, the productive inter-action between sovereign states and newly created European institutions.

It is the dialectic inter-action between these which constitutes the key to the EU's success. Without European institutions endowed with true power of decision and political action (European Council, Commission, Parliament, Court etc.) progress towards European integration would not have been possible. Powerful European institutions are, however, being tolerated by the states only because they rarely attempted to challenge the states' sovereign rights by way of direct confrontation. Such has been tried once, in the early 60s; it failed. Since then European institutions have learned to go slowly and softly, entering new areas only when the time was felt ripe and a consensus appeared possible.

Second, the pragmatic approach taken by all players.

The European regional system is a system *sui generis* and open-ended; it defies conventional constitutional definitions. It is neither a federation like Germany or Belgium, nor is it still a confederation of sovereign states, but rather a supra-national organisation.

Unlike most European states, it does not have a written constitution, the Treaties constitute a constitutional basis, but fall short of being formal constitutions. Nobody can really tell where the EU is heading in terms of its constitutional nature.

Different people express different views on the Union's 'final political objectives', its *finalites politiques*. Calling for a European federal state continues to be heresy in the United Kingdom, while in countries like Spain, Italy, Belgium or the Netherlands many people can live with such a goal as a long-term perspective. Political wisdom therefore suggests not to try and impose a 'Constitution' prematurely, but this should not prevent intellectuals, constitutional lawyers and even legislators from writing and discussing about this thorny issue.

What is essential is that there is a sufficient overall political consensus on the broadly defined nature and objectives of the European regional system, for policy makers to take the necessary short-term steps, and that in doing so Europeans are being guided by a healthy dose of political pragmatism, instead of allowing themselves to be bogged down by an excess of doctrinaire legalism.

Third, the evolutionary nature of the system.

Since its creation in the 50s, the European system has been subject to permanent adjustments and enlargements. The range of its policies, the measures taken and the priorities have changed constantly, so that everyone who may have revisited the system in five-year intervals must have had certain difficulties in recognising the 'animal': so much had it changed. Enlargements also led to significant institutional changes.

Essentially, the EU has always been reacting to problems popping up inside and outside: whenever it was felt that answers could be given in a more effective way by a common European approach, such answers were defined and, though often only after many years of internal discussion and even protracted internal disputes, implemented, whatever the legal basis. As it ought to be in any society, the legal base follows the political solution of the problem, not the other way round. But once the political solution has been accepted, it becomes an intrinsic part of the European legal system which thereby has been a constantly 'expending universe'.

The following three examples, all inter-linked, illustrate this typical EU approach.

In the middle of the 80s when the Union appeared to have gone out of steam, with the customs union and the common agricultural policy being put in place, the European Commission 'discovered' that the Treaty provisions had not been fully exploited, far from it, in areas like free movement of services, public procurement, free movement of persons and of capital, and that the maintenance of intra-European barriers in these fields constituted a severe handicap to European competitiveness in the global market: thus the single market concept was born. It led, thanks to a lot of persuasiveness and support from influential business groups, to the first major constitutional amendment of the Rome Treaties, i. e. the European Single Act (1987) which has turned out to be a vital key for future European developments.

In the early 90s, several member states were becoming increasingly aware that it would be impossible to advance on a Union-wide basis in the field of free movement of people and that therefore an essential part of the Single Act risked remaining *lettre morte*. This awareness led to the formation of the so-called 'Schengen Group' (France, Germany, Benelux) which decided to start implementing the principle of free movement of people within a smaller regional setting. Thus the principle and the practice of Europe moving at different speeds was born, which since has found another even more far-reaching application with the step by step introduction of European Monetary Union as of 1999. Indeed, the 'Schengen Group' served as a sort of spearhead in this politically very delicate area, which others joined progressively, as soon as the conditions were ripe.

Who would have dared to foresee, only 20 years ago, that at the turn of the century immigration, asylum, judicial cooperation in civil matters etc. would become matters of Union policy. Such an encroachment on one of the core functions of the modern state, i.e. internal security, is going to happen when the Amsterdam Treaty has have come into force, not because some very active European bureaucrats pushed for it, but because it was a logical consequence of free movement of persons provided by the Single European Act and the Schengen Agreement. Indeed, experience has shown that the management of free movement of people within Europe required more efficient rules and procedures than normal international treaties. This realisation made governments finally accept the gradual transfer of such a highly sensitive area into EU competence.

Fourth, the capacity by European institutions to fix long-term goals.

The EU has progressed in stages, by focusing on long-term objectives to be realised, in small steps, during long transition periods. Without the long -term horizons that were established again and again for putting into place environmental, agricultural, competition, structural and other policies, the single market and above all Economic and Monetary union (EMU), the EU would have failed a long time ago.

By projecting long-term objectives, obtaining consensus on these as well as on the broad strategies for attaining them, long before getting down into the more fastidious work of implementation and of overcoming the host of political and technical obstacles, the EU has consistently been able to muster support and create the necessary political momentum for changes to take place that, in the initial stages of the process, appeared beyond any realistic hope.

Thus, the boldest ever of its achievements so far, the EMU, will have taken more than 30 years to finally materialise, from the Werner Plan (1971), through the long and sometimes painful apprenticeship of the EMS (European Monetary System), to the Maastricht Treaty (1992) and the effective start of the new European money (Euro) in 1999 by 11 member states.

Fifth, the emphasis on legal rules.

Whatever the pragmatic nature of the European integration process, it would not have worked successfully without firm legal foundations. From the very start, the early promoters of the European Union have insisted on the need to build a strong legal base which over time has become the so-called *acquis communautaire*. Thousands of lawyers, professors, judges and lawmakers have contributed during the past four decades to compiling an impressive stock of European law that has progressively penetrated into national legal systems, in particular in areas like agricultural, environmental, competition, customs, transport law, but also into such realms as banking and finance, public procurement and technical standards.

This development in turn has had a remarkable impact on the legal profession. Today lawyers are not only required to study European law, but they also start, finally, regrouping themselves into European-wide law firms, in response to the creation of the single market for legal services. This in turn will help in accelerating the course towards even more European-wide legislation.

Towards More and More European-Wide Regulations

Very slowly and therefore hardly fully realised, national governments have seen their capacity of autonomous political action shrinking over the past 50 years.

This trend has been due to one overriding factor, globalisation, of wh0ich the EU has been both an integral part and a driving force.

There is hardly any single area of government policy left in Europe where national governments are still able to proceed without referring to EU regulations, directives, information or coordination procedures. This goes both for domestic and external affairs.

Nothing indicates that this trend might diminish during the coming two decades. On the contrary, one should rather assume a further acceleration, essentially for two reasons:

· On the external front, individual state governments will be less and less able to influence the growing number of decisions that, in the future, will have to be taken at a global level. The Kyoto Conference on Global Climatic Change (December 1997), at which the EU presented a common front, was just one important issue on which a sort of global consensus has been achieved because of the European countries acting jointly.

· On the internal front, the process of intra-European integration has reached a point where it will, henceforth, develop its own momentum, almost 'snowball-like'. The completion of the internal market and the emerging Economic and Monetary Union towards the beginning of next century will more than anything else accelerate the rush towards even more European-wide rules. This will be a natural consequence of business, banking, transport, research etc. being carried on increasingly at a continental scale and Europeans thereby developing progressively an identity of their own, over-arching traditional identities as citizens of a country, a region or a city. The ongoing wave of mergers shows that business anticipates the creation of a true single European market as a consequence of EMU.

Three recent examples, taken at random, demonstrate how far European-wide rules are about to influence everyday life of European citizens.

The first concerns the guarantees that industrial and trading companies ought to offer consumers on defective products. Should the consumer have the option of repair or replacement, or also of price reduction or even a refund?

National legislation on consumer protection varies widely. That is why it was felt necessary to replace whatever national legislation by a uniform EU - wide code of conduct, in line with and as a corollary of the single European market.

Only 10 years ago legislation on such a sensitive subject would have been unimaginable.

The second example appears to be even more extraordinary. It concerns weekend restrictions on lorries in the EU. Presently such restrictions exist in seven EU member states, but they vary as to the duration of the bans. For hauliers, operating European-wide routes, this lack of harmonisation amounts to an extra costs of US$ 1.6 billion per year. That is the reason why the European Commission has submitted proposals, in March 1998, for a uniform ban between 7 a.m. and 10 p.m. on Sundays. It demonstrates how national governments are being restricted in their capacity to legislate within national boundaries. The single market and the increasing importance of bans on national traffic leave little choice but to go for European-wide legislation.

The third example shows how the national independence in taxation matters is being progressively undermined by the single market. When the British government, in early 1998, decided to raise the excise tax on beer, bringing it to a level about ten times higher than in neighbouring EU countries like Belgium or France, British brewers protested vehemently, not the least because of the certainty of escalating beer 'imports' from across the Channel, and decided to take the matter to the European Court as being incompatible with a proper functioning of the internal market.

It therefore seems as if we are heading towards a new 'balance of power' between European institutions and national governments. However national governments may try to resist, their importance as independent political actors is bound to shrink further, as the European regional system continues to develop. In the future, their role in that system will be three-fold:

· in some areas, e.g. cultural, social and educational matters, they will continue to enjoy a high degree of autonomy within their respective constitutional powers;

· in some areas for which European-wide action is required, for whatever reasons, they will be partners in European policy making and therefore attempt to influence such policies in accordance with their national interests;

· finally, they will have to play increasingly the role of implementing agencies of European legislation or policies.

It appears probable that the second and third functions will absorb more and more of national political and administrative energies. Implicitly this means that the EU will, very slowly, develop towards a refined system of checks and balances between two main levels of governments, the one European and the other national.

Such a system may be compared to the German type of federalism (as opposed to US federalism) where the two levels of government (Bund and Laender) are interlocked by a sophisticated relationship of mutual inter-action.

Europe will progressively develop its own type of 'federalism' which will leave in place, at least for a very long time to come, 'sovereign states', but whose power to act independently will become increasingly curtailed by the need for European-wide action.

Such need may stem from technical or economic constraints, as in the case of common rules for inter-state traffic (weights of trucks, working hours of drivers, weekend bans, speed limits, taxation etc.). Or it may arise as a follow-up to earlier legislation, e.g. that related to the single market or to the introduction of a single currency which is likely to spurn off a host of European-wide rules in fields like banking and banking supervision, taxation, accounting, prices, wages and even employment.

But in the end, it will be the transformation of 15 national economies into a single one of truly continental dimensions that will progressively erode national governments' power to act as 'sovereign' states. They will no longer be able to pursue environmental policies by way of national 'eco-taxes'; their power to impose high corporate income taxes will be restrained because of competitive pressures from other member states. A national immigration or asylum policy is virtually impossible in a Union without borders. they have no longer any real possibility to fight unemployment through large-scale deficit spending etc. There remains hardly any matter in the area of economic and social policies where member states can legislate or decide as independently and freely as they could fifty years ago.

In a nutshell, the European regional system is likely to lead towards a progressive shift of focus of national government action, coupled with a steady increase of political action at the European level, with all the problems of a more efficient decision making process that this will increasingly raise.

The End of Intra-European Military Conflicts?

As Europe moves towards the turn of the millennium, it has all reason to rejoice. The EU countries will have lived in peace with each other for half a century, the longest period ever in European history without any military conflict having take place or even threatened to do so. What an achievement after centuries of wars, the European countries have, finally, learned to resolve whatever tensions, disputes or conflicts through peaceful means, by negotiations, diplomacy and compromise. A rule of law has replaced the rule of power and force in European affairs. The vast majority of today's population in Europe has never experienced any war, peace is being accepted as something normal to be almost taken for granted. No less than peace within the USA has become a matter of course.

Europe owes this wonderful state of affairs both to the EU and, though less and less, to NATO.

The existence of the EU for more than 40 years has profoundly changed our notions of national territory and national borders.

When citizens can peacefully and legally acquire any piece of land they want in any neighbouring country, there is no plausible reason to go to war in order to achieve territorial gains. When citizens can cross national borders without any controls and without even becoming aware, borders have lost their meaning. Similarly, the pursuit of national interest within the EU context has become quite a different operation from what it used to be in the traditional European diplomatic environment. It may mean using EU power against third countries, getting amendments passed on European legislation, or minimising contributions to the EU budget etc. Under no circumstances does national interest still aim at enlarging national territory, borders have become inviolable.

Similarly, the relations among the political classes of member countries have undergone a seachange. Whatever national interest they may have to defend at the European negotiation tables, they remain conscious of a common and often over-riding European interest. They know too well that whatever benefits one member country is also in the interest of all the others. There is thus an increasing sharing of interest as part of an emerging European identity.

Equally important, the traditional threat perceptions that have haunted European nations for centuries have ceased to exist. Belgium no longer feels threatened by a possible invasion from German or French armies, and the chiefs of staff of whatever national army have stopped preparing contingency plans for intra-EU military conflicts. Instead, they think about how to create and to make European brigades, composed of forces from different European countries, to effectively work together in possible international actions.

Within Europe, wars have lost their sense. They have become inconceivable, at least as far as the EU territory is concerned. In a dual meaning, from the point of view of their *finalite* and their technical means. What should Britain go to war for against say Germany? And how should such an imaginary war be fought technically, when it is no longer possible to mobilise 'national' resources against one's neighbours, when each of them is inextricably linked to the other by joint electricity grids, gas pipelines, banks, steel plants and, above all, joint defence industries.

Of course, one may think the unthinkable and imagine another 'Hitler' or 'Mussolini' seizing power in one of the bigger member states on an outrageously nationalistic platform and setting out to 'conquer' the rest of the continent as its 'supreme leader'.

But how far could such a maniac really seize political and military power in a totally transparent Europe where any political moves are closely monitored by the elites, the media and business throughout the continent and where the political sensitivity has been sharpened to the extreme. Not very far, it seems. Any such scenario therefore seems totally unrealistic.

Nato comes in as a reinforcing factor, both by its impact on the thinking of the military class within EU countries and, even more important, by having provided a shield of protection against external threats, i.e. from the Soviet Union, which otherwise might have impaired the peaceful process of European integration. Still, the recurring crises between two of its peripheral members, Turkey and Greece, escalating up to the brink of military confrontation demonstrate that Nato on its own may not be 100% able to ban military conflicts between its members.

But jointly, EU and NATO constitute undoubtedly the best possible safeguards against any military temptation among their members. As long as they remain in place as strong and healthy institutions it appears safe to rule out war within the EU.

Where Will the Outer Limit Be to the EU?

Since its start in 1951, with six member countries, limiting their cooperation to coal and steel, the European regional system has always been open-ended as to its geographical area.

This flexibility has served Europe well and it ought to be maintained as long as possible.

Geographical enlargement has taken place pragmatically, in stages, normally taking in groups of countries that were linked among themselves by geography or treaties: 1973 the first three EFTA members Denmark, Ireland, United Kingdom; 1981 Greece; 1986 the Iberian peninsula; 1996 the second group of EFTA members Austria, Finland, Sweden.

After the fall of the Iron Curtain in November 1989 it became clear that Central Eastern Europe would rapidly wish to join the European regional system. By early 1998 the enlargement process with the 10 countries of Central and Eastern Europe as well as with Cyprus had actively started and whatever the gigantic problems of absorption for the EU (funding, reforming of policies and institutions) and of adjustment for the newcomers (market economy, adopting EU legislation and policies), it seems quite safe to assume that by 2010 the number of EU member countries will have further increased to 26 countries with a population of roughly 500 million people, i.e. more than Russia and the USA combined and almost half of China.

Will the process of successive enlargements have come to an end by around 2010?

That is very unlikely. Indeed, the EU will be left with two

categories of European countries situated within the European regional system and closely inter-linked by various agreements, reaching from membership in the European Economic Area (Norway, Iceland, Liechtenstein) to free trade (Switzerland) and cooperation agreements (Balkan countries).

First, the remaining four EFTA member countries (Iceland, Liechtenstein, Norway and Switzerland) definitely remain possible candidates for future accession to the EU. They are so closely interwoven with the EU as to be considered quasi-members. But though they have to align on much of EU legislation and policies with only a limited say on them, their populations have so far resisted all attempts by their political elites to bring them fully into the EU system (e.g. two failed referenda in Norway on accession and one failed referendum in Switzerland on joining the European Economic Area).

How likely is it that this situation is going to change in any foreseeable future?

That will depend very much on how the Union's image will evolve in the next decade and on the 'political cost' for any European state to stay outside the European mainstream. Before 2010 their accession does not appear very likely, the more so as the EU will not do much canvassing for their membership. Switzerland and Liechtenstein appear somewhat more prone for accession than the two peripheral countries in the high north, with their special conditions and interests (oil, gas, fishing, mountain agriculture). But in the longer term all the four countries are likely to accede to the EU whose attraction will simply become too strong for any European country to be resisted.

Second, the countries of the Balkans (Albania, Bosnia, Croatia, Macedonia and Yugoslavia) will no less want to become part of the EU, as soon as they are able to fulfil the stringent political, economic and administrative conditions for membership. They are no doubt eligible for membership, but their integration into the European mainstream will prove very difficult in view of their history, their old-fashioned nationalism, as well as their lack of democratic tradition. Presently, none of these countries appear mature enough to join the EU in any foreseeable future, none being able to live up to the triple conditionality set for membership in Copenhagen (1993), i.e. respect of democracy and human rights, market economy and ability to adopt and implement past and future EU legislation.

But things will change, even in the Balkans. What appears excluded today, may become quite feasible 10-15 years down the road. What is essential, is to keep the option of membership open for these countries, even if it is too early to put the issue on the political agenda. Indeed, during the coming decade the EU must not be diverted from its overriding priority to digest the absorption of some 100 million people from Central and Eastern Europe.

But what about the EU's neighbours farther east, i.e. Turkey, Russia, Ukraine, Belorussia and Moldavia (not to speak about the Caucasian Republics)? Is there any chance of seeing these countries, even some of them, joining the Union within the next 20 years, or even beyond?

Among these, Turkey possesses the best credentials, by far. As early as 1964 it put its foot into the EU door and even possesses a certain legal claim, through the Association Agreement which expressly opens an accession perspective. Since that time, however, Turkey and the EU have been moving away from each other rather than coming closer, except in the economic field where the customs union has been completed, finally, in 1996.

Thus, the EU position on Turkish membership has become increasingly ambiguous, not to say hostile. The changing nature of the EU which has become immensely more 'political' than it had been in the early 60s has raised increasing doubts on whether Turkey, looked at as a whole and not just its more western parts, is really sufficiently European and 'Western' in its thinking and its value system to fit harmoniously into the EU family. In addition, major concerns are being expressed as to the possibility for the EU to absorb a relative giant country with a projected population of some 85 million in 2025 (Germany has 80 million), with all the problems that this raises, from immigration to financial burden and voting powers. All these considerations make the case for Turkish membership less attractive than 30 years ago, at the height of the Cold War and with an infinitely less complex EU.

It therefore seems wise to keep the Turkish case on hold, leaving both sides with the options open. In any event, accession is clearly ruled out before 2010 when the Union will have successfully absorbed the 10 Central and Eastern European candidates as well as Cyprus.

Is there any chance or hope, even in the wildest dreams, to imagine Russia, Ukraine, Belorussia or Moldavia as future EU members?

The Russian Prime Minister Chernomyrdin has, during a visit to Brussels in 1997, voiced such hopes, and shortly afterwards politically influential circles in Kiev have echoed these. But in the very same year President Yeltsin skilfully manoeuvred Russia into the world's biggest regional grouping, the Asian and Pacific Economic Community (APEC), that is set to establish an immense Asian-Pacific free trade area by 2020.

On the EU side, no political personality has so far dared to evoke publicly even the hypothesis of any EU enlargement beyond the borders of Finland, the Baltic states, Poland, Slovakia and Romania. There are very good reasons for such prudence. Imagine for a moment that the EU were to extend its rules for transport, environment, structural policy consumer protection, company law etc. to a vast, sparsely populated country, five times the size of the future 'EU 26', stretching to the shores of the Pacific Ocean, composed of dozens of nationalities with different languages and cultures, and one will immediately come to the conclusion that the EU would become totally unmanageable and cease to be a single legal and political area.

It therefore seems safe to assume, that the ongoing enlargement process will also fix the EU's eastern borders, for at least the next 20 years to come.

From a Regional to a Global Power?

During the past 40 years the EU has consistently had privileged relations with its immediate neighbours, i.e. the EFTA countries, until their progressive accession to the EU, the Mediterranean countries and, especially since 1989, the countries of Central and Eastern Europe, including the Balkans.

This emphasis on geographical neighbourhood stemmed from the simple desire to establish an optimum of peace, stability and prosperity in its 'backyard'. As a means to those ends, the EU has, in particular, facilitated trade relations through various types of free trade agreements.

This good neighbourhood policy has served both the EU and its neighbours very well, indeed. But with the progressive absorption of its traditional neighbours the question arises: what sort of relationship will the European-wide Union wish to establish in the future with the new set of neighbours in the east and south, but also with the USA as the close neighbour across the Atlantic, who are not able or likely to join the EU in a foreseeable future?

Does the traditional neighbourhood policy still make sense for the bigger Union? Will the EU, with its future status as one of the two leading economic and financial blocs in the world, not have to become much more global in its policy stance? Will it not have to shoulder, alongside the USA, much more global responsibilities?

To put it more sharply, will the EU, after having achieved its internal consolidation and defined its outer boundaries some time around 2020, not feel free to finally play once again a role as a world power, that some of its member states have played for most of the last 500 years of world history? And will geographical proximity continue to be an important factor of close relations, when human beings will increasingly communicate at extremely low costs through electronic media, via satellites?

It is likely that the future Europe will be forced to involve itself in world affairs with an intensity that few observers dare to envisage today. The next century will be marked by world-wide inter-action, with a few regional powers leading the show. In such a world it will be very hard to believe that the EU will content itself with the status of a 'regional power' that Henry Kissinger was generous to confer upon the Union in the early 80s when both the world and Europe were still divided by all sorts of fault lines. Indeed, as Europe moves towards an entity that will look more and more like one big country, with one currency, and EU citizenship parallel to the national ones, no internal borders, common ground - rules for most business activities, English as the *lingua franca*, EU - wide fight against criminality, drugs, EU - wide open university systems, free movement of people etc., EU external policy will increasingly concentrate on world affairs and relations with the other big actors in the emerging global system of world governance.

In such a world, the Euro-Mediterranean partnership concept, hailed in the early 90s as a major geopolitical factor, is likely to shrink to more reduced dimensions. Of course, Europe will have to continue to keep a close eye on what will go on in the Mediterranean, if only to prevent whatever turbulence from swapping over into its territory. Of course, some of the Mediterranean countries will continue to be important as providers of fossil and progressively solar energy. But at a world scale the relative importance of the Maghreb and Mashrek countries with their population of no more than 300 million people is bound to shrink, and Europe may therefore not be able to devote to them the same amount of energy as in the past.

Similarly, Russia should be seen less as a neighbour in the traditional sense, if only because of its sheer size. Rather it has to be understood as one of the key players in the future world system, linked very closely economically and politically to both Europe and the USA.

If one looks carefully, one is able to discern the first signs of the EU' s reach for a more global profile in today's external policies. The ASEM meetings, bringing together the heads of government of the 15 member states with those of the 10 major East-Asian countries; the EU' s active involvement in the WTO; its role in the G 8 Summit meetings; its search for a balanced partnership with both the USA and Russia, all these efforts can be interpreted as forebodings of the role the EU may be capable of playing at the global level when it will have established sufficient strength and coherence within Europe.

Will an Even Bigger EU Still Be Manageable?

Whatever the admirable capacity of the EU to adapt its institutional system, originally devised for only six member states, to ever-changing challenges and increasing membership, there are built-in limits to the adjustment capabilities of any social system.

Will the quantum leap form 15 to 26 members constitute such a strain that the European regional system will either collapse or undergo profound qualitative changes?

Nobody in a sensible mood anticipates the system's collapse. Otherwise the decision to enlarge would be suicidal, indeed. So the question is only what sort of qualitative change the EU will have to undergo when it absorbs 11 very poor countries which have been cut off from the European mainstream for half a century. Will the increasing economic, cultural, linguistic, political and even geographic heterogeneity of its members induce the EU to push for less EU-wide regulations and policies? In line with the principle of subsidiarity enshrined in the Maastricht Treaty? How profoundly will it have to revamp its institutional set-up in order to adopt EU-wide policies, corresponding to an overall European interest, without endless haggling?

Thinking on these vital issues for the future development of the EU as an efficient political entity is at a very preliminary stage.

One school of thought envisages a crisis scenario, seeing the Union diluted into a sort of loose free-trade association, lacking political punch and direction, unless the Treaty is radically amended and decision making procedures revamped.

The other school is much less horrified by the prospect of a Union with some 25 members or even 35, in due time. It puts more trust in Europe's capacity to always find practical solutions when it has to.

Of course, the enlarged EU will no longer resemble the 'EU 15', let alone the 'EU 6'. Priorities, working methods, working languages, political 'alliances' will have to change. The game will be different, the EU will become a new 'melting pot'. The relation between European Institutions and member states will undergo major changes. There will be more, but different haggling on budget allocations, appointments, environmental issues, agricultural issues etc., with new combinations of interest.

But the machinery will not come to a grinding halt. It may become more cumbersome, with 25 national parliaments to ratify certain, hopefully less, EU acts, or to transpose European legislation into national law, to work with more than 20 official languages etc. However, the machinery will still be able to adopt legislation and policies, the more so as most of the decisions within the EU are already being taken by majority voting, in a very expeditious way.

However, four major changes are required in order to make the system more effective and better adapted to 25 - 35 members.

First, the practice of co-decision among Council and Parliament has to be extended to all legislative acts. The EU has to evolve towards a bicameral system, e.g. comparable to the German one.

Second, the number of areas where decisions require unanimity among member states should be progressively reduced and eventually abolished. Qualified majority voting has to become the accepted rule, also for such highly sensitive fields as taxation, budget ceilings, treaty amendments or enlargements. Otherwise the EU is liable to becoming hostage to the sometimes eccentric political views of one or two, even very small, member states. In a Union with 25 to 35 members it becomes less convincing for individual member states to claim that 'vital' interests are at stake when the vast majority of member states can agree on a certain policy line.

Third, in the European Parliament the over-representation of the smaller member states must come to an end, maybe with minor derogations for tiny states like Cyprus or Luxembourg. Deputies must represent an equal number of voters, say 700 000, whether they are elected in Germany or in Denmark.

If this is achieved, the voting powers in the second chamber, the Council, may continue to contain a certain bias in favour of the smaller member countries, though somewhat less than at present.

Fourth, the members of the European executive, i.e. the Commission, should no longer be designated by the governments of member states but by the European Parliament. It must reflect the views and the strengths of the political parties represented in the European Parliament. A first but important step in this direction has been undertaken by the Amsterdam Treaty: the appointment of the Commission President is subject to approval by the Parliament.

These four institutional changes will constitute the basic menu for the European state system to become sufficiently flexible to cope with any number of member countries. They offer reasonable guarantees for efficient decision making, while preventing the EU from turning into a super-state. The political power play will become different from the past when Commission and Parliament, the two underdogs of the system, had to fight jointly for more powers against member states in the Council. With a Commission fully accountable to the Parliament, it may find itself more often at odds with a united front composed of Council and Parliament, especially if it were to try to enhance its own standing at the expense of the combined legislative.

In a much more heterogeneous EU, the Commission will have to restrain its temptation to introduce more and more European - wide rules. A Union with more than 20 members will have to learn how to harmoniously flourish with a minimum of government intervention and legislative rules from whatever source. It should accept guidance from the American federal system which leaves major regulatory powers to the individual states and relies more on market forces and competition between the states instead of excessive federal intervention. More than ever Brussels must in the future be guided by the simple rule: the less EU-wide regulation the better for all concerned.

EU institutions should concentrate their energy on three main priorities, i.e. to:

· formulate and defend European interests on the international scene. External relations, including security policy, will progressively have to become a European-wide concern otherwise Europe will never be able to play an international role commensurate with its combined economic and political power;

· assure a harmonious economic development which requires guidance in the macro-economic field, from budgets, to currency, exchange rates and employment as well as a constant monitoring of functioning EU-wide competition;

· but beyond these two conventional tasks EU institutions will have to initiate, much more than in the past, European-wide debates on the issues that are likely to confront Europe, and even the world, in the next century, from demography, to educational systems, social security, water, renewable energy, global food supply etc. European public opinion must be prepared for such and other issues that are likely to have an impact on our future way of life and that may require painful adjustments by society.

Conclusions

Three major conclusions may be drawn from the preceding analysis:

First, the EU is in the process of turning itself into a state-like entity. This is much more visible internally than externally. Internally the importance of EU-wide policies is bound to grow further. The introduction of a single currency for the entire EU as of 2002 will undoubtedly lead to a leap forward on the road towards harmonisation of legislation and a substantial melting of national interests, at least in the economic field. The EU will understand itself more and more as one single space of law and internal security, where military conflict between member states is virtually ruled out.

Second, on the external front the process will move more slowly. No rapid breakthrough towards a common foreign and security policy (CFSP) should be expected, as long as member states prefer to cling to their conservative foreign policy machines which will remain the last bastions of pseudo-sovereignty. But even these will be dismantled progressively, as the process of internal cohesion and the withering of national interests will gather momentum. The process will be further fuelled by the increasing impossibility to defend national interests outside the EU framework.

Third, for the coming two decades, EU foreign policy will remain focused on completing the enlargement process. This will be the single most important challenge. Only when essentially all European countries have joined the EU and when it will thus have become synonymous with Europe, will the EU finally have no choice but to seriously address issues of global nature and to undertake the necessary institutional changes to that end.

Europe will, however, most likely not have another grace period of 20 years during which to prepare for its future leadership in the world. Whether it likes it or not, the EU will have to assume much more international responsibility long before its complex process of enlargement will finally have come to an end, starting with the international spin-off of the EMU during the very first years of the next century.

3. The 'Nordic Model of Regionalism'

Bjørn Møller

'Norden' (tentatively defined as the region or subregion consisting of Denmark, Norway, Sweden and Finland) is, or at least was, special. Its high geostrategic importance notwithstanding, the Nordic countries throughout the Cold War managed to keep the level of tension in their part of the world manageable. Thereby they not only improved their own security situation, but also made a significant contribution to international détente.

The following pages analyze what was special of the region (if so it was) against the background of a preliminary analysis of regions and regionness. As a conclusion a number of 'lessons' are drawn from the Nordic experience that might presumably have a certain (at least heuristic) value for other parts of the world.

I. Regions and Subregions

1. Regions and Regionness

A region is a subset of the international system. However, the delimitation of such a subset is always a problem, if only because several criteria might be applied, each yielding a different result. None of them is, of course, more 'correct' than the others:[1]

The most obvious criterion of 'regionness' is that of geographical proximity, as a region is usually held to consist of contiguous states. This does, however, beg the question of where to draw the outer limit, unless there happen to be clear natural boundaries (such as oceans). Also, in the world of international relations 'proximity' is not so much a matter of distance as a function of topography, infrastructure and technology. What used to be insurmountable barriers may, for example, cease to be so as a result of a technological breakthrough. In some cases water divides, while in others it unites as has always been the case of the Baltic Sea. In comparison, 'difficult country' (such as mountains, deserts or forests) tends to divide.[2]

An alternative criterion of delimitation is the geographical distance from a centre. A region may thus be understood as a set of concentric circles.[3] This does, however, presuppose that there is a centre which is obvious as such to everybody, but this may be politically very controversial. Indeed, it is quite conceivable that there is not one, but several such centres. There is no *a priori* reason why the financial, economic, political, cultural, and religious centres of a region should be identical.[4] Rather than forming concentric circles, some regions may thus have a 'variable geometry' as has always been the case for Norden and the Baltic Sea region.

A variation on this theme is the notion that regions are analogous with 'empires' or 'suzerain' systems that have a centre, but where this suzerainty is based on tacit consent and 'fades out' gradually. An empire (region) in this sense thus has no outer limit, and it may overlap with other empires (regions).[5]

To the extent that one is interested in environmental issues (including 'environmental security'), the notion of ecosystem (characterized, e.g., by shared rivers and/or other sources of water supplies, etc.) may be the appropriate delimitation criterion, as is, at least in some respects, the case of the Baltic Sea region.[6]

A convenient political or legal criterion of delimitation might be membership of institutions defined as 'regional', e.g. by the UN.[7] However, in most parts of the world the density of institutions is much lower than in Europe. Furthermore, even in this most thoroughly institutionalized part of the world no institutions are all-inclusive.[8]

A 'softer' criterion is that of cultural affinity. This is, indeed, the distinguishing feature of the nine 'civilizations' (almost synonymous with regions), between some of which Samuel Huntington foresees a clash.[9] However, cultural homogeneity is usually greater seen from the outside (where it is viewed as 'otherness') than from the inside.[10] Furthermore, 'culture' has many aspects (e.g. religious, ideological, and ethnic) which do not automatically yield the same delimitation.

Related to this notion of cultural community is that of regions as 'imagined communities', in analogy with nations. Like the latter they may be constituted by the members 'imagining' themselves as belonging together, and the rest of the world acknowledging them as such, regardless of whether either has any 'objective' foundation.[11] In some parts of the world, however, a prevailing cosmopolitian orientation may cast doubt on such 'attitudinal regionness'. Indeed, one might argue that this will be the inevitable consequence of globalization and 'de-territorialization'. It may simply no longer be true that people's emotional affinities are inversely correlated with physical distance, because of the 'CNN effect'. There may also be discrepancies between how countries identify themselves, and how they are viewed by others. Greenland, for instance, presumably sees itself as part of Norden, but is reckoned as part of the Americas by the United States.

Regions might also be identified as such by a greater-than-average intensity of trade and/or other forms of economic interaction. This would, however, lead to a disregard of not only rather autharchic states, but also of states that produce mostly for the world market, i.e. which are not economically oriented towards any region.

2. Security Complexes

Finally, regions might be defined by an above-average intensity of security political and military interaction either benign, as in alliances or regional collective security systems, or malign, as in arms races or wars. Barry Buzan has suggested the term 'security complex' for such a region, defined as 'a group of states whose primary security concerns link together sufficiently closely that their national securities cannot realistically be considered apart from one another'.[12]

I shall take this latter criterion as my point of departure as it has the merit of singling out that particular aspect of interaction with which I am concerned on this occasion. It does, however, have three odd implications, and seems untenable in one respect: It presupposes a rather narrow concept of security,[13] as an expansion to include, for instance, 'environmental security' would make the edges of security complexes too blurred to be useful.

'Security communities' (between the members of which war has ceased to be regarded as a possibility, and where the attitude to military matters is one of benign neglect) cannot count as security complexes even though a security community is usually seen as the starting point for regional integration.[14]

In some parts of the world states may be so preoccupied with domestic ('security') matters, and have so insignificant power projection capabilities that states can constititute neither friends nor enemies to each other. Parts of Africa surely fall into this 'security complex-free' category.[15]

It makes little sense to draw (as Barry Buzan does) fixed borders between security complexes so as to rule out overlap and prevent states from being reckoned as parts of more than one security complex. This presupposes defining those states that seemingly transcend these borders (the United States, Russia, Turkey, and China, for instance) as 'buffers', where the term 'transmission cords' seems a much more appropriate metaphor.

By implication, it may have to be acknowledged that the borders of a security complex may be variable, depending on which issues are 'securitized'.[16] This may differ from region to region as well as over time. For instance, should the environment or the question of migration be securitized, some states may become parties to a security complex, while others may drop out of the picture if other issues are simultaneously 'desecuritized'. The latter may not happen automatically as there is no fixed limit for the number of securitized issues. On the other hand, as the security agenda cannot be boundless, some issues will eventually drop off it.

3.   Regions and Subregions

We have thus seen that the very concept of 'region' is not as clear as one might wish. Unfortunately the distinction between regions and subregions is not much clearer. Buzan, Wæver and de Wilde suggest defining a subregion as 'part of such a region [in its turn defined as 'a spatially coherent territory composed of two or more states'], whether it involves more than one state (but fewer than all of the states in the region) or some transnational composition (some mix of states, parts of states, or both)'.[17]

For all its merits, this taxonomy leaves open for further analysis the question of delimitation, e.g. whether something should count as a region or a subregion. For example, if Eurasia is counted as a region, Europe becomes a subregion and Norden a sub-subregion. If Europe is granted status as a region, Norden becomes a subregion. Neither alternative is more correct than the other, and their usefulness will depend on the context. We may thus end up with a very flexible categorization such as the following:

- a region is part of a whole, *in casu* the world;
- a subregion is part of a part of a whole, *in casu* a region;
- a sub-subregion is part of a part of a part of a whole, *in casu* a subregion
- etc. *ad infinitum,* or rather: to the level of disaggregation required by the analysis in question.

4. (Sub)Regional Structure

When trying to understand a particular (sub)region or security complex, the following (interrelated) questions immediately spring to mind, to which I shall venture some very tentative answers for the Nordic (sub)region in the following:

Definition, Designation and Delimitation
- Is the region well-defined or is its delimitation controversial?
- What are its defining criteria?
- Which states belong to it?
- Which other states are relevant to its internal dynamics?
- Is it internally homogeneous or heterogenous, and in which respects?

Structure, Dominant Strategies and Patterns of Interaction
- What is its structure: hierarchical or anarchical?
- Is it unipolar, bipolar, or multipolar?
- What is the level and nature of external 'penetration' or 'overlay'?[18]
- What is the degree and character of institutionalization?
- Is it a 'raw' or 'mature' anarchy, i.e. a conflict formation, an international society, a security regime or a security community?[19]
- What is the level of securitization and militarization?
- What are the dominant security strategies of its constituent parts?

II.   Norden During the Cold War

1.   *Definition, Designation and Delimitation*

Not only is it debatable whether Norden is a region, a subregion or a sub-subregion, both its proper name and its delimitation are, likewise, in dispute. The following table compares different conceptions of the Nordic and related, possibly overlapping, of region and subregions.

'Scandinavia' is the geographical notion which, stictly speaking, only includes the three states on the peninsula. However, it is often taken to also include Denmark, in which case it is synonymous with 'Norden'. 'Norden' also comes in several versions: as a minimum it includes Norway, Sweden, Finland and Denmark without their 'externalities', i.e. the Danish former colonies Greenland and the Faeroe Islands and without Svalbard/Spitsbergen, which is under Norwegian suzerainty, but circumscribed by a special arrangement with the USSR/Russia as are the Aaland Islands in the Baltic Sea.[20]

These externalities as well as Iceland are, of course, included in the more maximalist versions of Norden, but this implies an overlap between regions, as Greenland is reckoned by the United States as belonging to the Americas, hence also as falling under the 1823 Monroe Doctrine.[21] Finally, we have the term 'Northern Europe', including all of the above (with the occsional exception of Greenland).

To the extent that there was talk about Baltic regionalism (e.g. on the part of the GDR with its *Ostseewochen*), it was intended as ways of circumventing the block divisions, but this discourse was not really taken seriously in most other contexts. NATO was, for instance, concerned about presumed Soviet attempts to make the Baltic Sea a *mare nostrum*.[22] Since the end of the Cold War, however, Baltic Sea regionalism has flourished, however, almost to the point of replacing the image of Norden with that of a larger Baltic-Nordic community (*vide infra*).

There was also some talk of an Arctic region, reflecting two different trends. First of all, the growing geostrategic importance of the area produced by the spread of the 'tentacles' of the nuclear deterrence system (the BMEWS system on Greenland, for instance),[23] the growth of the Soviet Northern Fleet (homebased in Murmansk by the Barents Sea) and the US countermeasures planned for under the Maritime Strategy (*vide infra*). Secondly, the new assertiveness of the

DESIGNATION	COMPOSITION
'Scandinavia'	N, S, F
'Norden' (min.)	N (excl. SB), S, F (incl. AL), D (excl. Gr and FI)
'Norden' (max):	N (incl. SB), S, F, D (incl. G and FI), I
'Northern Europe'	N (incl. SB), S, F, D (incl. Gr and FI), I, (parts of) G, R
'Balticum'	D, S, F, (parts of) G, P, (parts of) R, Li, La, E
'Nordic/Baltic Subregion'	D, N, S, F, G, P, R, E, La, Li
'Arctic Subregion'	N, S, F, G, C, U, R

Legend: AL: Aaland Islands; C: Canada; E: Estonia; D: Denmark; F: Finland; FI: Faeroe Island; G: Germany; Gr: Greenland; I: Iceland; N: Norway; S: Sweden; SB: Svalbard; La: Latvia; Li: Lithuania; R: Russia; P: Poland; U: United States

indigenous people, manifested in the Innuit Circumpolar Conference.[24]

The very fact that the delimitation of the region(s) has been controversial reflects an important structural feature of Norden, namely its openendedness. There has of course been a 'core group' that has been regarded as being part of the region in any case, comprising Norway, Sweden, Finland and Denmark. Besides that, however, affiliations have been issue-dependent and/or the subject of political controversy. The core group has partly been identified as such through shared history, cultural and linguistic affinity, but even here there have been elements of 'variable geometry', as Finland does not belong to the same language group as the rest. One might thus question to what extent a Nordic identity has really been a fact, as well as to which extent this identity has overruled other, competing identities such as a European (for Denmark), a Baltic (for Finland and partly Sweden), an Arctic (for Greenland and parts of Norway, Sweden and Finland).[25]

In the following I shall concentrate on this core group, for which I shall reserve the term 'Norden', treating all the rest as externalities.

2.   *Structural Features and Dominant Strategies*

A remarkable feature of Norden has been its peculiar form of institutionalization, which one might label 'hi/low institutionalization': very high in low-politics fields (culture, for instance), but remarkably low in high-politics fields such as security politics. Hence, for instance, the failure of the post-war attempts at forging a Nordic defence community.[26] Since the demise of the Kalmar Union in the 14th century, there has thus never been any semblance of supranationality.[27] The highest political institiutions are the Nordic Council and the Nordic Council of Minsters, none of which amount to supranationality, hence Norden is, strictly speaking, distinctly anarchical.

   In comparison with other international anarchies, however, that of Norden has been exceptionally peaceful and orderly. First of all, even though it may appear self-evident today, it deserves underlining that Norden has been a security community for a very long time, perhaps since the Napoleonic wars. Since that time, none of the Nordic states have really taken the theoretical possibility of war with any of the others seriously, as they did in the past various unsettled territorial disputes notwithstanding.[28] Hence there has not only been a significant absence of war, but also of preparations for such intra-regional war, and an arms race between the Nordic countries has long been inconceivable. This 'significant insignificance' of military matters (which have thus become, probably irreversibly, 'desecuritized') is part of the explanation for the modest degree of militarization in all the Nordic countries throughout the Cold War period.

   Secondly, Norden was also a security regime, i.e. one where all actors (intra-regional as well as external) showed significant restraint in the expactation of reciprocal constraint by the others, thereby mitigating the security dilemma.[29] Non-provocation was thus an important theme in the security policies of all Nordic countries.[30]

   • No nuclear weapons were deployed in any of the Nordic countries (except, it turns out, in Greenland), which was remarkable considering the number of nuclear weapons deployed, for instance, in Germany.[31]

   • No foreign troops were permanently stationed here, except for Iceland and Greenland, which was equally exceptional, considering the strategic importance of Denmark and Norway.[32]

   • The military activities involving the Nordic countries were usually somewhat less offensive in their orientation than elsewhere, the more so the closer to the Soviet Union.[33] For instance, Denmark generally banned NATO military activities from Bornholm,[34] and Norway kept a low and distinctly defensive military profile in the northern parts of the country, bordering on the USSR.

- Finland, on the other hand, avoided whatever might be construed as 'anti-Soviet behaviour'.[35]

Not only were these instances of restraint generally accepted by both East and West, there was also little pressure on the Nordic NATO countries to increase their defence expenditures. Hence the rather low level of military spending as a percentage of GDP and the remarkable lack of correlation with the international climate.[36]

As a result, Norden was much less influenced by the ups and downs in East-West relations, even though its geopolitical and geostrategic importance remained very high. The term 'overlay' thus does not really seem appropriate, as it was never allowed to influence (sub-)region-internal relations.

There were, to be sure, challenges to this low tension regime:

- The Soviet naval build-up in adjoining areas through the 1970s and 1980s, when the USSR sought to become a fully-fledged sea power and had few other places to home-base its navies than the Barents Sea;[37]
- The more assertive reinforcement policy of NATO since the late 1970s, spurred *inter alia*, by the belief that wartime reinforcements via the transatlantic Sea Lines of Communications could be intercepted by Soviet attack submarines, hence that reinforcement in times of crisis was indispensable;[38]
- The Maritime Strategy of the Reagan administration, which envisaged (among other, less innocent, objectives) a protection of the above SLOCs by means of threats to the home base of the Soviet Northern Fleet, concretely entailing plans to go into the Barents Sea with nuclear submarines and even aircraft carriers, the defence against which would tie up the Soviet attack submarines;[39]
- The submarine incidents in the Swedish archipelago, which could be seen as rehearsals of Soviet counter-moves to the Maritime Strategy.[40]

All of the above developments threatened to make military tension in Norden commensurate with its geostrategic importance.[41]

However, none of these challenges resulted in an overturn of the low tension regime. According to some analyses, a means to this end was the so-called 'Nordic Balance'.[42] It has been aptly described as 'a balance of unused options' or of potential next steps, in which sense it was more akin to a balance of terror (conceived as a form of diplomacy) than one of power.[43] Indeed, the region-internal balance of power was close to irrelevant, hence none of the usual labels (unipolar, bipolar, multipolar) seems appropriate. The main 'ingredients' of the Nordic balance were:

- Denmark's and Norway's NATO membership, which amounted to less than a total commitment, not merely because of the above-mentioned deployment constraints, but also manifested in reservations about NATO strategy in general and nuclear strategy in particular (viz the so-called 'footnote policy' pursued by Denmark in the first half of the 1980s).[44]

- Sweden's policy of non-alignment, pointing towards neutrality in war, which made it the 'hinge' of the 'balancing act'. It was never interpreted as ruling out some military cooperation with the West, but neither did it preclude an activist critique of the United States, e.g. over the Vietnam War. Militarily it was expressed in a strategy of combined forward and in-depth defence, based on the assumption that Sweden would, at most, be a secondary target in an East-West war.[45]

- Finland's neutrality, which was defined in the Paris Treaty, and which had a slight inclination towards the East, mandated by the FCMA (Friendship, Cooperation and Mutual Assistance) Treaty with the USSR. More significantly, however, Finland remained a Western country, in spite of its having sided (for very good reasons, to be sure) with Germany during WWII. What is noteworthy about 'Finlandization' was thus not so much the Eastern bias, but the fact that Finland escaped the fate of the countries of Eastern Europe.[46]

The above could also be depicted as a set of inter-related restraints, each of which represented a voluntary, but conditional, concession to the respective adversary that might be reconsidered in case of perceived non-compliance with the unwritten rules:[47]

- restraint on the part of Denmark and Norway with regard to nuclear weapons and foreign military bases, as well as military activities, intended to reduce the threat to the Soviet bloc;

- restraint on the part of NATO (especially the US and UK) providing full security guarantees, but adopting a less offensive

posture than would have been adopted elsewhere;
- restraint on the part of Finland, committed to prevent an attack against the USSR from or via Finland by 'Germany or its allies';
- restraint on the part of the Soviet Union and the Warsaw Pact which neither sought to enrol Finland in the Warsaw Pact nor made use of the 'mutual consultantation and possible common steps' clause in the FCMA Treaty with Finland;
- restraint on the part of Sweden which remained in a swing position, wisely avoiding to lean too much (or too irreversibly) to either side, and which flirted with, but eventually abandoned, a nuclear option.[48]

Conceived as a normative concept, presumably guiding policy-makers, this Nordic Balance remained latent during most of its (presumed) existence. Only once was it allowed to more manifestly demonstrate its utility as a political tool for crisis management, namely during the 1961 'Note Crisis'. However, the absence of manifest applications during the remainder of the period cannot be taken as evidence of the concept's invalidity, since it has precisely been the purpose of the balance to prevent such crisis situations from emerging.

Such a conception, of course, inevitably presents the analyst with serious methodological problems, since the causality of non-events is an extremely elusive matter. I shall not pretend to be able to devise a method by means of which the hypothesis might be tested that the concept has in actual fact played a significant role in the deliberations of decision-makers. Neither do the underlying assumptions, however, appear to have been refuted by actual events, and we are hence left with arguments of intrinsic plausibility. Be that as it may, as a explanatory (or at least heuristic) device, the concept of the Nordic Balance seems able to put some order into the complex matter of Nordic security policies.

One might even see the discourse on the establishment of a Nordic nuclear weapons-free zone as a manifestation of the balance.[49] By some of its proponents, it was seen as a defensive move to stabilize a balance that was jeopardized by developments beyond the control of the Nordic countries (*vide supra*), by some critics it was charged with tilting the precarious balance in the East's favour.

3.   *The Post-Cold War Setting*

With the end of the Cold War, both the internal preferences and the context of Nordic security policies have changed quite dramatically. As the topic of the present paper is the situation during the Cold War, I shall limit myself to briefly enumerating some of these changes.

With the dissolution of the Warsaw Pact and subsequently the USSR itself, the entire Cold War edifice crumbled. Probably in an attempt to reap the fruits of the new détente, the Finnish government on 21 September 1990 unilaterally declared the Paris treaty 'obsolete', with reference to the developments in Germany. In a simultaneous declaration, President Mauno Koivisto also declared the FCMA treaty obsolete, whilst acknowledging the continued validity of its objectives. Nobody, not even the Soviet Union, seemed to take any notice of this peculiar instance of small-power unilateralism.[50]

Moreover, along with bipolarity went the foundations for neutrality which has become close to a meaningless concept, at least in the political versions represented by Sweden and Finland.[51] Both Finland and Sweden felt less constrained in their rapprochement with the West. As a result they both joined the EU (with fewer reservations than the old member Denmark) and established closer relations with NATO.[52]

Not much is thus left of the Nordic Balance, as most options have now been exercised and their inherent bargaining potential thereby expended. One might even argue that the balance has shifted from a very loose bipolar to a loose unipolar one where the most significant variation is with regard to the nature and tightness of relations with the West. Not even here, however, do we have an entirely clear picture, if we sub-divide 'the West' into NATO, the EU and the WEU:

- Denmark is the only state that is a member of both NATO and the EU. Its enthusiasm about the latter, however, is very modest,[53] and there is a distinct aversion against the WEU, where the Danish government only have the status of observers.

- Norway is a member of NATO, but not EU. Its relations with the WEU, on the other hand, are slightly closer than those of Denmark.

- Sweden and Finland remain outside NATO as such, even though they participate in its offspring, the Partnership for Peace. They have both joined the EU, where they are significantly more integration-minded than Denmark, also with regard to those dimensions that would seem to infringe most on neutrality, yet without joining the WEU.[54]

After the Cold War and the dissolution of the USSR, however, there has been a growing interest in the Baltic (sub)region,[55] probably reflecting the desire of the former Soviet republics for being part of a larger group just as much as the wish to remedy concrete perceived defence deficiencies. Not that the problems in this sphere are insignificant, but cooperation with Norden does not do much to solve the problem, as the Nordic countries could not possibly provide reliable security guarantees.[56] The problems facing Estonia, Latvia and Lithuania are amplified by the odd location of the Russian exclave Kaliningrad as well as by the fact that their being former parts of the USSR seems to push the date of their joining NATO way into the future, the Danish advocacy of their early admission notwithstanding.[57]

4.   Summary: The Nordic Setting and the 'Nordic Model'

To sum up what has already been mentioned along with some obvious facts, the Nordic setting during the Cold War was thus characterized by the following features:

- Norden consisted entirely of small and mini-states, which were not only culturally and ethnically relatively homogeneous but also alike in their economic and political nature (stable democratic welfare states) and in subscribing to policies of 'good world citizenship' (manifested in support for the UN, high levels of development aid, etc.).
- The area had a high geostrategic importance for both sides to the East-West conflict.

The Cold War 'Nordic Model' was characterized, *inter alia*, by the following features.

- A 'desecuritization' of military matters as far as intra-Nordic relations were concerned, perhaps even a desecuritization of Nordic relations as a whole.
- Non-provocation and confidence-building, based on the general understanding that there was nothing to gain by, but much to lose from, alienating the USSR, hence the need to take its security

concerns into account. Norden as a whole thus followed, however, unwittingly, the precepts of the Common Security philosophy propagated by the Palme Commission.[58]

- An 'indirect approach' based on a subtle exploitation of unexercised options.[59]
- Less than total alignment, as a way of combining security guarantees without 'entrapment'.[60]
- A reliance on several pillars. Rather than just NATO or their neutral stance, the Nordic countries thus also emphasized the United Nations, Nordic cooperation, the CSCE and, as far as Denmark was concerned, the European pillar, personified in the EU.
- Openendedness in that the Nordic community was so (deliberately) ill-defined, hence could not possibly be construed as directed against anybody. On the contrary, depending on the issue and concrete circumstances, almost any state might be involved.

III. Conclusion and Suggestions

We have thus seen that Norden during the Cold War was unique in several respects. It represented a successful balancing act between the two sides to the bipolar conflict, by means of which the Nordic countries succeeded in maintaining their security community within and a security regime involving both East and West. It is, of course, entirely possible that Norden was unique, hence that no lessons can be drawn for other regions, especially not for a different period.[61] However, certain elements of the 'Nordic model' would seem to be applicable to other regional settings, where they hold the promise of defusing conflicts. This is particularly the case of the policy of deliberate non-provocation that characterized the Nordic countries in their dealings with the Eastern superpower.

Such policies would, *mutatis mutandis*, seem quite appropriate for the former Warsaw Pact countries in their balancing between NATO and Russia and to other parts of the world, where small states confront a (regional-scale) great power such as Southeast Asia (in their relations with China) and the Gulf Region (where the GCC countries face both Iran and Iraq).[62] Just as the countries of East-Central Europe would be well advised to seek to strike a balance between balancing against and bandwagoning with Russia, e.g. by a voluntary 'self-Finlandization', the countries in Southwest and Southeast Asia would be better served by a kind of 'conditional semi-alignment' with the West (especially the United States) than by jumping the Western bandwagon, thereby alienating countries that will remain their neighbours and whose (actual or potential) strength is such that it is much preferable to have them as friends than enemies.

Notes

1. For various approaches, see Falk, Richard & Saul H. Mendlovitz (eds.): *Regional Politics and World Order* (San Francisco: W.H. Freeman and Company, 1973). Among the modern classics, one might mention Cantori, Louis J. & Steven L. Spiegel (eds.): *The International Politics of Regions: A Comparative Approach* (Englewood Cliffs, NJ: Prentice-Hall, 1970); Haas, Ernst B.: *International Political Communities* (New York: Anchor Books, 1966); Nye, Joseph S.: *Peace in Parts: Integration and Conflict in Regional Organization* (Boston: Little, Brown & Co., 1971); Russett, Bruce: *International Regions and the International System* (Chicago: Rand McNally, 1967). More recent studies include Taylor, Paul: *International Organization in the Modern World. The Regional and the Global Process* (London: Pinter Publishers, 1993), pp. 7-23; Wriggins, Howard (ed.): *Dynamics of Regional Politics. Four Systems on the Indian Ocean Rim* (New York: Columbia University Press, 1992); Daase, Christopher, Susanne Feske, Bernhard Moltmann & Claudia Schmid (eds.): *Regionalisierung der Sicherheitspolitik. Tendenzen in den internationalen Beziehungen nach dem Ost-West-Konflikt* (Baden-Baden: Nomos Verlag, 1993); Lawrence, Robert Z.: *Regionalism, Multilateralism, and Deeper Integration* (Washington, D.C.: The Brookings Institution, 1996); Holm, Hans-Henrik & Georg Sørensen (eds.): *Whose World Order? Uneven Globalization and the End of the Cold War* (Boulder: Westview Press, 1995); Singer, Max & Aaron Wildavsky: *The Real World Order. Zones of Peace / Zones of Turmoil* (Chatham, NJ: Chatham House Publishers, 1993); Tow, William T.: *Subregional Security Cooperation in the Third World* (Boulder, Col.: Lynne Rienner, 1990); Buzan, Barry, Ole Wæver & Jaap de Wilde: *The New Security Studies: A Framework for Analysis* (Boulder: Lynne Rienner, 1998), pp. 9-20, 42-45 & passim; Fawcett, Louise & Andrew Hurrell (eds.): *Regionalism in World Politics* (Oxford: Oxford University Press, 1995), passim; Lake, David A. & Patrick M. Morgan (eds.): *Regional Orders. Building Security in a New World* (University Park, Pennsylvania: Pennsylvania State University Press, 1997); Keating, Michael & John Loughlin (eds.): *The Political Economy of Regionalism* (Newbury Park: Frank Cass, 1997).

2. See Ward, Michael Don (ed.): *The New Geopolitics* (Philadelphia & Reading: Gordon and Breach, 1992), especially Diehl, Paul F.: 'Geography and War: A Review and Assessment of the Empirical Literature' (pp. 121-137); and Gichman, Charles S.: 'Interstate Metrics: Conceptualizing, Operationalizing, and Measuring the Geographic Proximity of States Since the Congress of Vienna' (pp. 139-158). On the importance of proximity for war-proneness see Goertz, Gary & Paul F. Diehl: *Territorial Changes and International Conflict* (London: Routledge, 1992); Siverson, Randolph & Harvey Starr: *The Diffusion of War. A Study of Opportunity and Willingness* (Ann Arbor: University of Michigan Press, 1991). For an analysis of the regionness of the Mediterranean see Calleya, Stephen C.: *Navigating Regional Dynamics in the Post-Cold*

War World. Patterns of Relations in the Mediterranean Area (Aldershot: Dartmouth, 1997).

3. On Europe, see Buzan, Barry, Morten Kelstrup, Pierre Lemaitre, Elzbieta Tromer & Ole Wæver: *The European Security Order Recast. Scenarios for the Post-Cold War Era* (London: Pinter, 1990), pp. 206-210.

4. On the Islamic conception of 'religious geopolitics' see, for instance, Fuller, Graham E. & Ian O. Lessler: *A Sense of Siege. The Geopolitics of Islam and the West* (Boulder: Westview, 1995), pp. 137-149 *& passim*. See also Charnay, Jean-Paul: 'Representation stratégique de l'Islam', pp. 7-18. Paper for the *Colloque Prospective des Ménaces* (Paris: Centre d'Étudues et de Prospective, 1996).

5. Wæver, Ole: 'Imperial Metaphors: Emerging European Analogies to Pre-Nation-State Imperial Systems', in Ola Tunander, Pavel Baev & Victoria Einagel (eds.): *Geopolitics in Post-Wall Europe* (London: Sage, 1997), pp. 59-93; idem: 'Europe's Three Empires: A Watsonian Interpretation of Post-Wall European Security', in Rick Fawn & Jeremy Larkins (eds.): *International Society after the Cold War. Anarchy and Order Reconsidered* (Houndsmills, Basingstoke: Macmillan, 1996), pp. 220-260. See also Watson, Adam: *The Evolution of International Society* (London: Routledge, 1992), pp. 3-4 *& passim*.

6. Westing, Arthur (ed.): *Comprehensive Security for the Baltic. An Environmental Approach.* (London 1989: SAGE/PRIO/UNEP). See also Prins, Gwyn: 'Politics and the Environment', *International Affairs*, vol. 66, no. 4 (1990), pp. 711-730; Thomas, Caroline: *The Environment in International Relations* (London: Royal Institute of International Affairs, 1992), pp. 115-151 *et passim*; Boulding, Elise: 'States, Boundaries and Environmental Security', in Dennis J.D. Sandole & Hugo van der Merwe (eds.): *Conflict Resolution Theory and Practice. Integration and Application* (Manchester: Manchester University Press, 1993), pp. 194-208.

7. On the role of regional organisations within the UN, see Gaer, Felice D.: 'The United Nations and the CSCE: Cooperation, Competition, Confusion?', in Michael R. Lucas (ed.): *The CSCE in the 1990s: Constructing European Security and Cooperation* (Baden-Baden: Nomos Verlag, 1993), pp. 161-206; Weiss, Thomas G., David P. Forsythe & Rogert A. Coate (eds.): *The United Nations and Changing World Politics* (Boulder, CO: Westview Press, 1994), pp. 33-36.

8. Clarke, Douglas: 'A Guide to Europe's New Security Architecture', *European Security*, vol. 1, no. 2 (Summer 1992), pp. 126-132; Rotfeld, Adam Daniel: 'Europe: Towards New Security Arrangements' (with appendices), *SIPRI Yearbook 1996*, pp. 279-324.

9. Huntington, Samuel: *The Clash of Civilizations and the Remaking of World Order* (New York: Simon & Schuster, 1996), pp. 26-27 *& passim*. The nine civilizations are the Western, Latin American, African, Islamic, Sinic, Hindu, Orthodox, Buddhist and Japanese. An earlier, and much less xenophobic version of the 'cultural approach' is Wallerstein, Immanuel: *Geopolitics and Geoculture. Essays on the Changing World-System* (Cambridge: Cambridge University Press, 1992), pp. 139-237.

10. Lapid, Yosef & Friedrich Kratochwill (eds.): *The Return of Culture and Identity in IR Theory* (Boulder: Lynne Rienner, 1995). See also Neumann, Iver B.: 'Self and Other in International Relations', *European Journal of International Relations*, vol. 2, no. 2 (June 1996), pp. 139-175.

11. Adler, Emanuel: 'Imagined (Security) Communities: Cognitive Regions in International Relations', *Millennium. Journal of International Studies*, vol. 26, no. 2 (1997), pp. 249-278. On 'imagined' national identities see Anderson, Benedict: *Imagined Communities. Reflections on the Origins and Spread of Nationalism* (London: Verso, 1991); Wæver, Ole: 'Identities', in Judit Balázs & Håkan Wiberg (eds.): *Peace Research for the 1990s* (Budapest: Akadémiai Kiadó, 1993), pp. 135-150.

12. Buzan, Barry: 'A Framework for Regional Security Analysis', in idem, Rother Rizwi & al.: *South Asian Insecurity and the Great Powers* (London: Macmillan, 1986), pp. 3-33; idem: *People, States and Fear. An Agenda for International Security Studies in the Post-Cold War Era*, Second Edition (Boulder: Lynne Rienner, 1991), pp. 186-229, quotation from p. 190. The delimitation of security complexes is illustrated by the map on p. 210. For an update see idem, Wæver & de Wilde: *op. cit.* (note 1), pp. 15-19 & *passim*. For a critique, see Haftendorn, Helga: 'Das Sicherheitspuzzle: Die Suche nach einem tragfähigen Konzept Internationaler Sicherheit', in Daase *et al.* (eds.): *op. cit.* (note 1), pp. 13-38, especially pp. 29-30.

13. On the expansion of the security concept see Nye, Joseph E. & Sean M. Lynn-Jones: 'International Security Studies: A Report of a Conference on the State of the Field', *International Security*, vol. 12, no. 4 (Spring 1988), pp. 5-27; Lynn-Jones, Sean M.: 'The Future of International Security Studies', in Desmond Ball & David Horner (eds.): *Strategic Studies in a Changing World: Global, Regional and Australian Perspectives*, Series 'Canberra Papers on Strategy and Defence', vol. 89 (Canberra: Strategic and Defence Studies Centre, Research School of Pacific Studies, ANU, 1992), pp. 71-107; Fischer, Dietrich: *Nonmilitary Aspects of Security. A Systems Approach* (Aldershot: Dartmouth, 1993); Møller, Bjørn: 'Security Concepts: New Challenges and Risks', in Antonio Marquina & Hans Günter Brauch (eds.): 'Confidence Building and Partnership in the Western Mediterranean. Tasks for Preventive Diplomacy and Conflict Avoidance', *AFES-PRESS Reports*, no. 51 (Mosbach: AFES-PRESS, 1994), pp. 3-49.

14. On security communities see Deutsch, Karl W. *et al.*: *Political Community and the North Atlantic Area. International Organization in the Light of Historical Experience* (Princeton, N.J.: Princeton University Press, 1957).

15. Ayoob, Mohammed: *The Third World Security Predicament. State Making, Regional Conflict, and the International System* (Boulder: Lynne Rienner, 1995).

16. The term is coined by Wæver, Ole. See, for instance, his 'Securitization and Desecuritization', in Ronnie Lipschutz (ed.): *On Security* (New York: Columbia University Press, 1995), pp. 46-86; idem: *Concepts of Security* (Copenhagen: Institute of Political Science, 1997); or Buzan et al.: *op. cit.* 1997 (note 1), *passim*.

17. Buzan *et al.*: *op. cit.* (note 1), pp. 18-19.

18. Buzan: *op. cit.* 1991 (note 12), pp. 219-221.

19. A raw anarchy is pretty much that described by Waltz, Kenneth N.: *Theory of International Politics* (Reading: Addison-Wesley, 1979). For a refinement see Buzan: *op. cit.* 1991 (note 12), pp. 146-185 *& passim*; and idem, Charles Jones & Richard Little: *The Logic of Anarchy. Neorealism to Structural Realism* (New York: Columbia University Press, 1993), pp. 19-80. On international society see Bull, Hedley: *The Anarchical Society. A Study of Order in World Politics.* Second Edition (Houndsmills, Basingstoke: Macmillan, 1995); and Fawn & Larkins (eds.): *op. cit.* (note 5), *passim*; Watson: *op. cit.* (note 5), pp. 299-310. On security regimes see Jervis, Robert: 'Security Regimes', *International Organization*, vol. 36, no. 2 (Spring 1982), pp. 357-378. On security communities see above, note 14.

20. On the special status of these territories in a comparative perspective see Lapidoth, Ruth: *Autonomy. Flexible Solutions to Intrastate Conflicts* (Washington, D.C.: United States Institute of Peace Press, 1996), pp. 70-77, 112-115, 143-152.

21. On the Monroe Doctrine see Perkins, Bradford: 'The Creation of a Republic Empire, 1776-1865', *Cambridge History of American Foreign Relations*, vol. 1 (Cambridge: Cambridge University Press, 1993), pp. 147-169. On the reactivation and application during the Second World War (when the Danish Ambassador to the United States unilaterally grated the US control of Greenland) see Lidegaard, Bo: *I Kongens Navn. Henrik Kauffmann i dansk diplomati 1919-1958* (Copenhagen: Samleren, 1996), pp. 172-216.

22. This was, for instance, the case of the Soviet advocacy of a Nordic nuclear weapons-free zone, including the Baltic Sea, but excluding Soviet nuclear weapons. See, for instance, SNU: *Dansk sikkerhedspolitik og forslagene om Norden som kernevåbenfri zone* (Copenhagen: SNU, 1983), pp. 19-20; idem: *Flådestrategier og nordisk sikkerhedspolitik*, vol. 1 (Copenhagen: SNU, 1986), pp. 214-239.

23. Arkin, William M. & Richard Fieldhouse: *Nuclear Battlefields. Global Links in the Arms Race* (Cambridge: Ballinger, 1985), pp. 220-221; Claeson, Paul: *Grønland - Middelhavets Perle* (Copenhagen: Eirene, 1983); Petersen, Nikolaj: 'Denmark, Greenland, and Arctic Security', in Kari Mötölä (ed.): *The Arctic Challenge. Nordic and Canadian Approaches to Security and Cooperation in an Emerging International Region* (Boulder: Westview Press, 1988), pp. 39-74.

24. Osherenko, Gail & Oran R. Young: *Age of the Arctic: Hot Conflicts and Cold Realities* (Cambridge: Cambridge University Press, 1989).

25. On its origins see Stråth, Bo: 'Scandinavian Identity: A Mythical Reality', in Nils Arne Sørensen (ed.): *European Identities. Cultural Diversity and Integration in Europe since 1700* (Odense: Odense University Press, 1995), pp. 37-58.

26. Udenrigsministeriet: *Dansk Sikkerhedspolitik 1948-1966* (Copenhagen: Udenrigsministeriet, 1968), vol. 1, pp. 21-43; vol. 2, pp. 29-84, 96-133.

27. Christensen, Aksel E.: *Kalmarunionen og nordisk politik 1319-49* (Copenhagen: Gyldendal, 1980).

28. Examples of inter-Nordic wars include: (I) The Seven Years War 1563-70, described in Gramrath, Helge: 'Perioden 1559-1648', in Aksel E. Christensen & al. (eds.): *Danmarks Historie* (Copenhagen: Gyldendal, 1977ff), vol. 2, pp. 443-450; Bech, Svend Cedergreen: 'Reformation og renæssance 1533-1596', *Politikens Danmarks Historie*, vol. 6, pp. 364-446; (II) the Kalmar War 1611-1613, described in Ellehøj, Svend: 'Christian Stidsalder 1596-1660', *ibid.*, vol. 7, pp. 199-207, 434-523; (III) the war over Skåne 1675-1679, described in Olesen, Gunnar: 'Den unge enevælde 1660-1721', *ibid.*, vol. 8, pp. 161-252; (IV) the Great Nordic War 1708-1721, described *ibid.*, pp. 381-510; (V) and the 1788 war, described in Vibæk, Jens: 'Reform og fallit 1784-1830', *ibid.*, vol. 10, pp. 168-174.

29. On the security dilemma, see e.g. Herz, John M.: *Political Realism and Political Idealism. A Study in Theories and Realities* (Chicago: Chicago University Press, 1951), *passim*; idem: 'Idealist Internationalism and the Security Dilemma', *World Politics*, vol. 2, no. 2 (1950), pp. 157-180; Jervis, Robert: *Perception and Misperception in International Politics* (Princeton, N.J.: Princeton University Press, 1976), pp. 58-93; idem: 'Cooperation Under the Security Dilemma', *World Politics*, vol. 30, no. 2 (1978), pp. 167-214; Buzan: *op. cit.* 1991 (note 12), pp. 294-327; Collins, Alan: 'The Security Dilemma', in Jane M. Davis (ed.): *Security Issues in the Post-Cold War World* (Cheltenham: Edward Elgar, 1996), pp. 181-195, pp. 171-201.

30. Clearly articulated, e.g., by Prime and Foreign Minister H.C. Hansen in the Danish Folketing, 21 January 1958, in Udenrigsministeriet: *op.cit.* (note 26), vol. 2, pp. 336-337. On the actual threat perceptions of the Soviet Union, pertaining to the Nordic region, see Nygren, Bertil: 'Distant Mirrors. Soviet Threat Perceptions of its Northwestern and Eastern Rim', *Research Report* (Stockholm: Swedish Institute of International Affairs, 1991). See also Bomsdorf, Falk: *Sicherheit im Norden Europas. Die Sicherheitspolitik der fünf nordischen Staaten und die Nordeuropapolitik der Sowjetunion* (Baden-Baden 1989: Nomos Verlagsgesellschaft); Zoppo, Ciro Elliott (ed.): *Nordic Security at the Turn of the Twenty-First Century* (Westport, Connecticut: Greenwood Press, 1992); Heisler, Martin O.: 'The Nordic Region: Changing Perspectives in International Relations', *The Annals of the American Academy of Political and Social Science*, vol. 512 (London: Sage, 1990).

31. Heurlin, Bertel: 'Dansk Kernevåbenpolitik', in idem (ed.): *Kernevåbenpolitik i Norden* (Copenhagen: SNU, 1983), pp. 91-113; Sæter, Martin: 'Norsk Atomvåpenpolitikk', *ibid.*, pp. 114-139. On the actual deployment of nuclear weapons in Greenland see DUPI: *Grønland under den kolde krig. Dansk og amerikansk sikkerhedspolitik 1945-1968*, vols. 1-2 (Copenhagen: DUPI, 1997).

32. Gunnarson, Gunnar: 'Continuity and Change in Icelandic Security and Foreign Policy', in Heisler (ed.): *op. cit.* (note 30, pp. 140-151; idem: 'The Impact of Naval Developments on Iceland', in John Kristian Skogan & Arne O. Brundtland (eds.): *Soviet Sea Power in Northern Waters. Facts, Motivations, Impact and Responses* (London: Pinter, 1990), pp. 91-100.

33. On Norway see Holst, Johan Jørgen: 'Norwegian Security Policy', in idem, Kenneth Hunt & Anders C. Sjaastad (eds.): *Deterrence and Defense in the North* (Oslo: Norwegian University Press, 1985), pp. 93-123; Brundtland, Arne O.: 'Norwegian Security Policy: Defence and Nonprovocation in a Changing Context', in Gregory Flynn (ed.): *NATO's Northern Allies. The National Security Policies of Belgium, Denmark, the Netherlands, and Norway* (London: Rowman & Allanhead, 1985), pp. 171-223; Ørvik, Niels: 'Norway: Deterrence Versus Nonprovocation', in idem (ed.): *Semialignment and Western Security* (London: Croom Helm, 1986), pp. 186-247. On Denmark see Holbraad, Carsten: 'Denmark: Half-Hearted Partner', *ibid.*, pp. 15-60.

34. The precise status of Bornholm is a somewhat delicate matter, since the USSR (according to their own reading of history) only left the island in 1946 on the precondition that no foreign forces would be stationed here. Denmark *de facto* acted as if she agreed with this proviso, but refused to accept any *de jure* commitments, and denied the USSR any *droit de regard* in this respect. See Udenrigsministeriet: *op.cit.* (note 26), vol. 1, p. 160; cf. the speech by Foreign Minister Ole Bjørn Kraft, 11 April 1952, *ibid.*, vol. 2, pp. 297-300; Børgesen, C.S.: 'Østersøen i aktuel dansk sikkerhedspolitisk betydning', in R. Watt-Boelsen (ed.): *Østersøen, i går, i dag, i morgen* (Copenhagen: Forsvarets Oplysnings- og Velfærdstjeneste, 1982), pp. 48-58; Petersen, Nikolai: 'Dansk sikkerhedspolitik i Østersøområdet', in Pertti Joenniemi & Unto Vesa (eds.): *Säkerhetsutveckling i Östersjöområdet* (Tampere: TAPRI, Forskningsrapport no. 35), pp. 54-67.

35. Iionen, Jyrki: 'Finland som model: Det finsk-sovjetiske forhold som et eksempel på fredelig Sameksistens', in Christian Mailand-Hansen & Ole Nørgaard (eds.): *Sovjetunionen og freden: en Debatbog* (Esbjerg: Sydjysk Universitetsforlag, 1983), pp. 162-173.

36. Wiberg, Håkan & Keld Jensen: 'Military Defence in Denmark: Expenditures and Conversion Problems', *Cooperation and Conflict*, vol. 27, no. 4 (December 1992), pp. 397-414; Gleditsch, Nils Petter: 'Defence Without Threat? The Future of Norwegian Military Spending', *ibid.*, pp. 397-414; Hagelin, Björn & Peter Wallensteen: 'Understanding Swedish Military Expenditures', *ibid.*, pp. 415-442.

37. Skogan, John Kristen: 'The Evolution of the Four Soviet Fleets, 1968-87', in idem & Brundtland (eds.): *op. cit.* (note 32), pp. 18-33; Taoka, Shunji: 'The Superpower Naval Build-Up: a Brief History', in Richard Fieldhouse & Shunji Taoka: *Superpowers at Sea. An Assessment of the Naval Arms Race* (Oxford: Oxford University Press, 1989), pp. 17-28; Tol, Robert van: 'A Naval Force Comparison in Northern and Atlantic Waters', in Clive Archer (ed.): *The Soviet Union and Northern Waters* (London: Routledge, 1988), pp. 134-163; Ries, Thomas: 'Soviet Military Strategy and Northern Waters', *ibid.*, pp. 90-133. On the strategic rationale, see e.g. MccGwire, Michael: 'Soviet Naval Doctrine and Strategy', in Derek Leebaert (ed.): *Soviet Military Thinking*, (London: George Allan & Unwin, 1981), pp. 125-184; Bathurst, Robert B.: 'The Soviet Navy Through Western Eyes', in Philip S. Gillette & William C. Frank, Jr. (eds.): *The Sources of Soviet Naval Conduct* (Lexington, MA: Lexington Books, 1990), pp. 59-80; Daniel, Donald C.F.: 'Alternate Models of Soviet Naval Behaviour', *ibid.*, pp. 237-248; Manthorpe, William H.J.: 'A Background for Understanding Soviet Strategy', *ibid.*, pp. 3-18; Rohwer, Jürgen: 'Alternating Russian and Soviet Naval Strategies', *ibid.*, pp.

95-120; idem: 'Russian and Soviet Naval Strategy', in Skogan & Brundtland (eds.): *op.cit.*, pp. 3-17.

38. Barth, Magne & Nils Petter Gleditsch: 'COB-aftalen i Norge - Et dyrt køb', *Militærkritisk Magasin Forsvar*, no. 8-9, 1982, pp. 12-16; idem: 'COB-aftalen. Amerikanske baser til lavpris', *ibid.*, pp. 10-11; Rasmussen, Søren: 'Skønt Dannebrog stadig blafrer..', in Bjørn Møller (ed.): *Forsvar - det bedste forsvar* (Egtved: Fredsbevægelsens Forlag, 1986), pp. 17-30; Winter, Judith: *De danske forstærkningsaftaler* (Copenhagen: Nej til Atomvåben, 1985).

39. The most authoritative exposition is Watkins, James D.: 'The Maritime Strategy', *U.S. Naval Institute Proceedings*, vol. 112, no. 1 (January 1986), pp. 2-17. See also Brooks, Linton F.: 'Naval Power and National Security. The Case for the Maritime Strategy', in Steven E. Miller & Stephen van Evera (eds.): *Naval Strategy and National Security. An* International Security *Reader*, (Princeton, N.J.: Princeton University Press, 1988), pp. 16-46. For a critique see Mearsheimer, John J.: 'A Strategic Misstep: The Maritime Strategy and Deterrence in Europe', *ibid.*, pp. 47-101. On the strategic anti-submarine warfare elements in the strategy see Rivkin, David B. Jr.: 'No Bastions for the Bear', *U.S. Naval Institute Proceedings*, vol. 110, no. 4 (April 1984), pp. 36-43; Pocalyk, M.N.: 'Sinking Soviet SSBNs', *ibid.*, vol. 113, no. 10 (October 1987), pp. 24-36; cf. Stefanick, Tom: *Strategic Antisubmarine Warfare and Naval Strategy* (Lexington, MA: Lexington Books, 1987).

40. Agrell, Wilhelm: *Bakom Ubåtskrisen* (Stockholm: Liber Förlag, 1986); Oldberg, Ingmar: 'Incidents in the Baltic: A Dark Side in Soviet-Swedish Relations Since 1945', *Nordic Journal of Soviet & East European Studies*, no. 1, 1987, pp. 15-48; Leitenberg, Milton: 'Soviet Submarine Operations in Swedish Waters 1980-1986', *The Washington Papers*, no. 128 (1986), pp. 24-107.

41. Joenninni, Pertti: 'Norden and the Development of Strategic Doctrines; From a Buffer Zone to a Grey Area', *Current Research on Peace and Violence* (Tampere: TAPRI), no. 1-2, 1986, pp. 54-73; Gleditsch, Niels Petter: 'Europe's Northern Region Between the Superpowers', *Bulletin of Peace Proposals*, vol. 16, no. 4 (1985), pp. 399-411; Tunander, Ola: 'Norden och USAs Maritima Strategi. En studie av Nordens förändrade strategiske läge', *FOA Rapport*, no. C 10295-1.4, September 1987; idem: *Cold Water Politics. The Maritime Strategy and Geopolitics of the Northern Front* (London: Sage, 1989).

42. Brundtland, Arne Olav: 'Nordisk Balanse før og Nå', *Internasjonal Politikk*, vol. 24, no. 5 (1966), pp. 491-541; idem: 'Den klassiske, den omsnudde og den fremtidige nordiske balance', in Ole Nørgaard & Per Carlsen (eds.): *Sovjetunionen, Østeuropa og dansk Sikkerhedspolitik* (Esbjerg: Sydjysk Universitetsforlag, 1981), pp. 83-99; idem: 'Den nordiska balansen anno 1987', in Bo Huldt (ed.): *Fred och säkerhet. Debatt och analys 1986/87* (Stockholm: Utrikespolitiska Institutet, 1988), pp. 36-46. For a critique see Wiberg, Håkan: 'The Nordic Countries: A Special Kind of System', *Current Research in Peace and Violence* (Tampere: TAPRI), no. 1-2/1986, pp. 2-12. See also idem & Ole Wæver: 'Norden in the Cold War Reality', in Jan Øberg (ed.): *Nordic Security in the 1990s. Options in the Changing Europe* (London: Pinter, 1992), pp. 13-34, especially pp. 23-26.

43. It might, e.g., be compared to the strategies of bargaining and independent decisions analysed in Schelling, Thomas C.: *The Strategy of Conflict* (Cambridge, MA: Harvard University Press, 1960), pp. 21-52 & *passim*; idem: *Arms and Influence* (New Haven: Yale University Press, 1966), pp. 35-91 & *passim*. See also Watson, Adam: *Diplomacy. The Dialogue between States* (London: Methuen, 1982), pp. 52-68. There is also a resemblance with Kissinger's 'linkage' strategies, intended to get the United States out of Vietnam without loss of face by means of the 'China Card', described in Kissinger, Henry M.: *The White House Years* (London: Weidenfeld and Nicolson and Michael Joseph, 1979), pp. 125-130; and in idem: *Diplomacy* (New York: Touchstone Books, 1994), pp. 703-732. It was based on the example of Metternich idolized in idem: *A World Restored. Metternich, Castlereagh and the Problems of Peace 1812-22* (Cambridge: The Riverside Press, 1957). See also Gaddis, John Lewis: 'Rescuing Choice from Circumstance: The Statecraft of Henry Kissinger', in Gordon A. Craig & Francis L. Loewenheim (eds.): *The Diplomats, 1939-1979* (Princeton, NJ: Princeton University Press, 1994), pp. 564-592.

44. Adler, David Jens: 'Fodnoteoprøret. Socialdemokratiets sikkerhedspolitik fra Hedtoft og H.C. til Anker og Ritt', in Søren Møller Christensen (ed.): *Man har et standpunkt... Socialdemokratiet og sikkerhedspolitikken i 80erne* (Kopenhagen: Eirene, 1984), pp. 49-63. On the background see idem: *Det europæiske teater. Bogen om raketterne og den nye Atomvåbenpolitik* (Copenhagen: Eirene, 1984), pp. 11-76, 348-414; Boel, Erik: *Socialdemokratiets atomvåbenpolitik 1945-88* (Copenhagen: Akademisk Forlag, 1988); Villaume, Paul: *Allieret med forebehold. Danmark, NATO of den kolde krig. Et studie i dansk sikkerhedspolitik 1949-1961* (Copenhagen: Eirene, 1995).

45. Roberts, Adam: *Nations in Arms. The Theory and Practice of Territorial Defence* (London: Praeger, 1976), pp. 62-123. For a critical analysis, see Agrell, Wilhelm: *Om kriget inte kommer. En debattbok om Sveriges framtida försvars- och säkerhetspolitik* (Stockholm: Liber Förlag, 1979).

46. Möttölä, Kari: 'Neutralitets og forsvarspolitik: finsk sikkerhedspolitik siden begyndelsen af 1970erne', in Bertel Heurlin (ed.): *Nordiske Sikkerhedsproblemer* (Copenhagen: SNU, 1984), pp. 139-173; Allison, Roy: *Finland's Relations With the Soviet Union, 1944-84* (New York: St. Martin's Press, 1985), pp. 174-175; Joennini, Pertti: 'The Underlying Assumptions of Finnish Neutrality', in Joseph Kruzel & Michael H. Haltzel (eds.): *Between the Blocs. Problems and Prospects for Europe's Neutrals and Non-Aligned States* (Cambridge: University Press, 1989), pp. 133-160; Mouritzen, Hans: *Finlandization: Towards a General Theory of Adaptive Politics* (Aldershot: Gower, 1988); Väyrynen, Raimo: 'Adaptation of a Small Power to International Tensions: The Case of Finland', in Bengt Sundelius (ed.): *The Neutral Democracies and the New Cold War* (Boulder: Westview, 1987), pp. 33-56. On the military aspects of this policy see Ries, Tomas: *Cold Will. The Defence of Finland* (London: Brassey's Defence Publishers, 1988), *passim*.

47. On the so-called 'note crisis', when these dynamics were presumably directly applied see Väyrynen, Raimo: 'Kernevåben og Finlands Udenrigspolitik', in Heurlin (ed.): *op. cit.* 1983 (note 31), pp. 18-57, especially pp. 22-32; Allison: *op. cit.* (note 46), pp. 43-57.

48. Quester, George: 'Unilateral Self-Restraint on Nuclear Proliferation: Canada, Sweden, Switzerland, and Germany', in Bennett Ramberg (ed.): *Arms Control Without Negotiation. From the Cold War to the New World Order* (Boulder: Lynne Rienner, 1993), pp. 141-157; Wallin, Lars B.: 'Sweden', in Regina Cowen Karp (ed.): *Security With Nuclear Weapons? Different Perspectives on National Security* (London: Oxford University Press, 1991), pp. 360-381; Prawitz, Jan: 'From Nuclear Option to Non-Nuclear Promotion: The Sweden Case', *Research Report*, no. 20 (Stockholm: The Swedish Institute of International Affairs, 1994); Cole, Paul M.: 'Atomic Bombast: Nuclear Weapon Decision-Making in Sweden, 1946-72', *Washington Quarterly*, vol. 20, no. 2 (Spring 1997), pp. 235-251.

49. SNU: *Dansk sikkerhedspolitik og forslagene om Norden som atomvåbenfri Zone* (Copenhagen: SNU, 1982), *passim*; *Nordic Nuclear-Weapon-Free Zone. Report of a working group appointed by the Ministry of Foreign Affairs* (Helsinki: Ministry of Foreign Affairs, 1987); Lodgaard, Sverre: 'Nordic Initiatives for a Nuclear Weapon-Free Zone in Europe', *World Armaments and Disarmament. SIPRI Yearbook 1982* (London: Taylor & Francis, 1982), pp. 75-93; idem & Marek Thee (eds.): *Nuclear Disengagement in Europe* (London: Taylor & Francis, 1983); Krohn, Axel: *Nuklearwaffenfreie Zone: Regionales Disengagement unter die Rahmenbedingung globaler Großmachtinteressen. Das Fallbeispiel Nordeuropa* (Baden-Baden: Nomos Verlagsgesellschaft, 1989).

50. The event went so unnoticed, that the present author (who does not read Finnish) had great difficulties in finding a reference to the event in non-Finnish sources. It is, however, briefly mentioned in *Europa-Archiv*, no. 20, 1990, Z-204.

51. Andrén, Nils: 'On the Meaning and Uses of Neutrality', *Cooperation and Conflict*, vol. 26, no. 2 (June 1991), pp. 67-84; Bebler, Anton: 'The Neutral and Non-Aligned States in the New European Security Architecture', *European Security*, vol. 1, no. 2 (Summer 1992), pp. 133-143; Binter, Josef: 'Neutrality in a Changing World: End or Renaissance of a Concept?', *Bulletin of Peace Proposals*, vol. 23, no. 2 (June 1992), pp. 213-218; Carton, Alain: *Les neutres, la neutralité et l'Europe*, (Paris: Fondation pour les études de défense nationale, 1991). See also Hakovirta, Harto: *East-West Conflict and European Neutrality* (Oxford: Clarendon Press, 1988); Sundelius (ed.): *op. cit.* (note 46), *passim*; Kruzel, Joseph & Michael H. Haltzel: *Between the Blocs. Problems and Prospects for Europe's Neutrals and Non-Aligned States* (Cambridge: Cambridge University Press, 1989), *passim*.

52. Arter, David: 'Finland: From Neutrality to NATO?', *European Security*, vol. 5, no. 4 (Winter 1996), pp. 614-632; Blomberg, Jaako: 'Finland's Evolving Security Policy', *NATO Review*, vol. 41, no. 1 (February 1993), pp. 12-16; Jalonen, Olli-Pekka & Unto Vesa: 'Something Old, Something New, Something Borrowed, Something Blue. Finland's Defence Policy in a Changing Security Environment', *Cooperation and Conflict*, vol. 27, no. 4 (December 1992), pp. 377-396.

53. The 1992 referendum on the Maastricht Treaty thus yielded a small but decisive majority against ratification: 41.7 percent voted no, compared with 40.6 percent in favour of the treaty. See Nielsen, Jørgen: 'Notat om afstemningen den 2. juni', *Arbejdspapirer*, no. 7 (Copenhagen: Institute for Political Studies, 1992); Lyck, Lise: 'Postscript: Denmark and the Maastricht Agreement - perspectives for Denmark,

EC and Europe', in idem (ed.): *Denmark and EC Membership Evaluated* (London: Pinter, 1992), pp. 236-243; Sauerberg, Steen: 'Parties, Voters and the EC', *ibid.*, pp. 60-76.

54. Laursen, Finn: 'The Maasticht Treaty: Implications for the Nordic Countries', *Cooperation and Conflict*, vol. 28, no. 2 (June 1993), pp. 115-142; Mouritzen, Hans: 'The Two Musterknaben and the Naughty Boy: Sweden, Finland and Denmark in the Process of European Integration', *ibid.*, no. 4 (December 1993), pp. 373-402; Bjørklund, Tor: 'The Three Nordic 1994 Referenda Concerning Membership in the EU', *ibid.*, vol. 31, no. 1 (March 1996), pp. 11-36; Ingebritson, Christine & Susan Larson: 'Interest and Identity'. Finland, Norway and European Union', *Cooperation and Conflict*, vol. 32, no. 2 (June 1997), pp. 207-222. On Norway see Eide, Espen Barth: 'Adjustment Strategy of a Non-Member: Norwegian Foreign and Security Policy in the Shadow of the European Union', *Cooperation and Conflict*, vol. 31, no. 1 (March 1996), pp. 69-104. See also Harden, Sheila (ed.): *Neutral States and the European Community* (London: Brassey's, UK, 1994).

55. Joenniemi, Pertti (ed.): *Cooperation in the Baltic Sea Region* (London: Taylor & Francis, 1993); idem (ed.): 'Neo-Nationalism or Regionality. The Restructuring of Political Space around the Baltic Rim', *Nord-Refo*, no. 1997:5 (Stockholm: Nordiska Institutet för Regionalpolitisk Forskning, 1997); Nørgaard, Ole & al.: *The Baltic States after Independence* (Cheltenham: Edward Elgar, 1996); Wellmann, Christian (ed.): *The Baltic Sea Region: Conflict or Cooperation? Region-Making, Security, Disarmament and Conversion*, Kieler Schriften zur Friedenswissenschaft, vol. 1 (Münster: Lit Verlag, 1992).

56. On the Baltic states' threat perceptions, see Jæger, Øjvind: 'Securitising Russia: Discursive Practices of the Baltic States', *Working Papers*, no. 10 (Copenhagen: Copenhagen Peace Research Institute, 1997); Park, Andrus: 'Russia and Estonian Security Dilemmas', *Europe-Asia Studies*, vol. 47, no. 1 (1995), pp. 27-45. On the evolving security policy see Petersen, Phillip: 'Security Policy in the Post-Baltic States', *European Security*, vol. 1, no. 1 (Spring 1992), pp. 13-49. On the NATO options see Asmus, Ronald D. & Robert C. Nurick: 'NATO Enlargement and the Baltic States', *Survival*, vol. 38. no. 2 (Summer 1996), pp. 121-142; Coleman, Fred: 'The Kalininggrad Scenario. Expanding NATO to the Baltics', *World Policy Journal*, vol. 14, no. 3 (Fall 1997), pp. 71-75. On defence policies see Jundzis, Talavs: 'Defence Models and Strategies in the Baltic States', *The International Spectator*, vol. 31, no. 1 (Jan-March 1996), pp. 25-37; Öövel, Andrus: 'Estonian Defence Policy, NATO and the European Union', *Security Dialogue*, vol. 27, no. 1 (March 1996), pp. 65-68; Skrastins, I.: 'The Armed Forces of the Baltic States: Current Status and Problems of Development', *The Journal of Slavic Military Studies*, vol. 8, no. 1 (March 1995), pp. 36-52; Zaccor, Albert M.: 'Problems in the Baltic Armed Forces', *ibid.*, vol. 8, no. 1 (March 1995), pp. 53-72. See also Nørgaard, Ole & al.: *The Baltic States after Independence* (Cheltenham: Edward Elgar, 1996).

57. On Kaliningrad see Oldberg, Ingmar: 'Kaliningrad-områdets framtid: Kasern, handelsplats ellefr stridsäpple', *Internasjonal Politikk*, vol. 5, no. 3 (1995), pp. 335-356; Wellmann, Christian: 'Market Place or Garrison? On the Future of the Kaliningrad Region', *PFK-Texte*, no. 28 (Kiel: Projektverbund Friedenswissenschaften Kiel, 1994); idem: 'Russia's Kaliningrad Exclave at the Crossroads: The Interrelation between Economic Development and Security Politics', *Cooperation and Conflict*, vol. 31, no. 2

(June 1996), pp. 161-184.

58. Palme Commission (Independent Commission on Disarmament and Security Issues): *Common Security. A Blueprint for Survival. With a Prologue by Cyrus Vance* (New York: Simon & Schuster, 1982). See also Väyrynen, Raimo (ed.): *Policies for Common Security* (London: Taylor & Francis/SIPRI, 1985); or Bahr, Egon & Dieter S. Lutz (eds.): *Gemeinsame Sicherheit. Idee und Konzept. Bd. 1: Zu den Ausgangsüberlegungen, Grundlagen und Strukturmerkmalen Gemeinsamer Sicherheit* (Baden-Baden: Nomos Verlag, 1986).

59. On the indirect approach in the military sphere see Hart, Basil Liddell: *Strategy. The Indirect Approach.* 2nd, revised, edition, 1967 (New York: Signet Books, 1974).

60. Ørvik, Niels: 'Introduction', in idem (ed.): *op. cit.* (note 33), pp. 1-14; Snyder, Glenn H.: 'The Security Dilemma in Alliance Politics', *World Politics*, vol. 36, no. 4 (1984), pp. 461-495; Sharp, Jane M.O.: 'NATO's Security Dilemma', *Bulletin of the Atomic Scientists*, vol. 53, no. 3 (March 1987), pp. 42-44.

61. See also Mouritzen, Hans: 'The Nordic Model as a Foreign Policy Instrument: Its Rise and Fall', *Journal of Peace Research*, vol. 32, no. 1 (February 1995), pp. 9-21; idem: *External Danger and Democracy. Old Nordic Lessons and New European Challenges* (Aldershot: Dartmouth, 1997), *passim*.

62. For an elaboration see 'Small States, Non-Offensive Defence and Collective Security', in Efraim Inbar & Gabriel Sheffer (eds.): *The National Security of Small States in a Changing World* (London: Frank Cass, 1997), pp. 127-154; idem: 'Preconditions for NATO Enlargement from a Common Security Point of View', *Working Papers*, no. 6 (Copenhagen: Copenhagen Peace Research Institute, 1997); idem: 'The Role of Arms Control and Defence Restructuring in the New South-Eastern Europe', *ibid.*, no. 13/1997); idem: 'Defence Restructuring in East Asia', *ibid.*, no. 24/1997); idem: 'Resolving the Security Dilemma in the Gulf Region', *The Emirates Occasional Papers*, no. 9 (Abu Dhabi: The Emirates Center for Strategic Studies and Research, 1997).

4. Subregionalism in South Eastern Europe

Sophia Clément

Introduction

The concept and implementation of regional cooperation in South-Eastern Europe are built on a range of paradoxes which underline at the same time the inherent limits of a regional approach as well as the main incentives in favour of its further development.[1] On the one hand, the increasing regional instability hampers attempts of regional cooperation. The ethnic and political tensions (Bosnia, Kosovo) and the successive economic crisis (Bulgaria, Albania, FYROM) have turned South East Europe into one of the most unstable regions in the European continent today.[2] The economic and political transition processes were slowed. The lack of regional definition and cooperative tradition further complicated the attempts to develop a cooperative framework. On the other hand, there are many incentives towards cooperative, if not integrative, paths: the development of common security concerns at a local level; the risk of marginalisation of the region from the broader European process of integration - as the enlargement process did not expand to the region while it needed it most, both in soft and hard security terms; the widening gap with neighbouring regions such as Central Europe; and finally the redefinition of the enlargement process as an open one.

The assessment of regionalism depends on the meaning it is given. The variables selected to assess potentially enhancing or uniting factors vary from region to region and often combine indigenous and exogenous factors. They are mainly economically driven in the Caucasus but more political and security related in South East Europe. Timing is another factor, as maturity is needed for cooperation to take place. The perception of regionalism is also important. If perceived positively, regionalism means shared common values and interests and leads to integration schemes. If assessed negatively, regionalism refers to conflict, difficult economic and political transition and nationalism, and leads to regional power centres and regional conflict formations, what might be called fragmented integration. Internal and external actors have different perceptions. Most outsiders tend to consider the region negatively in terms of history, elite behaviour, potential conflicts. Insiders are more divided. Some countries attribute credentials to a potential improvement of the region, while others dissociate themselves on a qualitative basis, as a different (geographically, historically, culturally) and a better (more politicised, i.e. western type of behaviour). A definition also appeals to the level and intensity invoked, i.e. bilateral, trilateral or multilateral interactions and various layers of integrations. In other words, does regionalism refer to a shift of structure towards a more specific and developed framework or does it simply imply the development of a something which is happening and taking form, giving rise to new regional power centres, integration schemes, regional conflict formations, or of derivations and extensions of constellations and potential conflicts? The answer depends on the level of integration required or sought, namely integration in view of the creation of a security system or a flexible model around a regional zone or area.

The regional cooperative initiatives which have been initiated by the international community and at the local level aim at enhancing good-neighbourly relations and achieve stability and security throughout the region by developing cooperation in the economic, political, and security fields. They however lack coordination, a coherent and strategic vision of South East Europe, and a linkage to the broader European setting. A rationalisation of all efforts is therefore needed.

1-Assessing Regionalism in South Eastern Europe
A Definition of a Region

Assessing subregionalism in South East Europe first implies to define to which extent a meaningful region exists or whether it is simply an external perception of disparate states. Such an attempt is problematic. First, geography, history and national criteria do not fit rigid definitions. Boundaries between regions are fluid and depend on the selected criteria. Geographic boundaries are either inclusive or exclusive depending on whether all-encompassing or strict geographic delimitations are chosen. The limits of regions themselves, or between them, vary accordingly. At times, South East Europe can include or exclude Croatia, Romania or Turkey. Second, a definition depends on perceptions. Geographic, historical and cultural criteria will serve as tools, and will be chosen accordingly, to present, interpret, or reinterpret, the perceived image of a region and distinguish it from adjacent ones. Cultural and historical dissimilarities are used to instil geographic differentiation, either entirely as belonging to a different regions or as occupying an in-between status. Consequently, there is a complex interaction between political relationships, social and historical background, and geographic factors.[3] Such a definition provides a tenuous and dynamic approach of a regions identity as it acknowledges a change of political and ideological factors, contrary to geographic boundaries and social factors. South East Europe does have a common recent past over this last century. The security and political issues which determine current political agendas are conditioned and determined by this legacy (former Yugoslavia). Interdependence (a change at one point affects the other point) and the proximate status of actors (but not necessarily contiguous) are the main variables of our analysis.

As a consequence of the multiple definitions and variable geometries attributed to the region, South Eastern Europe should be considered as a genuine region in the matter of security arrangements for the new Europe, and not simply as a collection of disparate states. A range of similar and deeply interdependent problems, such as common geographical and historical traits stemming from a recent common past, the necessity to jointly address common legacies which imply common solutions, and current common security threats and concerns make it, though not entirely coherent, at least distinct. Keeping in mind the fluidity of transregion borders as well as the negative perception granted by certain countries to the appellation Balkans, the term South East Europe is retained for the analysis and includes the following countries: Albania, former Yugoslavia (except Slovenia), Bulgaria, Romania, Greece and Turkey. Regionalism in South East Europe is understood not as a separate development from the European mainstream but as an integral part of the evolution of the broader European framework. Finally, in practice, there is no single way of organising regional cooperation and therefore no basis for imposing any model, other than to adapt it to local conditions.

The region has been heading towards a security vacuum, more in terms of perceptions than from a pure international relations approach. In general terms, the international relations theory advocates that the reduction of global politics has led to a diffusion of power from the core to the periphery of the international system towards a more polycentric world on regional relations, i.e. that the intrinsic dynamics of subordinate systems are becoming more significant features of the international system.[4] There is no consensus on their specific characteristics, on whether the advent of a multipolar system increases or decreases the likelihood of conflict and competition, and leaves more room to manoeuvre for regional powers. In reality, no specific patterns can be observed as they remain dependent on the nature of the subregional system. However, it is agreed that the uneven distribution of power conducive to the rise of regional politics has hampered the bottom layer of transnational interdependence at the local level where power is more evenly distributed. In already divided regions, the absence of constraint may increase the intensity of conflict as rivals attempts to settle old divergences as in Yugoslavia and may encourage external assistance for conflict resolution.[5] Since the end of the Cold War, South East Europe has undergone a series of in-depth changes and reshaping.

The Bosnian conflict, the revival of ethnic and political tensions and disputes, and the depth of economic crisis have considerably weakened the political, economic and social conditions in a region already characterised by a lower economic base and uneven economic development, weaker civil societies, a lack of tradition of statehood and fragile national identities, and a lack of cooperation at all levels. They have slowed the undergoing political, economic and social transition process and further weakened existing relations, by upsetting local ties, perceptions and past memories, altering the regional balance of power. The process of economic recovery and democratic consolidation will take longer than in Central Europe, which has promoted enhanced regional cooperative approaches and is heading towards integration into Western European structures. Finally, the direct pressure and interference of external powers have suppressed the usual security dynamics among local states. Former dividing lines had in reality helped to avoid conflict by freezing them. Paradoxically, artificial divisions had bolstered attempts to overcome the inter-block logic. The lift of the security umbrella and the opening of borders led back to renewed conflict.

Addressing subregionalism in South East Europe finally relates to the enlargement process in Europe: how to deal with regional cooperation within Europe's periphery and how it relates to enlargement, i.e. the consequences of enlargement - or non enlargement - and regional cooperation, and to which extent it promotes stability, inclusiveness or exclusiveness. South East Europe is linked to its northern part through a combination of direct and indirect interests. First, there are geographic proximity and a common shared history. It is also the region where all main European and Transatlantic international organisations regained their credibility and legitimacy, through the redefinition of their nature, the testing of their decision-making and operational mechanisms, and the establishment of regional structures promoting an integrative approach to security. Second, the level of conflict implies an enhanced presence of external powers through intervention, implementation of peace plans, internationalisation of conflict. Thus, South East Europe is understood here, not as a mere boundary, but as a subregional system of Europe which cannot be addressed independently of the evolution and integration process on the European continent.

In South East Europe, the diffusion of power from the core to the periphery is complex. Far from contributing to enhance local power (reorganisation of regional interests and activities) and keeping away external powers influence, the regional powers centre of interest is reoriented towards the centre. These uneven cross-interests between the core and the periphery of the European regional system are due to the diffusion of power and the parallel rise of local actors coupled with a growing dependency. South East Europe combines the advantage of being geographically close and historically linked to the rest of the European continent, and the disadvantage of being remote enough, at the periphery, not to affect direct interests and imply stronger commitments on behalf of external powers. This ambiguity of (in) direct interference coupled with the perceptions of local countries away from regionalism limits the inner dynamics in favour of regional cooperation. In South East Europe, the devolution of power to the periphery is mainly driven by an external voluntaristic will. This decentralisation process stems from various considerations from the core: a rational and practical need for internal reforms; more opportunistic reasons, such as European integration; a lack of funds;

and no real enlargement policy towards its southern part. Consequently, the development and evolution of regionalism in South East Europe will depend on how the concept will be thought through and presented: its aims and objectives, its specific *rationale* in the region.

The Security Paradox in South East Europe

South East Europe presents a range of limits and incentives to regional cooperation. A first series of negative variables seems to prevent any kind of regional approach. First, it is one of the most diversified subregions on the European continent with multiple degrees of integration, as the region encompasses countries with very different status in the Western political and economic organisations. During the Cold War, they were two NATO members (Greece and Turkey), two Warsaw Treaty members (Bulgaria and Romania), and two independent countries (Albania and Yugoslavia). This fragmentation continued after 1990: within the Western political and economic organisations such as EU, WEU and NATO, there are full members, associate partners and associate members, as well as countries without any form of agreement. There are important disparities at all levels among states of the region. Second, the gap is widening with neighbouring subregions, especially with Central Europe, more coherent and unified and where parallel regional cooperative initiatives have been undertaken. Ties have been strengthened which have helped these countries to catch up with the economic and political criteria of the West while South East Europe is still dominated by the absence of any institutionalised regional framework. Thirdly, South East Europe remains by far the most unstable subregion of the European continent. Political instability, current and potential conflict areas (Bosnia, Kosovo, FYR of Macedonia) and economic instability (Bulgaria, Albania, FYROM) have generated difficult and painful economic and political transitions in all of them.

Fourthly, the Balkan countries are not part of the enlargement process in Europe. They have been the left-outs of NATO and EU enlargements while needing membership most both in terms of soft and hard security. They fear it could lead to further marginalisation from the broader European political, economic and securitarian arrangements in the making. As their main goals remain the development of market economy, security concerns, as well as the need to escape from what is perceived as a problematic area, integration within European political and security organisations remains the main objective. This tension between enlargement and regional cooperation is a key factor to assess the former.[6] As a consequence, a range of regional initiatives has been undertaken reflecting the necessity of addressing in an appropriate manner the problems at the regional level. Thus, regional cooperative attitudes and initiatives in the region are voluntaristic political processes aiming at initiating the development of multilateral links at all levels, economic, political, social, and military. Whether there are top-down or bottom-up, these initiatives are essentially externally driven.

2-Subregional Cooperative Frameworks in South East Europe
An Historical Overview

In the past, there have been continuous attempts to set up cooperative frameworks in the region. The majority of them were initiated in the aftermath of periods of political instability, essentially in the inter-World War period and after WWII, in order to decrease tension and promote the development of mutual relationships. Limited by the range and depth of regional problems, they adopted a purely functionalist approach and exclusively addressed the lowest common denominator, i.e. low politics matters, such as economic, transport, energy and environment. However, a spillover effect towards more controversial matters of high politics (political, security, military), was expected.

The Balkan Conferences in the 1930s were initially limited to economic, industrial and environmental issues although they ambitiously aimed at creating a Balkan Federation which would have stemmed from the spillover of low issues into higher ones and into political integration. However, the same political divergences and conflicts around territorial and minority issues further deepened the existing dividing lines and blurred the common goal of regional cooperation. For instance, the resolution of minority issues was considered as a precondition for participation by two countries, Albania and Bulgaria, which had lost the Balkans wars and WWI. The formation of alignment and axis like the Balkan Pact (security agreement between Greece, Romania, Yugoslavia and Turkey in 1934 against Bulgaria and Albania) and the Little Entente (between Yugoslavia, Romania and Czechoslovakia in 1933) revealed the persistence of antagonistic blocs along traditional lines in the thirties.

The attempts to reach a regional *rapprochement* during the Cold War had an entirely different starting point within the framework of the antagonistic blocs. They focused on the security dimension, as the countries of the region aimed at overcoming military alignments in the region. They were also essentially motivated by the former's will to endorse a political initiative which would allow them to overcome internal (either national or intra bloc) constraints. Lacking effectively evolving and mature internal forces and conditioned by the broader Cold War inter-bloc logic, they failed like previous attempts, or had a somehow limited impact at best. For instance, in the late 50s, the Romanian initiative, or Stoica Plan named after the then Romanian Prime Minister, proposed the creation of a Balkan Nuclear Weapons-Free Zone which aimed to create a Peace zone based on a regional disarmament treaty. Along the above mentioned causal pattern, it was motivated by the Romanian government's intention to follow an independent foreign policy. It stumbled upon bipolar considerations and divisions: NATO members like Greece and Turkey objected to any withdrawal of American weapons from the region which would have opened the way to a consolidation of Soviet influence; unaligned Yugoslavia was not in a position to adopt a decisive stance on the issue. Finally, the period of *détente in* the 70s and 80s paved the way for renewed attempts.

Greek initiatives, supported by other Balkan countries, concentrated, as in the 30s, on low politics to provide a forum for regional consultation and cooperation at a political and experts level. Like earlier attempts, internal considerations were the driving force. The then Greek Prime minister, Constantine Karamanlis saw it as an occasion to improve Greece's regional relations in the framework of the country's future membership of the European Union. A decade later, the Papandreou government adopted, along more or less the same lines, a more independent policy vis-à-vis the United States and the European Union, trying at the same time to balance tense relations with Turkey over the Aegean and Cyprus, through an equal distance policy in the region. Again, a dissociation of the region from inter-bloc politics and external influence stumbled on mutual disagreements and bilateral conflicts. The dissolution of Yugoslavia finally ended the series of Balkan Conferences.

Some lessons might be drawn from previous attempts. The regional initiatives could succeed because they focused on practical and concrete low security issues such as transport, infrastructures, communications. They avoided high security issues like politics and security, which would have prevented short term agreements and longer term perspectives for cooperation. Subregional initiatives are also bound to fail if they exclude or are directed against one or more countries of the region, or if they are motivated by alignment with an external power. It might only contribute to upset the regional balance of power and increase dividing lines as well as internal competition.

New Regional Cooperative Frameworks
The Evolution of Mutual Perceptions

Mutual perceptions concerning a regional approach have evolved over the last few years. Since 1991, integration within European political and security organisations has remained the ultimate goal for the countries of the region. Current and potential conflicts contributed to limit the development of multilateral links. The fact that the countries of the region were not part of the enlargement process was perceived as an exclusion and a marginalisation both individually and regionally. Consequently, regional cooperation was considered as nothing more than an alternative or a substitutive framework offered to them as a consolation prize, which would have limited prospects for further integration and constitute a waiting room impeding or delaying accession. The increasing regional instability, the need for security guarantees, and the evolution of the concept of enlargement towards a more inclusive approach (defined as an open process with the regional approach as a basic conditionality) slowly modified these considerations. The regional approach was then assessed as an accommodation to enlargement, a possibility to fill the political and security vacuum in the region, avoid further marginalisation, and provide channels for closer cooperation and interaction with Western organisations. Furthermore, as the enlargement processes, especially those of the EU's, have been explicitly defined as open, provided all the required predefined criteria for accession were met, its development might provide for the economic, political and security conditions which would help meet them. Lastly, European organisations defined it as part of a conditionality approach linked to integration, a top-down explicit obligation. Regional cooperative frameworks were thus understood as an integral part of the wider European integration process, and as such, are promoted.

The concrete reasons behind regional countries interests and motivations to promote regional frameworks are manifold. All support the goals of democratic institutions and market economy but diverge on the role regional cooperation acquires in meeting them. Some, like Bulgaria and Turkey, as well as Greece, openly support the development of regional cooperation initiated at a local level, independently of the integration issue: it is a means to provide confidence-building measures and the development of economic links. Quickly aware that it would not be part of NATO enlargement, Bulgaria supported all local frameworks able to enhance confidence-building measures in the region.[7] Greece, as the only EU, WEU and NATO member, saw an opportunity to play a regional role and improve the bad relations of the past few years. Others, like FYROM, have been more reluctant to subordinate to regionalism as they felt their case might be made stronger, were they to act alone. But its leadership heavily supports top-down approaches such as Royaumont. The strong international presence on its territory and the country's importance to regional security and stability initially led its leaders to dissociate themselves and promote the country's own integration. Other countries, like Romania, and more specifically Croatia, dissociated themselves from the Balkans, claiming their exclusive belonging to Central Europe on the basis of historical and cultural (and religious for Croatia) criteria. They also believed that their better economic situation and the support of historical allies, respectively France and Germany, would include them into the happy few of the first wave of enlargement. Their exclusion from negotiations (from NATO for Romania and both for Croatia), the difficult access to the Central European market, but above all external pressure such as the conditionality argument of the EU's regional approach and American pressure, convinced them to join South East European cooperative frameworks.

Western European countries approach to the region evolved as well. Most perceived South East Europe negatively as mainly driven by politic and economic instability, democratic weakness, and prone to conflict. As a consequence, a strategic approach towards the region which would have linked it to the broader integration process was not on the agenda. In the light of the Bosnian crisis, it was however understood that any instability would have economic, political, psychological and security costs on the Western part of the European continent. It might weaken Western organisations' integration and reform process, i.e. internal coherence and cohesion at a time when they are trying to set up and consolidate decision-making and institutional mechanisms. It might increase economic aid towards the area (reconstruction, refugees). Regional cooperation was considered as an essential tool of confidence-building measure for the region and made a conditionality for future accession. A range of initiatives, promoted both at the international and at the local level, stemmed from this change of perceptions.

The Top-Down Initiatives[8]

In view of the problems of the region, externally and politically driven regional approaches have a central role to play. The Royaumont process for Stability and Good Neighbourliness in South East Europe was launched by the EU in February 1996 after the adoption of the Royaumont Declaration at the Paris peace Conference in December 1995. Intergovernmental and political in nature, it follows the guidelines of a regional approach recommended by the European Council, in articulation to the Dayton Agreement, as a forum for the implementation of its civilian provisions. It was based on a French proposal presented at the OSCE Budapest Ministerial Council. Initially, it was limited to Bosnia-Herzegovina, Croatia and the FRY and constituted a sub/subregional cooperative framework to implement the civilian dimension of the Dayton agreement in Bosnia (return of refugees and displaced persons, common democratic institution-building) for a long term stabilisation of the region. It is important as the only regional framework including FRY by its linkage to the Dayton Agreement. It later expanded to include all the countries of the region, as well as Russia.

EUs regional approach coupled economic aid and conditionality to promote integration and avoid partition. To succeed, regional stability might promote the normalisation of mutual relations, the development of transborder cooperation and good neighbourliness, and civil society-building approaches. In practice, this means the consolidation of borders, the promotion of good neighbourliness, the peaceful resolution of minority issues through regional round table meetings, and the development of cross-border projects. Its inclusion within the OSCE and its merge with the Stability Pact - for the moment subordinated to an agreement on the FRYs reintegration within the organisation - remains the longer term objective. It would permit to rationalise these two initiatives by combining and centralising the politico-economic and the securitarian approaches of the EU/OSCE towards the region and grant it concrete political as well as regional dimension, especially through the enhancement of article V of the former dealing with a regional approach. To this effect, a general Coordinator, Ambassador Roumeliotis, was appointed by the EU in early 1998.

The South East European Cooperative Initiative (SECI) was initiated by Ambassador Richard Schifter, President Clinton's political advisor, in December 1996. This approach exclusively provides economic and financial assistance through private-funded projects in order to support the modernisation of the local private sector and reintegrate the region into European and broader Western structures.[9] The multiple tools available are economic and financial projects, border crossing issues, infrastructure, energy, communications, and environmental protection. It was named South East European Initiative in order to encompass all the countries of the broader region, with the exception of the FRY, especially those reluctant to be part of it like Slovenia and Croatia. Hungary, Italy and Austria are observers. Willing to give it a political basis, the United States wished to merge it with the European Union initiative and the Stability Pact under an OSCE umbrella. This proposal was however rejected by both organisations unwilling to subordinate to the American leadership and to weaken the coherence of the EU and the OSCE political initiatives with an exclusively private-funded approach. Furthermore, SECI was initially perceived as a competing project which lacked both funds and transparency. However, there has been an important convergence of interests over the past years which led to greater coordination and complementarity between the two initiatives.

In late 1995, NATO set up the Partnership for Peace (PfP) programme. Based on a bilateral and a voluntaristic basis, it provides for military assistance to non-NATO member countries in order to modernise the military and defence sectors such as a reform of the military and of defence budgets in view of enlargement, and prepare their armed forces to peace-keeping requirements in Bosnia. While each country defines its own needs, NATO gives advice and practical assistance. The Euro-Atlantic Partnership Council (EAPC), which replaced the North Atlantic Cooperation Council (NACC) in 1997, provides the political dimension. A multilateral fora for political consultations, it aims at enhancing coordination among participants. After the Albanian political and financial crisis in Winter 1997 which witnessed the falling apart of the Albanian Army and police forces, NATO set up an enhanced PfP for Albania. Provisions for FYROM might be upgraded after the outbreak of the Kosovo crisis, but without reaching the level of Albania which is still considered as a special case.

The Bottom-Up Initiatives

The locally initiated frameworks have two main characteristics. First, they are intergovernmental in nature. The still weak civil societies, the hectic economic and political transition processes, the defensive mutual perceptions and the high level of conflict in the region do not predispose for a development of cross-border relations at the societal level. The patterns of regional transformation provide for three ideal regional type classifications: transnational cross-border interaction between states at the societal level; intergovernmental regional model of government-led interaction; and combination of both where policies are introduced after a consensus between the government and the private sector thus allowing a comprehensive regional model. South East Europe currently corresponds to the second model. It is only with the development and evolution of reforms, long term, that it might reach the potential to match the first model. Second, they put an emphasis on the security dimension as conflict management remains the main internal preoccupation of this conflict-ridden area. The predominance of conflict has led to the promotion of local initiatives which mainly focus on security aspects of peace-keeping exercises and training (Rapid Reaction Force, Conflict Prevention Centre...).

Originated at the local level after a Bulgarian proposal in February 1996, the Conferences on Stability, Security and Cooperation of the Ministers of South East Europe, were initiated in Sofia and Thessalonika,[10] and followed by a third Experts meeting in March 1998 in Turkey.[11] They include all countries of the region but Croatia.

Aiming at stability, security and cooperation in the region, they focus on low security issues: good neighbourly relations; democratisation and human rights; economic cooperation; liberalisation of trade; infrastructure projects; cooperation in the field of justice, terrorism, drugs and arms trafficking. Although non-binding, non-institutionalised and somehow limited by the depth of disputes, they provide a fora for discussion and a common framework where common positions and joint declarations on the problems of the region can be taken. The Crete Summit, in Greece, in early November 1997, did not address the main political issues. But it gave all regional leaders the opportunity to meet, for some after decades, and to address the situation of the region, thus breaking the ice both of reluctancy and isolation. The debates around a minimal institutionalisation to create a series of coordinating bodies in the regional capitals dealing with the respective fields (Council, Central Bank etc...), and to set up regular ministerial meetings, show the will to develop the regional approach as well as to use all means available to provide channels for discussion and cooperation.

In March 1998, in Ankara, five countries - Albania, Bulgaria, FYROM, Romania and Turkey - joined by Greece later on, agreed in principle to create a Multinational Balkan Rapid Reaction Force - renamed Multinational Peacekeeping Force in Southeastern Europe - to address current and future crises. A letter of intent to develop the force within NATO's PfP framework was signed by nine countries[12] during a Defence Ministers meeting in Tirana in May 22, and its creation was officially announced for September 26, in Skopje.[13] It promotes the enhancement of security through the creation of joint military units, contingent upon a case-by-case basis by the participating nations. This local initiative reveals the existence of common concerns, if not of common interests. According to the official document which was issued after the meeting, the force should not be assessed only in a regional context but will be available for NATO or WEU-led conflict prevention and peace support operations having a UN or an OSCE mandate. It might assist in bridging divergences or to discuss them politically before effective action is taken. It lays the ground for cooperation mentality and consultation, especially between countries which might have certain interests in a rapprochement. It could also reduce clear-cut dividing lines between regions and bridge the north and the south of the South East European peninsula. For instance, the presence of Romania is extremely important for the sustainability and the coherence of the initiative. Romania has initiated a policy of openness towards regional cooperation using its position as a bridge positively as having both a Southeastern and a central European dimension, thus using to the full its multiple and multilayered memberships. However, divergences already appeared concerning the location of potential future HQ[14] or some reluctance concerning the possibility of this force to interfere in the internal affairs of neighbouring countries.[15]

The interdependence with neighbouring regional initiatives is another important factor. The existence of parallel initiatives such as Royaumont, SECI, BSEC, creating additional opportunities for active regional cooperation was explicitly assessed during the Thessalonika meeting in July 1997. Geopolitically, South East Europe is linked to Central Asia, as it stands at the crossroads between Western Europe and the Black Sea, and its main oil and gas pipeline routes. Consequently, economic and political events in the Central Asian region have a concrete impact and consequence on South East Europe. South East Europe might not be considered as a boundary of Europe but as an integral part of it. It remains at the forefront of emerging subregional cooperation frameworks in Europe's boundary zones like BSEC, Caucasus, Central Asia.[16]

Substate bilateral or trilateral transborder cooperation, based on the Euroregion model, might also have an important development potential in the long run and can contribute to develop economic interdependence and concrete solidarities which might contribute to a decrease of political and ethnic tensions. They concern infrastructures, business-type relations, environment, exploitation of natural resources and cultural and educational exchanges. However, in spite of the fact that they embed a strong potential for economic and political development, these initiatives are recent and concrete realisations have not been achieved to a greater extent. The subregional framework remains weak to cope with all the needs and financial means are scarce. Countries do not realise yet the longer term benefits of such an approach. The difficulties raised by transborder cooperation between Bulgaria and Romania in their attempts to build a bridge over the Danube bring to light the obstacles and misperceptions. Similarly, the debates over the different transport routes and corridors running East-West and North-South corridors reveal a sense of competition rather than intensive cooperation or a search for complementarity.

3- An Assessment of Regional Cooperative Frameworks in South East Europe
Limitations

However, at the top-down level, such a plethora of initiatives does not hide the lack of an encompassing and coherent approach to the region. While they should promote complementarity, their implicit competitiveness enhanced duplication and a lack of coordination. Originally, some, like Royaumont and the SECI, gave priority to economic issues without defining common strategies and projects. They were, and still are to a certain extent, loosely defined. They do not provide adequate goals, nor substantial financial means, to address the real needs and problems in order to provide a coherent conflict prevention approach. Most approaches are non-binding as they are not clearly linked to the wider integration process. Consequently, they lack the main incentive to implementation and leverage. Furthermore, as most have developed on a bilateral basis, between the organisation and the country concerned like Royaumont or the PfP, they do not contribute to promote a sense of regionalism. Finally, there is also an imbalance between the involvement and commitment of certain countries to regional cooperation.

The range and the depth of regional disputes, among others the Kosovo conflict, the fragility of the Bosnian peace process, or the strained relations between Greece and Turkey, inevitably limit political flexibility and constitute barriers to effective regional cooperation as well as to its further enhancement. Low political issues alone cannot by themselves help to overcome the political obstacles in the absence of a parallel confidence-building process and real conflict prevention approach to each conflict separately as well as towards the region as a whole. Already, the core countries of the Royaumont initiative, with the exception of FRY willing to develop bilateral and multilateral economic and political relations with all its neighbours[17] fear a consolidation might re-establish the former Yugoslavian space. The FYR of Macedonia had not initially signed the Declaration of Stability, Security and Cooperation, resenting local initiatives which might delay its claims for accession. Bosnia-Herzegovina sent an assistant minister for foreign affairs to the Crete meeting instead of a head of state and of government, to indicate its reluctance to enter any local cooperative scheme where it might lose its political leverage for the implementation of the Dayton agreement. Greece had not initially joined the Balkan Rapid Reaction Force, giving priority to established Western military alliances. Furthermore, no regional framework might be sustainable in the long run in the absence of FRY lying at the centre of the peninsula.

There are hardly any cases where economy has allowed a spillover to political issues.The political economy of regionalism remains rather poor in the case of South East Europe. The countries are going through painful economic transition. Trade relations are low and Western countries, external to the region, still remain the main trading partners. As a result, the overall trade is more important with the European Union than at the regional level. With neighbours, trade relations are often lower than 1%, showing that geographic proximity does not automatically lead to intra-regional trade.[18] Similarly, trade with the EU is far more important than with countries of the region.[19] Furthermore, economic measures alone might not address the essentially structural problems of the region. GPD amounts to only 25% of the average in the European Union and there is an important discrepancy of economic growth compared with Central European countries, which will increase after the latter become members of the EU. These developmental gaps between different subregions as well as within South East Europe appeal for an increased dependance on external assistance, essentially the EU, and interaction between regional and top-down European cooperative initiatives. Countries which might have a more direct interest in the region (Austria, Italy, Greece) can play an essential role as South East European countries do not have the economic means, the financial resources nor the available infrastructures to invest into and promote transborder or regional projects. The last report of the EU Commission in April 1998 which assesses the economic situation in each country concerned and the respect of the political and economic conditions set by the Union clearly states the low pace of reforms and development, although to various degrees.[20] Therefore, a further institutionalisation of the different existing frameworks cannot by itself compensate the lack of resources and infrastructures. Secondly, and more important, the perception is anchored that direct links with Western economic markets are more advantageous than poor economic regional relations lacking complementarity. Short term, the prospects of a rapid development remain poor and might succeed only in the long term. However, the lack of openness of Western markets and the difficult integration into Western political and economic organisations could favour the development of economic links, free trade, and transnational forces. Economic and trade relations between certain countries reveal an important potential for development as shown for example by the balance of trade between and FYROM.[21] Such an evolution will be more a consequence of reforms and of an improvement of bilateral relations than a precondition to it. Therefore, longer term development of regional cooperation at the societal level should remain a major objective.

Analysis patterns of interaction within and between regional systems establish ideal types of regionalism using factors such as symmetry and asymmetry to measure the existence or not of similarity or dissonance in ideology which might encourage or constraint cooperation. They aim to address to which extent certain regions stimulate regional formation and which types of foreign policy interaction are more likely to nurture these trends. In doing so, they assess two types of attitudes: either the threat effect, i.e. the perception that regional formation lies against their self interests, leading to rejection; or the demonstration effect, i.e. that regional formation increases their international weight, leading to imitation. The current pattern prevailing in South East Europe is evolving from the first to the second. The attraction dimension has become all the more important. But the causal link established between a sense of attraction and the creation of regionalism is not verified here. On the contrary, the attraction effect of the other regional subsystem, especially since it belongs to the same subregional (European) system, hampers the efforts towards enhanced regional cooperation. The difficulty to integrate subregionally stems from the existence of a *dominant* system within the regional (European) system. Instead of becoming an incentive, it established a relationship based on dependency: the power of attraction increases the will to integrate within the other main subsystem instead of creating a parallel one. This is all the more strong since it is based on asymmetry and would recreate the binoma symmetry/asymmetry between two subsystems, a centre/periphery scheme within the (European) system, instead of erasing barriers. Consequently, a redefinition of integration appears to be at the core of establishing a linkage between enlargement and regional cooperation. As shown by the Nordic example, regional cooperation, far from being a natural development, can be created, as a consequence. Contrary to Central European states, South East European states are not inclined to *replicate* the process of European integration but to *integrate* within it. All the recent integration efforts exclusively aim at meeting the criteria for further integration within the EU as a conditionality element. The unique objective remains integration within existing frameworks and not a creation of parallel structures, perceived as being external and not complementary.

Since it is a long term process, a sense of regional cooperation, both in terms of perceptions and interests, might develop, although without superseding the EU integration process. It would only *coexist* in parallel, as has been the case for Nordic regional cooperation, which was however prior and developed gradually. While the former developed as a *complement*, in South East Europe it emerges after and might develop *instead*. Perceptions might be altered if it were understood as a complement, although there are no specific patterns observable.

In South East Europe, there is a total absence of a symmetry pattern, such as mutual involvement, common interests and mutual participation. The asymmetry is dominant: external powers intervene in the region (conditionality policy, interference into regional conflict) while the local countries are in a subordinate position of demand; the uneven development between the two regions does not create a conflict of interests pattern; the potential for participation is exceptionally high as there is a possibility (enlargement as an open process), a potential (local development), a perception (part of the same European system) and a will (determination, more or less confirmed, to be defined as such and to meet criteria) to participate in the dominant formation, and thus integrate, in the future. The need to coordinate policies and find a consensus on how to maximise their comparative advantages thus drastically decreases.[22]

The efforts to develop subregionalism in South East Europe create a basic paradox: EU subsystem aims at enhancing subregionalism in its immediate periphery while its very existence contributes at the same time to weaken the former. South East Europe totally fits the contrast pattern: it is weakened by the EU regional subsystem as its interests are directly hurt by the uneven development and the level of asymmetry; the EU subsystem is reasonably strong and offers rewards for participation (economic development, political cooperation, security in the traditional sense); participation or access in it is an option for the South East European subregional system as the enlargement process remains open, provided they meet the required criteria. The contribution of the EU in weakening the prospects of regional movements in its vicinity, such as the Mediterranean, described by Stephen C. Calleya, applies even more to South East Europe: the opportunity of direct association to a certain number... of states to participate in the benefits of this comprehensive international region is enough to discourage the states concerned from pursuing the establishment of their own internal region by offering sufficient enough rewards and remaining open through membership, association, or special arrangement a reasonable alternative, the European Union has hindered other regional efforts.[23] For the abovementioned reasons, there is no dilemma in South East Europe in joining or not the EU regional system. Attitudes are clearly in favour of integration. Consequently, far from strengthening their own grouping, they opt for direct accommodation with the core region. Subregional cooperation becomes a way to overcome the security dilemma. In the best case, instead of being strictly limited to its own dimension, it is intrinsicly perceived as part of enlargement and related to the future development of EU and NATO.

Future Prospects For Regional Development

However, there are many arguments in favour of a workable framework of regional cooperation in South East Europe. It is precisely because there are so many internal conflicts as well as intra- and inter-regional political and economic imbalances that a regional approach is particularly needed. Without being the solution to all ends, it might be a useful, if not essential, complementary dimension to address the problems of the region within different frameworks and levels. At the economic level, the lack of resources, the absence of competitiveness of their products constitute incentives to develop economic relations regionally.

The emergence of common strategic concerns might paradoxically be one of the major incentives. Geopolitically, Albania, Bulgaria, FYROM and Turkey on one side, and Greece, Bulgaria, FYROM, and Yugoslavia on the other, are respectively the main transit corridors running East-West and North-South. Bulgaria and Yugoslavia have an interest in exploiting the Danube River. Although for different reasons, a number of countries similarly support regional status quo: FRY and FYROM fear an emancipation of their Albanian communities might lead to secession; Greece is reluctant to any further fragmentation along its northern borders; Turkey objects to autonomist waves which might bolster its internal Kurdish issue. For FRY, regional cooperation remains a unique opportunity to rebuild strained relations with neighbours and end the country's isolation.[24] Finally, the Kosovo crisis might be a major test for the potential of South East European countries to cooperate peacefully and constructively.[25]

This common threat perception to security constitutes a uniting factor but does not presuppose the emergence of a feeling of a regional common identity. With the re-emergence of conflict, local leaders have started to develop an increased awareness of the interdependence between the various crisis points: they share common principles (territorial integrity, border inviolability); internal concerns (borders, minorities) and common objectives (peaceful resolution of conflict, no spillover effect). The creation of a Balkan Rapid Reaction Force directly stems from such considerations. In that case, Buzan's security complexes paradigm, where a group of states whose primary security concerns link together sufficiently closely that their national securities cannot realistically be considered apart from one another, entirely fits.[26] According to this approach, regional transformation results from shifts in the internal dynamic of the security complex and the external dynamic associated with the global rivalry. In a purely functionalist approach, the region creation might stem from the emerging existence of common political interests, but also from a prior formal organisation. To put it differently, the emergence of common concerns might lead, in the future, to formal organisation in the sense of an institutionalisation which will in turn contribute to the regional dynamic. The enlargement issue not being (re)defined to address their needs adequately, unity at the regional level might become a long term asset. In view of the above mentioned priority of integration within broader frameworks, this *rapprochement* might not be perceived as a consolidation of particularism, a higher national unity, a cultural and political entity seeking to promote and safeguard indigenous culture and foster autonomous political institutions at a regional level.[27] The South East European model suits a more functional approach to interdependence and interaction, where regions might be defined at various levels, either geographical, social, organisational, historical etc. Translocal political, military, economic and social bounds stem from the inherent interdependence, and mutual relations can be either cooperative or conflictual, but either way, and constitute a form of regional complex.[28]

Regions are international subsystems that can be distinguished from the whole by the particular nature and intensity of their interactions with each other.[29] The region then becomes united by more than only an ad hoc problem. It can be either geographic proximity (although by itself this variable might not be explicative of the countries retained), political interdependence and interaction (as security concerns), and the future creation of a regional institutional framework, either it is bound to remain loose, flexible and transitional.[30] Consequently, a region shall be loosely defined as a pattern of relations among basic units in world politics which exhibits a particular degree of regularity and intensity of relations as well as awareness of interdependence among the particular units.[31] The regional frameworks objective, in distinguishing a distinct area and then identifying the patterns of interaction within it, makes the definition of a region operational in the sense that such a definition is essentially understood as an analytical apparatus for separating certain traits perceived as relevant.[32] Variables such as actors self-awareness within regions of social and cultural homogeneity are too restrictive a definition. The variables retained by Stephen C. Calleya thus fit our analytical needs: the states' pattern of cooperative or conflictual relations or interactions exhibit a particular degree of regularity and intensity to the extent that a change in their foreign policy actions has a direct influence on the policy-making of neighbouring actors, described as regional patterns of interaction; the existence of proximate states; the influence of external states.[33] This definition takes into account the evaluative and political, thus arbitrary, decision of defining borders between regions, as assessed by Braudel, and advocates that the intimacy of interaction among the participating states decreases as the edge of one region and the start of the next one is approached.[34] Finally, South East Europe is defined as a distinct group of states which is part of an international region. It is considered as an inherent part of the broader European region, to which the enlargement issue is an integral part, and which comprises, Northern, Western, Central, and South East Europe.

The linkage of regional countries to the broader European integration process remains the main reason for their participation. Regional frameworks are perceived as the available tools or means, and as a first step towards further integration. External top-down initiatives thus have a central role to play in the build-up of regional cooperation. The enlargement door should therefore be kept open for regional cooperation to work. The future effectiveness of regional cooperation frameworks, either top-down or bottom-up implies a clearer (re)definition of regionalism by Western European countries, as well as its linkage to the broader European security context, i.e. whether regionalism is perceived as a substitute, as an alternative security structure, or as a means to fulfil European integration. In general terms, the linkage between enlargement and regional cooperation might be enhanced, and the process clarified and made unambiguous. Since security on the European continent is understood as being inclusive and not exclusive, South East Europe, far from being at the periphery of Europe and marginalised, might be assessed as being of direct interest to European organisations involved in the region, which might commit to gradually integrate them. The conditionality aspect might then be reinforced to provide both incentives and obligations for the implementation of policies and reforms as a binding process. Leaving a security vacuum in South East Europe might increase instability and a *posteriori* crisis management cost for Western Europeans. For all the above mentioned reasons, regional cooperation might be promoted and institutionalised up to a certain level within the framework of top-down initiatives. Bottom-up initiatives might be developed in accordance with and in complementarity to the broader existing frameworks, while a separate institutionalisation will remain unlikely.

As a consequence of regional instability and uneven development within the region, any preferential treatment or discrimination could prove dividing. South East European political, economic and security cooperation can be established only on the basis of a global approach to the region, including all states, i.e. the successor states of Yugoslavia and Turkey. They should not be considered, and thus instrumentalised, by external countries as assets in the realm of broader political and securitarian considerations. Equality of membership and participation is a condition for regional cooperation to work. The lack of interests of one state towards regionalism would automatically limit incentives. By harming regional coherence and intensifying divisions instead of bridging them, it would promote exclusivity and competitiveness and prevent the poorest states from coping with requirements. Splitting off the South East European states into the Central European sphere constitutes a second limit. The specificity of problems, and thus of solutions, should be addressed in common, as any split would weaken the regions internal coherence and its bargaining capability towards major international organisations. This would ensure a coherent policy implementation at the regional level and promote a sense of regional identity.[35] However, a differentiation approach might be considered regarding the compliance of criteria, as a basic conditionality to integration.[36] An overexpansion of membership to unprepared countries might weaken the coherence, not only of regional cooperation, but also of the enlargement process as a whole.

The depth of problems in the region, economic, political and securitarian in nature, justify major outside involvement, a real entry strategy and a strategic approach for international organisations. The political and security vacuum in South East Europe will not be filled by large numbers of interlocking networks of security arrangements unless they have political and economic coherence. International organisations could then promote a better division of labour and coordination. The European Union could rationalise economic aid and reconstruction plans and promote transborder projects aiming at integration. The OSCE might address softer security issues such as border and minority, and transborder cooperation. The Stability Pact could be extended to South East Europe. Its article V providing for a regional approach could be extended to arms control measures including the CFE Treaty, provided some adaptations. The OSCE has an important and useful experience in the region. It has been involved in FRY, with long term spillover monitoring missions in 1992 (in spite of a withdrawal in 1993 due to the Serbian veto within the OSCE), FYROM since 1993, and Albania since 1997 as the main coordinating organisation for foreign assistance, within the framework of cooperative security in Europe.[37] NATO might work out a PfP Plus for the region, intensifying joint exercises over bilateral relations and linking the enlargement issue to regional cooperation.

NATO and EU enlargement to Central Europe brings to the fore the importance of an inter-linkage and interaction between subregional cooperative initiatives to avoid an increased gap and future marginalisation which could lead to new dividing lines. It might help South East European countries to prove their commitment to a regional approach in view of integration while at the same time increasing its political significance. However, such cross-participation should not be over-enhanced as it might lead to a dilution of South East European cooperative frameworks into neighbouring ones and prevent the development of a coherent regional structure able to successfully address the problems of the region. Relations with the Central European Initiative (or its follow-up) and BSEC (five of its eleven members originating from South East Europe) should be explored, especially after NATO and EU enlargement. BSEC projects are essentially based on the same fields of economic cooperation such as infrastructure, energy and communications, and it would rationalise and better coordinate the regional initiatives and reinforce mutual relations with the broader European frameworks.

Conclusions

The likelihood of South East Europe becoming a region *stricto sensu* is not a basic precondition for regional cooperation to work. Flexible definitions based on interaction and proximate status prevail in this case. The deep economic, political and social problems have essentially privileged intergovernmentally-led regional cooperation without a real regional identification being on its way. Thus, regional cooperation in South East Europe provides for alternative patterns of interaction at various levels and in different sectors.

The views on how to address the multiple crisis in the region are many and do not allow to draw specific conclusions. There remain only options, ways forward and potential avenues. However, the situation in South East Europe is specific: it remains crisis ridden, economically backward with weak civil societies. Consequently, the success of regionalism remains based on outside interest to inspire regional cooperation. Especially since the driving force of regional cooperation remains external, namely integration within broader European structures and conditionality. Multiple memberships are not incompatible with subregional cooperation, nor is a combination and coexistence of top-down and bottom-up initiatives. They must however not be further divisive, exclude certain countries and provide a preferential treatment as a certain degree of regional coherence might be preserved for regional cooperation to work. Furthermore, the former should focus on security issues which might constitute the field for the development of common concerns and objectives aiming at avoiding increased instability, further fragmentation, and promote peaceful conflict resolution.

Regional cooperation initiated locally is a precondition for the success of top-down frameworks. Externally imposed solutions can hardly be sustainable unless they are undertaken by the countries themselves, and promoted locally as a precondition to cooptation. They might be clearly understood as part of a security-building process aiming to support and assist, and provide long term solutions. An extensive use of available mechanisms within international organisations should be made. For regional cooperation to work, a necessary balance between top-down and bottom-up approaches is needed such as coordination and transparency to promote interdependence.

Notes

1. Some points have been presented by the author in "Emerging Sub-regional cooperation in South-Eastern Europe" in Alyson Bailes and Andrew Cottey. Regional cooperation frameworks, Macmillan, London, April 1998.

2. By "Balkan region" or "South-Eastern Europe", we imply Albania, former Yugoslavia (except Slovenia), Bulgaria, Romania, Greece and Turkey.

3. See the definition by Cantori and Spiegal, in Stephen C. Calleya, "Navigating Regional Dynamics in the Post Cold War World", Dartmouth, Aldershot 1997, op. cit. p.30.

4. Barry Buzan. "People, States and Fear: An Agenda for International Security Studies in the post-Cold War Era", Hemel Hempstead, Harvester Wheatsheaf. p. 298.

5. Ibid. p. 208.

6. Sophia Clément. *"L'Europe du sud-est après les élargissements de l'Union européenne et de l'OTAN"*, in Les Balkans, deux ans après les Accords de Dayton, Sophia Clément and Thierry Tardy (eds.) Relations Internationales et Stratégiques, Paris, December 1997.

7. Jeffery Simon, "Bulgaria and NATO: 7 lost years", Strategic Forum, n.142, May 1998.

8. Sophia Clément, "Emerging Subregional Cooperation...", op. cit.

9. Southeast European Cooperative Initiative - SECI, Activity Report 1997, Vienna.

10. Sofia Declaration on Good-Neighbourly Relations, Stability, Security and

Cooperation in the Balkans, Conference of the Ministers of Foreign Affairs in Sofia on 6-7 July, 1996, of the Ministers of Foreign Affairs of seven Balkan countries of countries of South Eastern Europe (Albania, Bosnia-Herzegovina, Bulgaria, Federal Republic of Yugoslavia, Greece, Romania and Turkey). Thessalonika Declaration on Good-Neighbourly Relations, Stability, Security and Cooperation in the Balkans. Conference of the Ministers of Foreign Affairs of countries of South Eastern Europe, 9-10 June, 1997.

11. They are based on the model of the Balkan Conferences of the 30s. They draw upon two previous conferences in Belgrade in 1988 and Tirana in 1990.

12. Albania, Bulgaria, FYROM, Romania, Slovenia, Turkey, Greece and Italy, as well as the United States.

13. "Balkan countries to set up peacekeeping force", SWB, EE/ B/1, 25 May 1998.

14. "Ministers say setting up of Balkan Force is more important than location", SWB, EE/3226 B/3, 14 May 1998. "Conference marred by dispute between Greece and Turkey", SWB, EE/ B/1, 25 May 1998.

15. Declaration of the Macedonian Defence Minister, Lazar Kitanovski. "Minister says NATO Rapid Intervention Troops should not train in Macedonia", SWB, EE/ 3193 A/11, 4 April 1998.

16. Security and Integration in Eurasia's New Boundary Zones: The Role of Subregional Cooperation, Macmillan, 1999.

17. "Trust at the cornerstone of cooperation", Serbian Bulletin, September 1996.

18. Vladimir Gligorov, "Trade in the Balkans", paper prepared for the seminar on "South east Europe after NATO and EU Enlargement: Towards Inclusive Security Structures?", Institute for Security Studies, Western European Union, Paris, 11-12 December 1997. To give but a few significative examples, in % shares of exports and imports, Slovenia reaches 10.34/6.18 with Croatia, 3.17/0 with B&H and 2.05/0.75 with Macedonia but less than 1% with all the other countries. Albania: 4/3.5 with Macedonia, 9.9/26.8 with Greece and 6.2/4.1 with Turkey and below 1% with others. Greece: 1.3/0.4 with Yugoslavia, 0.8/0.4 with Macedonia, 1.75/1.05 with Bulgaria, 1/2 with Turkey and lower with the rest of the countries.

19. For example, in % shares of exports and imports for Croatia: 18.61/20.57 with Germany, 21.03/18.25 with Italy; for Macedonia: 18.7/14.75 with Germany, 4.48/6.75 with Italy; for Bulgaria: 9.13/10.67 with Germany, 9.65/5.89 with Italy. Ibid.

20. Agence EUROPE, *n.7201,* 16 April 1998, p.6.

21. The exchanges have increased from US$ 92.8 million in 1992 to US$ 271.3 in 1996. Greek investments have increased from US$ 13 million in 1992 to US$ 63 million in 1995. Balance of trade. Source: Greek Ministry of Economy, October 1997.

22. Stephen C. Calleya. op. cit. p.8.

23. Ibid.

24. Predrag SIMIC. Post conflict settlement and regional cooperation in South Eastern Europe: the role of Yugoslavia (Unpublished).

25. See declaration by European Affairs Minister Andreas Papandreou, "Kosovo a test for Balkan cooperation", International Herald Tribune, 2 April 1998.

26. Barry Buzan. People, States and Fear: An Agenda for International Security Studies in the post-Cold War Era. Hemel Hempstead, Harvester, Wheatsheaf. p.190.

27. Stephen C. Calleya, op. cit. p.27.

28. Stephen C. Calleya, op. cit. p.33.

29. Barry Buzan et al. "Regional Security: A Post-Cold War Framework for Analysis", Working Paper, Center for Peace and Conflict Research, Copenhagen, 1994. p.7.

30. Stephen C. Calleya, op. cit. p.29-30.

31. Karl Kaiser, "The Interaction of Subregional Systems: Some Preliminary Notes of Recurrent Patterns and the Role of the Superpowers", World Politics, vol.21, n.1, October 1968. p.86.

32. Stephen C. Calleya, op. cit. p.27.

33. Stephen C. Calleya, op. cit. p.36.

34. Ibid. p.37.

35. Spyros Economides. The Balkan Agenda: Security and Regionalism in the New Europe. London Defence Studies, Center for Defence Studies, Brassey's, 1992.

36. Sophia Clément, "South East Europe: Towards a Differentiated Process?", WEU-ISS News Letter, December 1997.

37. Sophia Clément. "The OSCE Involvement in the Albanian Crisis" in The Albanian Crisis and the International Community, Andrea de Guttry (dir.) 1999.

5. The OSCE and Regional Cooperation in Europe

Monika Wohlfeld[1]

1. Introduction

Subregional cooperation has been an integral component of Western European cooperation and integration since 1945. The Benelux and the arrangements between the Nordic countries provide excellent examples of such cooperation. The post-Cold War years saw both a further development of existing subregional groupings, and the emergence of several new ones, voluntarily entered into by OSCE participating States in Central and Eastern Europe, the Baltics, and in South Eastern Europe and reflecting a new concept of security and new opportunities to enhance security. Observers began to note that 'the new subregional groups are not only products of but also significant contributors to the positive changes in Europe's security environment in recent years.'[2] They help strengthening democracy and market economies, as well as stabilising relations among neighbouring states and facilitating the process of European integration. They also help to promote and implement OSCE principles and objectives.

Many observers argue that to be successful, subregional cooperation frameworks, particularly those in Central, Eastern, and South-eastern Europe, should be included in the process of building a pan-European security order. International organisations (particularly the OSCE and the United Nations, but also the Council of Europe and the European Union) already provide the principles on which these groupings and frameworks are based. However, it is often observed that so far the links between the subregional organisations and international organisations in Europe (OSCE, the WEU, NATO, but also the EU with its Common Foreign and Security Policy) are still rather weak. Some consider the OSCE to be best suited for the task of supporting and coordinating subregional efforts: 'The OSCE with its inclusive, pan-European membership, its broad definition of security, its focus on prevention and its cooperative approach has an important role to play in the various subregions of the OSCE area as a whole.' [3] Arguably, although the OSCE played an, admittedly mostly indirect, role in setting some of these groupings up, its working relations with them are not very well developed. Thus the argument is put forward by some observers that further institutional links between the OSCE and subregional groupings are needed.

This paper focuses on the issue of OSCE's cooperation with formalised, and occasionally institutionalised, subregional frameworks, that is intergovernmental frameworks established by subregional groups of States within the OSCE area (such as the Council of Baltic Sea States (CBSS), the Central European Initiative (CEI), the Black Sea Economic Cooperation (BSEC), the Royaumont Process, and the Southeast European Cooperative Initiative (SECI)), and discusses expectations versus reality of this form of links. However, it also briefly considers two other dimensions of subregional cooperation relevant to the organisation: informal intergovernmental coordination of positions by groups of States within the OSCE on various political issues; and aspects of OSCE's work which have a subregional dimension, one example of which is the implementation of subregional agreements concluded elsewhere (the Stability Pact, and the Annex 1B of the Dayton/Paris Agreement). The two dimensions highlight the opportunities for, and limitations of, cooperation between subregional frameworks and the OSCE. This chapter is not a history of subregional cooperation, nor a description of the current functions or memberships of these groupings.

Some words about terminology and definitions: To define the concepts of 'region' and 'subregion' in the context of the OSCE poses some problems. The 1997 OSCE Copenhagen[4] documents refer to both regional and subregional groupings without specifying the difference between those. One should note also that the OSCE is itself a regional arrangement under Chapter VIII of the United Nations Charter, and that therefore any geographically defined groups of States within the OSCE space can be understood as subregions. For the purpose of this chapter, a subregion is understood to refer to a geographically (and often also historically) coherent area within the OSCE space as a whole. However, in some contexts, particularly arms control and CSBMs, and regional round tables, the accepted usage is to refer to groups of States as regions rather than subregions and to speak, for example, of regional CSBMs. For the purpose of this chapter, where common usage is to speak of 'region' and 'regional' rather than, as defined above, of 'subregion' and 'subregional', for reasons of clarity this common usage will be maintained, but marked in italics (*regional*).

The membership of the OSCE and the comprehensive nature of its mandate suggest the usefulness of coordination and cooperation on a subregional basis. States with similar subregional interests tend to join together on an *ad hoc* basis.

In the decision-making process, several groups of States coordinate their positions within the OSCE on a regular basis: in addition to the largest and formalised caucus of the European Union States and the ten associated States (which reflects their commitment to a Common Foreign and Security Policy), and - on a case-by-case basis - the North Atlantic Treaty Organisation, there are smaller and more flexible subregional groups of States which coordinate their positions on an *ad hoc* basis. The so called GUAM group (Georgia, Ukraine, Azerbaijan and Moldova), the three Baltic States, four Central European States (Poland, Hungary, the Czech Republic and Slovakia), and occasionally some or all of the five Central Asian states coordinate depending on relevance of issues.

The coordination of positions among OSCE participating States based on common interests reflecting geographic proximity highlights that in a consensus-based organisation, the process is as important as the result, meaning that consensus-building on a subregional basis is considered overall a positive phenomenon. Simultaneously, some countries may approve of flexible, *ad hoc* subregional caucuses, but may feel left out, or confronted with the emergence of 'power blocs' in the OSCE, if faced by inflexible, dogmatic subregional groups. In this context, formalised links between the OSCE and subregional frameworks may be considered difficult by some OSCE participating States.

Significantly, multilateral coordination of positions among subregional groups of States in the OSCE context has so far not lead to creation of more formalised subregional frameworks, or to involvement of existing frameworks in the coordination of positions in the OSCE.

2.Subregional Aspects of OSCE's Work

In the field, no OSCE mission has a mandate providing for a clear subregional dimension. Because OSCE missions are intended to offer cost-effective, timely and flexible responses to a broad range of issues, and are in all cases deployed with the approval of the host country, the OSCE participating States place emphasis on developing 'tailor-made' and therefore different mandates. However, pragmatic and goal-oriented cooperation on specific issues of subregional concern (such as refugees) takes place between some missions, often with contributions from other international organisations.

The subregional dimension is also subject to debate in OSCE's arms control fora, but here the common usage of terminology is to refer to *regional* aspects. For reasons of clarity, the common usage is maintained in the context of this chapter. As a 1995 OSCE seminar concluded, "the present OSCE and arms control agreements (sic) constitute an important tool and a sound basis for ensuring security and stability. However, they do not always meet specific regional concerns."[5] To take these *regional* concerns into account, the OSCE's Forum for Security Cooperation (FSC) has on its regular agenda a discussion of participating States' experience in the area of bilateral and *regional* issues. The result is a regularly updated informal listing of voluntary agreements that deepen existing common commitments, prepared by the OSCE Secretariat.

The issue of *regional* arms control commitments also found its way onto the agenda of the *ad hoc* working group for the review of the Vienna Document 1994 (3rd edition) on the Negotiations on Confidence- and Security-Building Measures and Disarmament in Europe. However, even though there is some support for *regional* approaches to arms control, a number of countries find the concept difficult: arms control is indivisible, it is argued, and countries oppose special *regional* arrangements, particularly when they are suggested by third states.

An example of a specific *regional* issue on the agenda of the FSC are proposals regarding confidence- and security-building measures (CSBMs) for the Baltic region. If accepted, *regional* proposals such as these could theoretically be incorporated in the form of a chapter in a planned revision of the Vienna Document. According, for example, to Wolfgang Ischinger, Political Director of the German Foreign Ministry, specific CSBM commitments codified in the Vienna Document could be complemented and strengthened through specific *regional* measures decided in the context of a *regional* table, with the participation of both Russia and the United States.[6]

The OSCE also has experience in implementing subregional agreements concluded elsewhere. The OSCE's contribution to the Stability Pact, and the involvement in the implementation of Annex 1-B of the Paris/Dayton Agreement are two recent and important cases. In the case of the Stability Pact, the common usage is to refer to *regional* round tables; the situation under the Annex 1-B is more complicated, as the Annex refers overall to an 'Agreement on Regional Stabilisation', the Article IV to 'Subregional Arms Control Measures' (for the Republic of Bosnia and Herzegovina, the Republic of Croatia, the Federal Republic of Yugoslavia, the Federation of Bosnia and Herzegovina, and the *Republika Srpska*) and Article V to 'Regional Arms Control Agreement' ('in and around former Yugoslavia'). The difference between 'regional' and 'subregional', in this case, is pragmatically defined and distinguishes a group of States from that same group plus surrounding countries.

Under the Stability Pact, *regional* round tables (for the Baltic region and Central and Eastern Europe) were convened to focus on particular *regional* challenges and to identify concrete projects and relationship-building activities that might contribute to *regional* stability. The Pact on Stability in Europe was adopted and signed in Paris on 20-21 March 1995. Monitoring of compliance with and implementation of the specific agreements outlined in the Pact was entrusted to the OSCE. The OSCE offered to provide "involvement with regard to the observance of OSCE principles and commitments in the implementation of the... agreements or arrangements" of the Stability Pact, and described the experience of the *regional* tables as useful for dealing with *regional* issues.[7] The experience of *regional* round tables has since been reflected in debates on subregional initiatives in the OSCE context, but neither the possibility of requesting OSCE assistance with the implementation of projects and activities decided upon in the Stability Pact nor the possibility of using *regional* round tables in the OSCE context has so far been used.

Another of the Organisation's current experiences is the negotiation and implementation of the progressive measures for arms control and regional stability provided for in articles II, IV and V of the Annex 1-B of the Dayton/Paris Agreement. Article II on Confidence- and Security-Building Measures in Bosnia and Herzegovina was signed in Vienna on 26 January 1996. Article IV on Measures for Subregional Arms Control, aimed at establishing a stable military balance at the lowest levels of armaments, was signed in Florence, Italy on 14 June 1996. Both of these articles are considered a success for the OSCE. The next step for the OSCE is the negotiation of Article V (Agreement on Regional Stabilisation), which deals with *regional* arms control agreements and has as its goal the establishment of a *regional* balance in and around the former Yugoslavia.[8] The processes are considered to be complementary to the work undertaken by subregional groupings in Southeast Europe, such as the Royaumont Process or the Southeast European Cooperative Initiative (SECI).

The OSCE's activities undertaken on a subregional rather than on a comprehensive basis, these are accompanied by debate and occasionally controversy. While the subregional approach lends itself to many of the OSCE's goals and principles, the concept of comprehensive security which is at the base of the OSCE's work makes pursuing subregional activities complex and for some participating States troublesome. As in the case of coordination of positions on a subregional basis, flexibility, transparency and access may prevent these kinds of problems. Significantly, so far, the experience of subregional aspects of OSCE's work has not led to either the creation of more formalised subregional frameworks, or to involvement of existing frameworks in this dimension of the OSCE.

3. OSCE's Cooperation with Formalised Subregional Groupings

Prior to the decisions of Copenhagen, references have been made to subregional cooperation in OSCE documents. It was in 1996 in Lisbon that a direct link was established between the OSCE and subregional frameworks. The Lisbon Summit Declaration states that 'the OSCE could contribute to using fully the potential of the various regional cooperative efforts in a mutually supportive and reinforcing way.'[9]

In 1997, in Copenhagen, the OSCE participating States agreed that: they will further strengthen non-hierarchical cooperation between the OSCE and other organisations within a Platform for Cooperative Security to be elaborated as an essential element of the Document-Charter. ... Based on the provisions set put in the

Common Concept, they will offer the OSCE as a potential forum for interaction of regional and subregional groupings in the OSCE area, with the aim of facilitating exchanges of information and of developing a pragmatic approach to addressing challenges, including those in the field of post-conflict rehabilitation.[10]

The Copenhagen documents refer to the Platform for Cooperative Security, which is one of the proposed elements of the Document-Charter on European Security, aimed at developing a concept for synergies between the OSCE and other organisations, including subregional groupings, in a non-hierarchical manner. To date, a focused debate on the subregional dimension of the Document-Charter has not yet taken place, although a number of unofficial papers on that subject has been introduced in the working group of the Security Model Committee dealing with the Platform.

On the side of the subregional groupings, the documents and declarations express willingness to implement OSCE's principles, pursue close general links with the Organisation, and cooperate in a number of specific areas. The member States of the various subregional groupings repeatedly have reaffirmed their commitment to the implementation of the relevant documents of the OSCE. In a recent example, the Council of Baltic Sea States (CBSS), at its 7th Ministerial Session in Nyborg on 22-23 June 1998, reiterated that "cooperátion and security are in particular based on common principles and adherence to the OSCE as well as on commitments of the states to the UN Charter."[11] Similar declarations have been made by other subregional groupings.

Not all of these groups have decided to take on a security role. Instead, a number of them, particularly those with a more diverse membership, such as the Black Sea Economic Cooperation (BSEC), which has identified economic cooperation "as a contribution to the OSCE process",[12] have chosen either not to pursue security initiatives, or to pursue them on an informal basis, and focus on other areas. Others however, without taking on a 'hard' security role, acknowledged the role of contacts with the OSCE in this sphere. For example, the Central European Initiative (CEI) Foreign Ministers' meeting, held in Sarajevo in June 1997, stressed the need to intensify cooperation in the sphere of security, stability and confidence-building measures through regular contacts with the OSCE and other relevant organisations in Europe.

Some specific areas for cooperation have been identified by subregional groupings. The CBSS, for example, "welcomed the intention of the CBSS Commissioner to give priority to and coordinate his efforts in the media field with the EU, the High Commissioner on National Minorities and the OSCE Representative on the Freedom of the Media". [13] The OSCE and the Council of Europe cooperated with the CEI working group on national minorities in drafting the CEI Instrument for the Protection of Minority Rights.[14] CEI experts participated in monitoring the national elections in Albania in June 1997, which were held under the auspices of the OSCE.

Another specific case are the two most recent subregional initiatives aimed at Southeast Europe, the Royaumont Process and the Southeast European Cooperative Initiative (SECI), which, in their conceptual stages, were intended by their "architects" to be, or to become in time, integral parts of the OSCE. The "Process of Stability and Good Neighbourliness in South-East Europe", called the Royaumont Process, an EU initiative that emerged from the Stability Pact, began in late 1995 and was signed together with the Paris Peace Agreement. It deals with problems of stability and good-neighbourliness in Southeast Europe. In the initial declaration of the process, the Southeast European States participating in it emphasised that they "consider that this reflection should take place in the framework of the OSCE, repository of the Pact on Stability. To this end, we propose to give it, in due time, the form of a regional table for strengthening stability, good neighbourliness and cooperation in south-east Europe', where all States of the region will be represented on an equal footing, consistent with the relevant OSCE decisions."[15] This principle of equal footing, which gives the Federal Republic of Yugoslavia (FRY), which does not participate in the OSCE, access to the forum, has not allowed the OSCE to coordinate the process as originally intended. A temporary solution was found in having the EU Presidency serve on a provisional basis as a point of contact and coordinator of the initiative, with the OSCE attending meetings. The issue of Yugoslavia's participation in the OSCE has so far not been resolved. In the concept paper for the SECI (but not in its subsequent documents), the OSCE is seen as the framework within which SECI will function. In neither case has this been possible, since any such moves requires the consensus of OSCE participating States, but practical arrangements for cooperation with the SECI have been developed: the SECI Coordinator has been designated by the OSCE Chairman-in-Office; the OSCE has begun to provide technical support; and SECI representatives participate in seminars and conferences organised by the OSCE.

4. Assessment of Factors Promoting and Hindering the Development of OSCE's Cooperation with Subregional Frameworks

Subregional frameworks would clearly benefit from more political and practical support from international organisations, which would give them visibility, credibility, and political weight and possibly also the expertise and resources they need.

The potential for increased cooperation between the OSCE and subregional frameworks exists in a number of areas. They include the discussion of CSBMs (see above), the economic and environmental dimension, and the human dimensions (human rights, issues pertaining to freedom of media, election monitoring and support for civil society, including NGOs). In the economic dimension, the Lisbon Summit Declaration already commits the Organisation to further enhancing its ties to mutually reinforcing international economic and financial institutions. In the same paragraph, the Organisation commits itself also to enhancing its "interaction with regional, subregional and transborder cooperative initiatives in the economic and environmental field" because of their contribution to the promotion of good-neighbourly relations and security. [16] It is an area in which subregional groupings are interested - for example, the incoming Danish Presidency of the CBSS also made environmental and nuclear safety a priority area. The appointment of the Coordinator of OSCE Economic and Environmental Activities can be expected to improve interaction with subregional groupings. However, although subregionalism is challenged by lack of resources to deploy on cooperative projects, the OSCE cannot provide financial and project-oriented support, and cannot be used as a forum for, for example, infrastructure programmes - a prominent aspect of subregional groupings' work. Here, other organisations and institutions, particularly the European Union, are of importance. In the human dimension, some links exist already between subregional groupings and the High Commissioner on National Minorities as well as the Office for Democratic Institutions and Human Rights, and could be further developed. Furthermore, the recently established institution of the OSCE Representative on the Freedom of Media may be of interest to subregional frameworks. The Representative intends to pursue close links to these groupings.

More far-reaching, OSCE's activities with a subregional

character and also to some degree the possibility to coordinate positions on a subregional basis on various issues within the OSCE decision-making process may be considered as ready-made opportunities ('plug-ins') for the involvement of more formalised subregional frameworks.

But as most States participating in subregional frameworks shy away from taking on a security dimension, they may not wish for strong formalised links to an organisation like the OSCE, but which, unlike them, deals among others with aspects such as arms control and conflict management. The nature of the OSCE however may give the best indication of the opportunities and obstacles for its relations with subregional frameworks.

The fact that 54 States participate in the Organisation implies that all European States, members of subregional groupings, are also represented in the OSCE. This implies opportunities for cooperation between the OSCE and these groupings. Furthermore, both the OSCE and subregional cooperation frameworks can facilitate cooperation between States that are members of treaty-based organisations, such as NATO, and those who are not, or not yet, members of such organisations. They can thus help overcome dividing lines, in accordance with the OSCE concept of indivisible security.[17] Both the OSCE and subregional groupings will have an increasingly important role to play in cushioning the impact of slow enlargement.

There are, however, participating States that are hesitant to create or to participate in special arrangements on a subregional basis and/or formalised subregional groupings, either because they see them as imposed by others or because they are apprehensive either of arrangements that do not ensure equal possibilities and rights to all their members or of being marginalised by or within these frameworks. Others prefer not to give such frameworks a direct security role because they believe that this could be detrimental to their efforts at integration in Euro-Atlantic structures. But the most important consideration, and one that has to be addressed adequately, is the fear on the part of a number of States that the OSCE, this unique pan-European framework, might be fragmented.

The OSCE is a consensus-based organisation, reflecting the principle of cooperative security. It implements this principle by encouraging the growth of mutual understanding and promoting the mutual accommodation of other States' interests - goals also pursued by subregional groupings.[18] The consensus-rule also creates certain limitations. For example, it is not always easy or even possible to reach consensus on formalising links with other international institutions and organisations, and that may also apply to subregional groupings. It is often easier to work within the OSCE in a low-visibility, pragmatic and flexible manner, reflecting an implicit agreement on benefits of cooperation.

The OSCE is an organisation based on a comprehensive understanding of security. Its philosophy reflects an approach focusing on traditional security aspects as well as on the human dimension, democracy-building, the economic dimension, the environment and humanitarian dimensions. Subregional groupings as well have the potential to deal with a wide range of non-military security issues and respond sensitively to their members' actual "soft" security needs, thus also reflecting the concept of comprehensive security. There is scope for sub-regional groups to address soft security issues, such as organised crime, drugs and illegal migration. To date however, except maybe in the context of initiatives in the Baltic region, practical cooperation in this area has been developing rather slowly. In this sphere, there may be room for cooperation between the OSCE and subregional groupings.

The existing subregional groupings have had little success in removing bilateral tensions and problems among their members. They have however occasionally prevented such problems from dominating all aspects of the bilateral relationship. It is clear that bilateral problems may prove to be an obstacle in the various countries' attempts to develop closer relations or to integrate with international organisations. Significantly, the OSCE, jointly with subregional groupings, may be able to provide the appropriate tools for dealing with such bilateral issues. The OSCE can assist subregional groupings by addressing concrete problems on the ground as they arise by carrying out its tasks of early warning, crisis prevention, crisis management and post-conflict rehabilitation - monitoring, mediating and sending missions - which no subregional grouping is able to carry out by itself. The OSCE undertakes these tasks as a rule in close cooperation with other organisations, which could also include subregional groupings.

5. Conclusion: Possible Future Developments

The declaratory policies of both the OSCE and of subregional frameworks on cooperation are often quite ambitious. This is a reflection of the fact that the principles and commitments of the OSCE are also goals of subregional groupings. However, the implementation of political declarations does not always correspond to them, in particular, the more ambitious plans, such as to actually embed subregional frameworks in the OSCE, have not been implemented, as they require consensus among participating States. Probably the most important obstacle towards developing closer links between the OSCE and subregional groupings is some participating States' fear of working against the concept of common security. Clearly, the development of regionalism and contacts with subregional frameworks must be well integrated into the OSCE framework in order to avoid the danger of fragmentation of European security. Another obstacle is the subregional groupings' reticence and/or inability to take on a clear security role, which makes the relations between the OSCE and the groupings uneven.

But the relations are evolving. The most important current development in the relations between the OSCE and subregional groupings is the Document-Charter for European Security, now being negotiated, in particular the Platform for Cooperative Security. To date, it is not certain how the issue of subregional cooperation will be brought into the Document-Charter. However, the OSCE could offer to provide a conceptual framework for cooperation and a forum for an interinstitutional exchange of views, a function which could be used to support subregional cooperation - and one for which the OSCE, because of its geographic reach, is probably best suited among European institutions and organisations. Communication and interaction between subregional groups and international organisations and institutions can provide a useful tool in shaping the European security environment. For example, it can help in developing shared agendas and joint projects and prevent competition between subregional groups, particularly for EU support.

The longer term development of links between the OSCE and subregional groupings will depend primarily upon the capabilities, and the further development of the role of the Organisation in the European security architecture. The nature of enlargement processes of NATO and the EU will surely play a role in this context, as it will for the development of subregional frameworks.

The new European system will be multi-institutional and multi-functional. The OSCE and subregional groupings will both play an important role in this architecture, whether they are linked or not. However, stronger relations may make both more able and capable of dealing with security challenges in Europe.

Notes

1. Dr. Monika Wohlfeld is a Diplomatic Adviser at the OSCE Secretariat. This contribution is based on a chapter on 'The OSCE and subregional cooperation in Europe' she contributed to the *OSCE Yearbook 1998*. Nomos Verlag, forthcoming 1998.

2. Anders Bjurner, 'European Security at the End of the Twentieth Century: The Subregional Contribution', in *Subregional Cooperation in the New Europe: Building Security, Prosperity and Solidarity from the Barents to the Black Sea,* Andrew Cottey (ed.). Macmillan Press, 1998, p. 8.

3. Ibid., p. 8.

4. Paragraph 5 (e), Decision no. 5 on "Guidelines on an OSCE Document-Charter on European Security", Copenhagen, Sixth Meeting of the OSCE Ministerial Council, 19 December 1997.

5. 'FSC Seminar on Regional Arms Control in the OSCE Area: Chairman's Summary", 18 July 1995.

6. Wolfgang Ischinger, "Nicht gegen Rußland. Sicherheit und Zussamenarbeit im Ostsee-Raum", *Internationale Politik* 2/1998 p. 39.

7. Decision no. 63, 31 Plenary Meeting of the OSCE Permanent Council, 25 July 1995.

8. The Special Representative of the Chairman-in-Office (CiO) for Article V Negotiations was appointed in Copenhagen in December 1997.

9. Lisbon Document 1996, Lisbon Summit, 3 December 1996.

10. Paragraph 5 (e), Decision no. 5 on "Guidelines on an OSCE Document-Charter on European Security", Copenhagen, Sixth Meeting of the OSCE Ministerial Council, 19 December 1997.

11. Communique of the 7th Ministerial Sessions of the CBSS, Nyborg, 22-23 June 1998.

12. Summit Declaration on Black Sea Economic Cooperation, 25 June 1992.

13. Communique of the 7th Ministerial Sessions of the CBSS, Nyborg, 22-23 June 1998.

14. In 1990, CEI countries agreed it was essential that the democracy, rules of law, human rights, including the rights of persons belonging to national minorities, should be respected, promoted and guaranteed. The CEI Working Group on Minorities carried out discussions on this topic. By November 1994, the Foreign Ministers of the CEI had approved the CEI Instrument for the Protection of Minority Rights, a political declaration. [http:/www.digit.it/ceinet/ceibroch/polit.htm]

15. Declaration on the Process of Stability and Good Neighbourliness (Royaumont, 13 December 1995).

16. Lisbon Document 1996, Lisbon Summit, 3 December 1996.

17. Alyson JK Bailes, and Andrew Cottey, "Multi-layered Integration: The Subregional Dimension. An Interim Report with Recommendations addressed to the Chairman-in-Office of OSCE and OSCE Participating States", Warsaw, October 1996, p.2.

18. Ibid., p. 3.

Section Three

Global Regionalism

6. Regional Dynamics in the Mediterranean

Stephen C. Calleya

Introduction

Developments around the Mediterranean area in the post-Cold War years have underlined the fundamental fact that this geo-strategic location continues to be dominated by a mosaic of distinct sub-regional constellations, each evolving according to their own indigenous pattern of relations.

Given such a heterogeneous cluster of regional dynamics, is a multilateral initiative such as the Euro-Mediterranean Process (EMP) the correct mechanism to contend with the plethora of security challenges largely emanating along Europe's southern periphery? If so, what can be done to make this process more effective and sustainable than it has been to date?

Geo-strategic Setting

An analysis of the society of states which are geographically proximate to the Mediterranean basin reveals two prominent international regions: the geographical space which borders the north-west sector of the Mediterranean which is labelled the European Union, and the geographical area covering the south-eastern flank of the basin which is labelled the Middle East.

The four sub-regions encompassing the Mediterranean are southern Europe, the Balkans, the Maghreb, and the Mashreq. Each of the sub-regions continue to follow different evolutionary patterns and there is very little to indicate that any of them will integrate with their counterparts across the Mediterranean any time soon. Relations across Southern Europe are largely cooperative dominant, with this group of countries increasing their intergovernmental and transnational ties with the rest of Europe on a continuous basis.

In contrast, conflictual relations have consistently hindered closer cooperation between countries in the Balkans, North Africa and the Levant. Relations in these three sub-regions of the Mediterranean remain primarily limited at an intergovernmental level, with cross-border types of interaction across the southern shores of the Mediterranean limited to the energy sector and Islam. [1]

The geopolitical shifts that have taken place throughout the Mediterranean since the Barcelona conference in November 1995, particularly the slowdown in Middle East peace talks and the escalation of hostilities in the Kosovo conflict, have forced Euro-Mediterranean strategists to reconsider what policy mechanisms should be introduced to ensure that the goals outlined in the Barcelona Declaration are attainable. This includes paying more attention to specific sub-regional trends that are currently manifesting themselves around the Mediterranean.

The thaw in cold war relations in the Levant which systematically spread to other parts of the Middle East after the historic Israeli-Palestinian peace agreement of 1993 came to a practical halt with the election of Benjamin Netanyahu in late 1995. Aspirations that the Middle East peace process would become more comprehensive with the inclusion of both Syria and Lebanon were largely replaced by efforts to preserve the fragile peace process.

Neither the Europeans nor the Americans were able to influence Israeli Prime Minister Netanyahu's more hard-line approach to the peace process that resulted in a freezing of peace negotiations. The suspension of the MENA process in 1998 was the result of a concerted effort by the majority of Arab League members to terminate normal relations with Israel and revive the economic boycott against Israel. [2]

Any hope of revitalising the peace process took a back seat in the last quarter of 1997 and throughout 1998 and the first half of 1999 as Middle East leaders became more preoccupied with the possibility of another showdown between the United Nations and Iraq or Israel and its Syrian neighbours. The election of Ehud Barak as Israeli Prime Minister in May 1999 offers a window of opportunity to reactivate the dormant Middle East peace process.

In the Maghreb, efforts to promote more cooperative relations have also been at more or less of a standstill in recent years. Internal strife in Algeria and international sanctions against Libya have stifled attempts to reactivate the notion of a more integrated Maghreb as was outlined in the Arab Maghreb Union Treaty of 1989. [3] The European Union's more active policy towards Algeria in 1998 and the United Nation's decision to suspend the sanctions regime against Libya in 1999 have helped create a more conducive climate to remove some of the numerous political stalemates that continue to prevent further intra-regional cooperation across North Africa.

Along the northern shores of the Mediterranean, Southern European countries have also had to contend with an increase in turbulent relations in their vicinity. Animosity between Greece and Turkey reached quasi-hostile intensity in early 1996 when a dispute over the sovereignty of a number of Aegean Islands resulted in an escalation of military movements on both sides. Diplomatic initiatives to formalise a set of good neighbourly principles since have largely failed to move Greece and Turkey towards a more cordial relationship. [4] Despite diplomatic interventions by the European Union and the United States, Athens and Ankara also remain stalemated as a result of their failure to broker a peaceful resolution to the Cypriot issue. [5]

Since January 1997 Turkey has further strengthened its strategic alliance with Israel conducting a series of joint maritime search and rescue exercises. Operation Reliant Mermaid took place off the coast of Israel and included the participation of the United States and Jordan. The naval manoeuvres demonstrated this alliance's ability to dominate the pattern of relations in the eastern sector of the Mediterranean. The subsequent balance of power shift has resulted in an occasional outcry from Iran, Syria and Iraq who perceive the intensification of military cooperation as a direct threat to their sovereignty. [6]

Further West, stability in the Balkans has blown hot and cold. Regional relations received a boost in December 1997 when U.S. President Clinton announced that U.S. troops would remain stationed in the region until a more secure peace was achieved. Paradoxically, instability again emerged when the neighbouring country of Albania appeared to be on the brink of fragmentation. The increase in tension in Kosovo throughout 1998 and the outbreak of war between NATO and Yugoslavia in March 1999 once again plunged the Balkans into turmoil. The fragile peace that has emerged with the creation of a western Kosovo protectorate in no way guarantees that the decade of instability across the Balkans has come to an end.[7]

Prospects for the Future: A Regional Assessment to 2010

A number of indicators extant today can be used to project the strategic environment in the Mediterranean to 2010. Unless these indicators change significantly, the environment for the first ten years of the next century will be set by the year 2000. The speed with which the events in Europe and the Middle East are moving makes it likely that the shape this part of the world will take by 2010 will be clearly discernible by the end of this century. The United States and Europe will continue to depend on the Persian Gulf and North Africa for much of their energy supplies. They will however be joined by the likes of China and India who will need to satisfy their growing energy demands and therefore access to these areas will remain a high foreign policy priority.

In the first half of the 1990s the Mediterranean showed signs of becoming a cooperative dominant area. But the past four years has witnessed an increase in conflictual relations throughout the Mediterranean and a resultant shift to an indifferent type of region. Fault-lines along a north-south and south-south axis have become more apparent, with no sign of a process of regional transformation taking place.

As relations stand, two scenarios are possible: the first is one in which a number of Mediterranean countries manage to integrate at both a regional and international level, while the rest continue to go through a process of fragmentation. The second is one in which the majority of countries in the Mediterranean are not able to integrate into the international political economy and gradually become failed states.

As patterns of relations across the Euro-Mediterranean area stand, the majority of littoral countries in the Mediterranean seem unlikely to integrate into the global political economy that is emerging. Transnational ventures remain limited, with states in the area more concerned with intra-state and inter-state conflictual issues than with promoting inter-state types of cooperation.

If European Union efforts to foster inter-Mediterranean political and economic cooperation are to succeed they must be complemented by initiatives that Mediterranean states themselves initiate as part of a process that aims to create a transnational network upon which cross-border types of economic and financial interaction can take place. To date, the Mediterranean has not succeeded in creating an environment where people, products, ideas and services are allowed to flow freely. At the moment there are too many bottlenecks in the system and this will prohibit the region from competing and prospering in the global village of tomorrow.

In contrast to the more cohesive and cooperative South-East Asian and Latin American developing regions, the Mediterranean currently consists of a number of sub-regional constellations, i.e., Southern Europe, the Maghreb, the Mashreq, and the Balkans, that are evolving along separate and distinct paths. Perhaps the label that best describes the pattern of relations in the area is "fragmegration" which denotes the integration efforts being pursued by the EU Southern European countries and the fragmentation type of relations that continues to dominate the southern and eastern shores of the basin. In fact, the lack of cohesion and unity achieved to date somewhat mirrors regional dynamics manifesting themselves across central Africa. [8]

During the first ten years of the new millennium the United States will shift its foreign policy concerns in the region further east, focusing on the management of relations in the Mashreq and the Persian Gulf. The rest of the Mediterranean will become a European Union sphere of influence once a common foreign and security policy is operational. In the interim, the EU will continue to contain instability that may emerge along its southern periphery. In the short-term, its priority will be to achieve internal cohesiveness through the successful implementation of economic and monetary union. In the medium term, the EU's objective will be to integrate as many central and eastern European countries as is feasible.

The EU has an opportunity to further strengthen its external relations in the Mediterranean by strengthening its ties with the three European Union Mediterranean candidates of Malta, Cyprus and Turkey. Relations with the three countries are currently proceeding at different levels and different speeds.

Malta is currently gearing up for EU accession negotiations and eventual membership by conducting a screening process with the EU. The Maltese Islands hope to commence actual accession negotiations early in the year 2000. Malta has been playing a proactive constructive role in the Euro-Mediterranean process since its launching in Barcelona in 1995. In addition to hosting the second Euro-Mediterranean ministerial meeting in April 1997, Malta is also actively promoting the idea of a stability pact for the Mediterranean.

Cyprus has already commenced accession negotiations with the EU, with half of the thirty-one chapters already open. By the end of the Portuguese Presidency in mid-June 2000 Cyprus is expected to have opened all EU chapters for negotiation. Any EU aspirations that accession negotiations would have a positive impact on Turkish-Greek relations and the division of the Mediterranean Island have however failed to materialise.

Turkey's sheer size, religious and cultural traits, and human rights record continue to prevent it from becoming an EU member. The European Union's indifferent attitude towards Turkey at the Luxembourg summit of December 1997 cast a cold shower on EU-Turkish relations that could become permanent unless Brussels introduces a more cooperative framework of relations in the near future. The stalemate between Greece and Turkey over Cyprus is another factor that continues to hinder EU-Turkish relations and unless resolved in the near future could delay the next round of EU enlargement altogether, given Greece's veto status. Despite EU pronouncements to the contrary, the EU is unlikely to adopt the Cypriot stalemate as it stands.

The Euro-Mediterranean Summits: From Malta to Stuttgart

The EMP is certainly the most important regional process that currently exists in the Mediterranean as it brings together all of the European Union member states and twelve Mediterranean countries which are Morocco, Algeria, Tunisia, Egypt, Jordan, Israel, Syria, Lebanon, the Palestinian Authority, Turkey, Cyprus, and Malta.

Given the more indifferent patterns of regional relations that exist in the Mediterranean than those that existed in November 1995, it was no small feat that the second EMP meeting, the first ministerial meeting of its kind that took place in the Mediterranean, could take place. The high turnout of foreign ministers at the EMP meeting in Malta, particularly the presence of Syria, Israel and the Palestinian Authority, illustrates the importance that the participating countries attach to the process that offers the possibility of extending cooperative patterns of relations at several levels.

In addition to strengthening north-south relations as the EU becomes more active in the Mediterranean, a high priority is also being given to nurturing south-south relations that are to date lacking. Specific efforts are being made to assist Mediterranean countries to become more aware of the opportunities that exist in their neighbouring states, and offering the Mediterranean countries involved in the EMP with incentive packages to pursue trans-Mediterranean ventures. After dedicating the majority of its external resources to Central and Eastern Europe at the start of the 1990s, the EMP is an EU attempt to revitalise its outreach programme towards the Mediterranean in an effort to spur cooperative relations in the area.

At the first Euro-Mediterranean Conference which took place in Barcelona in November 1995 the twenty-seven partner countries established three principal areas of cooperation. The Barcelona Process set out three basic tasks:

•   a political and security partnership with the aim of establishing a common area of peace and stability;

•   an economic and financial partnership with the aim of creating an area of shared prosperity;

•   a partnership in social, cultural and human affairs in an effort to promote understanding between cultures and exchanges between civil societies. [9]

The main task at the Euro-Mediterranean meeting in Malta in April 1997 was for the member states to elaborate more specifically on implementation of the partnership programme and to set up short term action plans so that tangible cooperative ventures could commence.

Top of the agenda was the endorsement, or at least elaboration, of a security charter that will lay the foundations for the peaceful resolution of crisis situations and conflicts throughout the Euro-Mediterranean area. Such a charter would enable the partners to identify the factors of friction and tension in the Euro-Mediterranean area and to carry out an assessment of how such destablising focal points can be managed.

In actual fact the Malta Declaration indicates that very little headway was registered in moving ahead with implementing such a goal.

The Participants take note of the work of Senior Officials on a Charter for peace and stability in the Euro-Mediterranean region, and instruct them to continue the preparatory work, taking due account of the exchanged documents, in order to submit an agreed text at a future Ministerial Meeting when political circumstances allow, (Malta Declaration, May 1997, p.4).[10]

The vagueness of the above phrase is a clear indication of the lack of progress that has been achieved in conceptualising a framework for setting up a pan-Euro-Mediterranean security arrangement. The partner countries found it difficult to commit them to an incremental work programme that would at least seek to create the necessary cooperative relations that would allow for the introduction of such a charter. They also failed to hammer out a specific timetable within which such a framework of analysis could be introduced. The stalemate in the Middle East made it all but impossible to even contemplate moving ahead in such a direction.

The Euro-Mediterranean Process was given a new boost of confidence at an informal gathering of foreign ministers of the participating countries in Palermo in June 1998 during the British Presidency of the EU. The meeting helped to chart a less ambitious work plan in an effort to assist EMP countries in defining a practical package of confidence building measures that would create the necessary atmosphere within which a more elaborate mechanism, such as a security charter could be fleshed out. [11]

The third Euro-Mediterranean Foreign Ministerial conference that took place in Stuttgart in mid-April 1999 provided another opportunity to examine how the EMP had progressed since its launching in Barcelona in November 1995. [12]

The Stuttgart conference served the purpose of injecting another dosage of realpolitik into the Barcelona Process. Whereas the second Euro-Mediterranean ministerial meeting in April 1997 in Malta was overshadowed by the stalemate that was developing in the Middle East peace process (MEPP), the Stuttgart conference was constantly overtaken by diplomatic overtures that were unfolding in the Kosovo crisis. It is now clear that the EMP is not a cooperative security initiative that should be viewed in isolation of regional dynamics unfolding simultaneously in the vicinity of the Euro-Mediterranean area.

Geopolitical shifts that have occurred in the Mediterranean since the launching of the Barcelona process and the course of events surrounding subsequent high level Euro-Mediterranean ministerial meetings have made it blatantly clear that a strategic reassessment on how to implement the goals outlined in the Barcelona Declaration is necessary.

The Stuttgart conclusions again support the continuation of the Middle East peace process (MEPP). While this in itself is a welcome development, the EU has not succeeded in doing much more than pay lip service to the goal of revitalising the MEPP. The fact that the Euro-Mediterranean Process did not have a significant positive impact on the MEPP throughout Benjamin Netanyahu's term as Prime Minister of Israel underlines the basic fact that while the success of the EMP is dependent upon advancement of the MEPP, the EMP has had very little influence, if any at all, on the MEPP.

It is therefore worth seriously considering whether it makes sense for Euro-Mediterranean policymakers to dedicate as much time and effort as they have been to the MEPP in future. Perhaps it would be better if the concept of conditionality is applied more consistently when it comes to dispersing political and economic resources to the Middle East region. It is also important to consider whether more attention should be given to enhancing cooperative relations in other sub-regions of the Mediterranean such as the Maghreb.

This is particularly the case now that regional relations in the Middle East are more conducive to a resumption of peace talks with the election of Labour Party leader Ehud Barak and Maghrebi relations have taken a turn for the positive with the suspending of sanctions against Libya. Taking into consideration the particular sub-regional trends that are currently manifesting themselves in the Mediterranean area is a prerequisite to spurring sub-regional and intra-regional cooperation.

Elaboration of the political and security chapter of the EMP took a step forward at the Stuttgart Euro-Mediterranean foreign ministerial meeting with a renewed commitment to support already existing partnership building measures. This includes developing further the Euro-Mediterranean information and training seminars for diplomats and activities of the Euro-Mediterranean Study Commission (EuroMeSCo) that are both contributing to the shaping of a culture of dialogue and cooperation through informal exchange and open discussions between practitioners involved in the implementation of the EMP.

The inclusion of guidelines for elaborating a Euro-

Mediterranean Charter for Peace and Stability is also a positive development. Identifying the framework within which a security charter can be spelt out is essential if progress is to be registered. It is however clear that a Euro-Mediterranean Security Charter remains a long-term goal. In the interim, the guidelines are a good exercise in taking stock of what security concepts have been discussed up to now. It will also assist in identifying those areas of cooperation where incremental steps can take place when the political atmosphere permits.

At the Stuttgart meeting the EU also committed itself to continue financing the Euro-Mediterranean process between 2000 and 2006, although no precise funds were earmarked. When the EU and the European Investment Bank come to unveiling the MEDA II programme they should make it clear that the primary role of this financial mechanism is to act as a catalyst when it comes to promoting financial and economic cooperation. This will help avoid raising expectations of an economic windfall too high within the Mediterranean partner countries. It is also essential that bureaucratic bottlenecks of financing are eliminated with the introduction of simpler funding procedures. Otherwise interest in participating in cooperative Euro-Mediterranean ventures is sure to wane.

The Stuttgart conference also provided a number of positive inputs that could boost the EMP partnership if properly harnessed. The invitation to Libya to attend the Foreign Ministerial meeting was a first step towards integrating this geo-strategically important North African country into the international community of states. The gradual integration of Libya into the EMP framework will facilitate the task of furthering transnational cooperation across the southern shores of the Mediterranean in general and the Maghreb in particular. It could even facilitate re-launching efforts to activate the dormant Arab Maghreb Union (AMU) process that sought to emulate the European experience of integration.

Stuttgart also identified a number of important events around which the EMP will evolve at the turn of the century. The decision to organise an investment conference and informal Foreign Ministerial conference during the first half of 2000 during the Portuguese Presidency of the EU will allow policy-makers to monitor developments on a regular basis. The citing of the fourth Euro-Mediterranean Foreign Ministerial meeting that is scheduled to take place in the second half of 2000 during the French Presidency of the

EU also demonstrates a clear EU commitment to further implement the Barcelona Declaration objectives.

Time to Evaluate

When it comes to the direct tangible endeavours that the Euro-Mediterranean process should seek to realise these can primarily be classified into three specific time-oriented categories: the short term, the medium term and the long term.

In the short term, the twenty-seven partner countries must introduce a basic type of confidence building measure network that will enable them to manage and contain the large number of security challenges that risk upsetting stability across the Euro-Mediterranean area. The long list of "soft" security issues that could derail the EMP include maritime safety, environmental pollution, narcotics trafficking, and the flow of illegal migration.

A confidence building initiative that can be introduced as part of an exercise that aims at the nurturing of a Euro-Mediterranean profile within the framework of the EMP is that of establishing a Euro-Mediterranean Development Centre (EMDC). The EMDC's principal objective would be to promote the dissemination of information relating to the Euro-Mediterranean process in an effort to enhance the level of transparency when it comes to taking decisions about the allocation of funds. Given the fact that DG1B is currently in the final stages of appropriating the EURO 5 billion earmarked for MEDA I and has already commenced preparations for the unveiling of MEDA II for the period 2000-2006, such a measure should take place as soon as possible. [13]

As further progress is registered in each specific chapter of the EMP it is clear that there will be a need to monitor closely the large number of intra-regional cooperative ventures that will be endorsed. Apart from its intrinsic value, such a coordinating centre will help overcome inconsistencies in the process and facilitate informal exchanges of views on a wide variety of subjects of common interest.

In line with the general framework of cooperation envisaged in the Barcelona Declaration of 1995, the EMDC's chief objective will be to encourage development in the following sectors:

• at a macroeconomic level, with the maximum degree of convergence between economic, monetary and budgetary policies;

- promoting investment by standardising trade regulations and customs legislation;
- systematic monitoring of initiatives that the EMP is seeking to operationalise such as industrial zones and centres of special services;
- enhancing cooperation in sectors as diverse as science, technology, education, infrastructure, environment and tourism;
- strengthening dialogue on social issues, including the narco-industry, migratory trends and cultural exchanges.

The overall objective of the EMDC will be to assist in upgrading sectoral cooperative arrangements that currently take place in the energy, tourism and infrastructural sectors. Such measures are an indispensable part of the procedure that will have to be established if the overall goal of creating a free trade area is to become a reality.

The EMDC will in the first instance become a clearing-house of EMP information. Its main goal will be to build a Euro-Mediterranean community of values by strengthening the cooperative regimes that were outlined in the Barcelona Declaration.

In the medium term, the societal issues that the EMP will need to address if socio-economic conditions are to improve, include the promotion of food production, trade exchanges, industrial cooperation, debt rescheduling and relief. An upgrade also needs to take place in investment capital, particularly, in the communication, transport and tourism sectors, which are the very growth areas of the economies of most developing countries across the Mediterranean. Closer cooperation between the countries concerned will also facilitate the promotion of alternative sources of energy such as solar and wind energy which would make production costs cheaper and more sustainable.

In the longer term, the creation of a flexible security framework that is already addressing soft security issues as those outlined earlier will set the stage for tackling more sensitive security challenges which include intolerant fundamentalism, demographic expansion and outright conflict.

Early Warning: EMMA

At the moment there are no elaborate mechanisms to contend with security crises such as an accidental collision at sea between transport tankers crossing through the choke points such as the Straits of Sicily, or the alarming rate of degradation which is currently taking place in the environmental sector. One must also mention the proliferation of drug consignments which are reaching ever deeper into the civil societies of the Mediterranean, and the accentuation of illegal migratory flows from south to north which risks destablising the legal structures of the state.

At this point in the partnership process a concerted effort should be made to immediately take incremental steps towards setting up an information mechanism that can assess the significance of such security issues and their likely impact on Euro-Mediterranean relations in the near future. Once this has been realised the cooperative maritime security network can be instructed to draw up policy positions on security issues that are regarded as the most serious.

Ideally, at a later stage one should also investigate the feasibility of setting up a Euro-Mediterranean Maritime Agency (EMMA) that would be mandated to coordinate the cooperative security network with objectives similar to those carried out by a coastguard. The EMMA should initially carry out stop and search exercises in two principal areas: maritime safety and maritime pollution. This phase could be enhanced at a later stage by monitoring other aspects of security that include narcotics trafficking and the transport of illegal migrants.

Such an early warning mechanism should be open to any of the Euro-Mediterranean partner states that wish to participate. In order to ensure that such a security model can become operational in the shortest period possible, the EMMA should consist of sectoral types of soft security cooperation.

Any two or more EMP members can start cooperating in specific sectors, such as that pertaining to maritime safety without having to wait until all partners are ready. This will enable the EMMA to evolve along sub-regional lines before it becomes feasible to establish a fully-fledged Euro-Mediterranean Coastguard at a later date.

In addition to strengthening political and security channels of communication, the establishment of such a Euro-Mediterranean early warning network will assist in cultivating more intense crisis management mechanisms in an area where these are lacking. Areas where cooperation can be strengthened include conducting simulation exercises of oil spills, ensuring that international standards are observed during the cleaning of oil tankers, and monitoring the activities of non-Mediterranean fishing boats that are operating in the Mediterranean with a particular emphasis on over-fishing.

Conflict Prevention: Empowering EuroMarFor

The maritime security arrangement of EuroMarFor should open its doors to southern Mediterranean countries (at least offer observer status in the short-term). This will help dispel the negative perceptions that have been generated since the establishment of this maritime security force. At a later stage, this force can then become the actual confidence building enforcer of EMMA.

In order to ensure that such a flexible security arrangement moves beyond the conceptual stage in the shortest time-frame possible, its primary mandate may be limited to the following codes of conduct: fact-finding and consultation missions, inspection and monitoring delegations. Such traditional rules of engagement may also be supplemented by operations that include the facilitation of humanitarian relief particularly in times of natural disasters. At a later stage, situation centres may be set up around the Mediterranean to monitor activities under this mandate. The long list of security issues that would require consistent attention include: maritime safety, environmental pollution, narcotics trafficking, terrorism, organised crime, flow of illegal migration.

In the medium to long term, the creation of a flexible security framework that is already addressing soft security issues as those outlined above will set the stage for tackling more sensitive security challenges which include intolerant fundamentalism, demographic expansion and outright conflict.

Functions of the Euro-Mediterranean Conflict Prevention Network

• Monitoring political, military, and economic matters of interest to countries and the Euro-Med Partnership process itself.
• Supervising and operating communications among focal points which have already been established as a CBM.
• Maintaining and updating background information for crisis prevention and management.
• Being prepared to provide facilities in case a contingency staff is set up with respect to a given crisis or conflict.
• Supporting briefings to the public and private bodies.

- Providing a continuous flow of information to members according to mandates.
- Providing information to media.

A decision will have to be taken on what the scope of instruments will be at the disposal of the network. These would range from fact-finding and observer missions, diplomatic and economic forms of pressure and the deployment of troops. The introduction of economic and diplomatic sanctions can be supplemented by the use of force if there is an escalation of violence.

In a region as heterogeneous as the Mediterranean area is, the main sponsor of the Euro-Mediterranean conflict prevention network, the European Union, should only act as a mediator, leaving decision-making and action to the main actors directly involved in a crisis. The EU has a wide range of mechanisms in the economic, political and social domains that will enable it to influence decision-makers at the local level when it comes to complying with preventive measures. It is only once the majority of local actors, both at governmental level and the public at large, perceive that more will be gained by compliance, that preventive measures will be able to attain their true objective.

It is only after such a threshold has been arrived at should a concerted effort be made to spell out the parameters of a security charter which will include both confidence building and crisis prevention measures that seek to further advance regional disarmament. The introduction of a Euro-Mediterranean security charter will also assist in creating a climate where the partner countries can develop command and control mechanisms to intervene as early as possible in crisis situations. Acting only after an aggressor has acquired territory or access to natural resources is to force the unwelcome choice between a massive military response and a major strategic debacle. The later the international community and security organisations intervene, the larger the cost and the less chance to restore stability.

The Political Dimension

The positive steps registered between the Palestinian Authority and Israel during the Euro-Mediterranean conference in Malta in April 1997 and thereafter shed light on the positive influence the European

Union can have on the outcome of regional relations. What are the prospects for a more active and effective EU external policy towards the Mediterranean and the Middle East?

To date, the European Union remains an economic hegemon in the Mediterranean area. All the countries in the basin are highly dependent on conducting trade with Western Europe. The aspiration of creating a Euro-Mediterranean free trade area by the year 2010 as stipulated in the Barcelona Declaration of 1995 and the negotiation of "association agreements" with the Mediterranean partner countries in the interim augur well for a more assertive EU economic role in the Mediterranean.

Whether this process will enable the EU to establish a more proactive political role with its southern periphery is however no foregone conclusion. Such an outcome will depend largely on how successful Brussels is in implementing its goal of establishing a common foreign and security policy (CFSP) as envisaged in the Maastricht and Amsterdam Treaties. The appointing of such a prolific individual as Javier Solana to the post of High Representative of the (CFSP) and the creation of a policy planning unit for security policy are certainly welcome developments in this respect. Harbingers of a more active EU foreign policy towards the Middle East would be wise to recall that European attempts to influence regional dynamics in their vicinity have met with limited success in even the recent past: the Bosnian fiasco and the Kosovo conflict are valid cases in point.

On the other hand, European Union diplomatic overtures leading up to the Malta, Palermo and Stuttgart foreign ministerial meetings tend to suggest that EU member states are gradually realising more effectively their goal of pooling their diplomatic resources into a single decision-making process. Although national interests continue to supersede the notion of a collective security approach to regional affairs, the Euro-Mediterranean process is at least providing the EU with a mechanism through which it can interact with the Mediterranean in a more coherent and systematic manner.

Nevertheless, the European Union will have to advance carefully if it is not to upset the concept of "balancing" in relations between Mediterranean states and their external patrons. If the EU is perceived to be attempting to dominate intra-Mediterranean patterns of interaction, the latter could retaliate by becoming less cooperative in their dealings with specific EU member states that have substantial political and economic interests in the area. The consequences of such a turn of events would be very high if such a trans-Mediterranean backlash were to include the key oil and gas producers.

The European Union must also formulate an external affairs strategy towards the Middle East that does not appear to be duplicating Washington's endeavours to broker a peace settlement in the region. Failure to adopt such a policy will only result in a wastage of already scarce resources and could also lead to a situation where the European involvement in the Middle East is regarded more through a competitive lens than a complementary one.

The fluid nature of contemporary international relations in the Middle East certainly offers the European Union with an opportunity to upgrade its influence in this geo-strategically proximate region. One option that could assist the EU in becoming more effective in the region is to introduce a political mechanism that will allow it to adopt a more regular, rapid and flexible type of involvement in the Middle East.

This could take the form of creating a specific ad hoc committee that would assist the EU's special envoy to the Middle East. This committee would be mandated to constantly update the EU Commission and the Council of Ministers about regional patterns of relations and peace process developments. The introduction of such a committee would also facilitate communication flows between Europe and the Middle East protagonists, a confidence building measure in itself.

The Middle East stalemate is not only detrimental to the region itself but is also having a negative impact upon regional relations across the Mediterranean area. International initiatives such as the MENA process and the Euro-Mediterranean process that have attempted to spur intra-regional cooperation are being held hostage as a result of the lack of progress in peace talks.

If a breakthrough does not emerge in the near future the international community under the leadership of the United States should step back from the current stalemate and conduct a complete re-assessment of the Middle East situation. The European Union must also do more than simply accept its subordinate role in the region – it is a major economic player in the Middle East and should seek to play as important a political role. For some reason the EU has not realised that the Mediterranean area which includes the Middle East is its backyard and until it seeks to play an important role in this geo-strategic zone its aspiration of projecting a common foreign and security policy will remain a fallacy.

When it comes to re-thinking how to accommodate both the Israelis and the Palestinians a number of strategic models could serve as a useful guide. A Westphalianization blueprint would call for the immediate recognition of a Palestinian state. A Finlandization model would establish a neutral Palestinian state. A Vaticanization model would lead to the establishment of a religious trusteeship. A Sinaification approach would call for an international peacekeeping force to monitor agreed upon borders. A Bosnification model would seek to replicate some of the provisions adopted in the Dayton peace plan, while a Brusselization approach could be considered when it comes to discussing the future of Jerusalem, with the disputed city perhaps becoming the administrative capital of both Israel and Palestine. [14]

Given the direct bearing the Middle East peace process is already having on the evolution of the Euro-Mediterranean process, it certainly seems a logical course of action for the Europeans to consider in the run up to the next millennium.

The Economic Dimension: Geo-economic Realities

By about 2010 the EU will have become by far the biggest single market and the world's most concentrated area of economic prosperity and internal stability. It will comprise essentially all of Europe, east and west, more than 90% of total European population. i.e. almost 500 million people, (half of China or India) and have a combined GDP of some 12 000 billion USD, an almost unimaginable figure.

How will the 12 non-EU riparian Mediterranean countries, from Turkey to Morocco, adapt to these profound geopolitical changes that will take place north of them in the next 12 years? How will they coexist with the future European giant? To what extent will they be drawn into its economic and political orbit? To what extent will they have to integrate with the European and consequently the world economy? These are questions of vital importance for both the EU and each its Mediterranean neighbours.

Do the Mediterranean countries still have a real alternative? Could they try to stay in a sort of splendid isolation within their tiny national economies, surrounding themselves by high walls of protection and ignoring the profound technological arm economic changes taking place around them? To date, Mediterranean trade with Europe is marginal. The majority of Mediterranean countries are dependent on European markets. If Mediterranean countries are to increase their ability to penetrate the global market they must diversify and improve their export capabilities.

Economic development always starts at home. It can never be imposed from the outside. It is a matter of the right mixture between individual freedom of action and the right government policies. This goes for each and every country of the globe, small or big, rich or poor.

It is important to keep these basic considerations in mind when asking about the role that one very specific, and not the most important, economic policy, the one related to trade with the rest of the world, can play. Or, to put it more directly, what is the case for free trade between a Mediterranean country such as Egypt and the EU on the one hand, its Mediterranean neighbours on the other?

The answer is straightforward: the Egyptian economy is far too small to satisfy its increasingly sophisticated needs for cars, food, computers; planes and computers on its own, i.e. to be essentially self-sufficient. Egypt therefore has to export goods and services in order to be able to buy from others what they can supply more efficiently. But for whatever Egypt may wish to export to the world market it needs to be able to compete with a myriad of competitors from Europe, Asia or America. The only way to become competitive is to expose national producers or providers of services to those elsewhere, as if there were no borders with artificial barriers like customs duties or administrative controls (licenses, quotas, currency restrictions etc.).

This has been the recipe tested successfully in Europe, the USA and Japan during the past 50 years, since the end of the 2nd World War, which has allowed these countries to become the dominant economic powers at the end of the 20th century.

It was this basic philosophy, the conviction that prosperity is best enhanced in a climate of competition and free trade, that induced the EU and its Mediterranean neighbours three years ago, in Barcelona, to envisage the setting up of a vast Euro Mediterranean free trade area. This free trade area will be a zone where goods and progressively also services should be traded free of any restrictions, as if within national borders. Deregulation and liberalization are therefore very much the name of the game.

This objective has been laid down in a comprehensive policy document, the Barcelona Declaration, in November 1995. The 27 foreign ministers of the signatory states, that is, all fifteen European Union member states and twelve Mediterranean countries, agreed to work towards establishing a Euro-Mediterranean free trade within 15 years, by about 2010.

The State of Play

Where do we stand presently with the implementation of that ambitious long-term objective? What remains to be done? What are the obstacles on the way? And what are the chances of the target date of 2010 being respected?

From the EU side, the situation looks as follows:

• with five Mediterranean countries (Israel, Turkey, Malta, Cyprus, Palestine), covering almost 50% of all EU trade with the Mediterranean free trade has been essentially completed (totally for manufactured products, partially for agricultural products);

• with three countries (Tunisia, Morocco and Jordan) free trade has been agreed; it will be progressively established during a 12 year transition period and should essentially be completed by the target date of 2010;

• with four countries (Egypt, Lebanon, Algeria and Syria) negotiations are still under way. Assuming optimistically that these will be concluded by the end of 2000, followed by two years of ratification, free trade might be completed by 2015 only.

Free trade between Mediterranean countries and the EU will open the way for free trade among the Mediterranean countries themselves. Indeed, it is difficult to contemplate that at some stage Egypt will freely import furniture or metals from Greece, while subjecting those same products from Jordan or Tunisia to high import duties or other import restrictions. Intra-Mediterranean free trade therefore follows as a logical corollary from Euro-Mediterranean free trade.

Presently Mediterranean countries do less than 10% of their total trade among themselves. This is clearly insufficient for neighbouring countries. The trade potential is insufficiently exploited because of high, sometimes even prohibitive trade barriers, every country attempting to protect its tiny manufacturing sector as well as it agriculture.

Enhancing horizontal trade patterns across the Mediterranean is therefore one of the central goals of the Barcelona Process. The EMP has so far failed to seriously financially support intra-regional economic cooperation in the region. Only 10% of the overall MEDA I funding budget (1995-1999) was allocated to regional initiatives. The remaining 90% has been earmarked for bilateral cooperative agreements between the EU and its southern partners. If anything, this is likely to lead to an increase in vertical trade.

A more logical alternative would be to dedicate a larger proportion of the forthcoming budget, MEDA II (2000-2006), to regional projects. Such projects should aim at assisting Mediterranean partner countries establish industrial sectors in areas where they already have a comparative advantage. This will avoid wasting the already limited funding which is available and simultaneously ensure that a more diversified Mediterranean economic base is created.

The logic of Mediterranean or even all-Arab free trade has been clearly recognised by policy makers for more than 50 years, since the very start of the Arab League in 1948. But action has failed to follow until very recently. The Euro-Mediterranean initiative has given a new impetus to Mediterranean free trade.

In 1997, spectacular progress towards Mediterranean free trade was achieved, when Turkey and Israel, the two economic 'giants' in the Mediterranean agreed to go for bilateral free trade. The Arab countries around the Mediterranean have not yet clearly decided on how to proceed.

They have, for good reasons, concentrated on the EU front, assuming that they would more easily achieve a breakthrough among themselves once they were tied by free trade to their giant neighbour in the north whose competition they have to fear much more than that of immediate neighbours.

Thus they have kept hesitating between a bilateral approach, with Egypt, Jordan, Morocco and Tunisia agreeing on reciprocal tariff concessions for specific products, and an all-Arab approach.

Indeed, in 1997, in reaction both to the Euro Mediterranean and the Turkish-Israel Initiative, the Arab League has decided (once again) to launch an all Arab free trade agreement (AFTA). 18 of the 22 Members of the Arab League have signed the agreement that provides for the reciprocal elimination of all duties by 2008. But only 12 of the 18 signatories have effectively proceeded with the cutting of duties by 10% by 1ˢᵗ January 1998, as provided; moreover more than half of the products were put in exemption. Thus, however good the intentions to finally organise all-Arab free trade, the results look anything but promising.

Free trade must be transparent and comprehensive, if it is to have the desired impact on the patterns of trade and production. If it is to be realised during a transition period, of 5 to 10 years, the calendar must be clear and absolutely trustworthy. The agreed tariff cuts must be implemented 100%, and they must not be replaced by other even more restrictive trade obstacles. Monitoring and policing of the agreements has to be seen as absolutely indispensable for the credibility of the whole enterprise. For economic operators must firmly believe in the process, they must anticipate its results and help to bring it about. All this has so far not been the case for the Arab countries' efforts to establish free trade among themselves.

One should therefore carefully monitor what is going to happen when it comes to forthcoming tariff cuts as envisaged under the AFTA agreement. If implementation is as poor as on 1st January 1998, when only two-thirds of the signatories acted at all, but only on half of the product coverage, the all-Arab initiative would be better replaced by a more limited but serious and well-prepared approach by those Arab Mediterranean countries that have signed free trade agreements with the EU. This should be complemented by similar agreements with the Gulf Cooperation Council States (GCC) that have already successfully implemented free trade among their six members states. These 10 core countries should form the basis of what may progressively become a vast European-Mediterranean free trade area, with Turkey and possibly Israel to be included when the time is ripe.

Stability across the Mediterranean is crucial if the necessary investment capital required to ameliorate economic conditions in the area is to be successfully attracted. The difficulty in attracting private investment to the Mediterranean area in the current uncertain climate is clear. This helps to partly explain why the Mediterranean has so far only succeeded in attracting less than 2% of international investment.

In this respect it should be noted that growing disparities between per capita incomes on the Northern and Southern shores of the Mediterranean have continued to increase, even in states such as Morocco and Tunisia, where stringent economic reforms and structural adjustment programmes have been introduced. The significant extent of economic disparities in the Mediterranean along a north-south axis is evident when one compares the 1994 annual average World Bank figures of $18,000 per capita income to the North, and only $700 per capita to the South.

The 4.6 billion ECUs agreed at the Cannes Summit in July 1995 to fund the Euro-Mediterranean initiative over a five year period still only represents about half of the 7.4 billion ECUs earmarked for East and Central Europe over the same period, where the population totals 96 million people, as opposed to 230 million people in the Mediterranean basin. Moreover, the funds the EU have dedicated to the Mediterranean for the 1995-1999 period is less than one third of the trade surplus it achieved with the 12 Mediterranean partners and Libya in 1995 (13.7 billion ECU) and less than half the trade surplus it registered with the same area during 1993 (12.1 billion ECU) and a little more than half the surplus obtained during 1994 (9.3 billion ECU), (see Appendix Two, EUROSTAT, 1997). [15]

If the Euro-Mediterranean Process (EMP) is therefore to be regarded as a credible initiative it will have to identify and operationalise a series of cooperative cross-border projects that will act as a catalyst to increase the interest of international investors to this part of the world. Otherwise, the objective of establishing a more economically balanced Euro-Mediterranean area will not transpire. Although free trade in itself is likely to increase the level of trade between the northern and southern countries of the Mediterranean, there is nothing to guarantee that this will necessarily reduce the wide level of economic disparities that currently exist. In fact, an increase in EU exports to the Mediterranean would only exacerbate the negative balance of payments which countries in the south are experiencing.

The harsh economic realities that Mexico has had to confront since signing up to the NAFTA agreement is indicative of the negative impact the introduction of free trade measures can have upon developing countries. In effect, the creation of a free trade area could end up reinforcing current North-South and South-South divides as riparian states of the Mediterranean find it more and more difficult to attract international investment.

The creation of a free trade area is nevertheless certain to boost trade. But there should be no reason for euphoria. Even supposing the Mediterranean countries will be successful in streamlining and restructuring their manufacturing industries and in developing competitive export opportunities, this will not transform all of them into Mediterranean 'tigers'. Turkey's example shows, however, that the intensity of trade between Europe and individual Arab countries can grow enormously, especially for countries like Egypt, Morocco, and Tunisia, provided more entrepreneurs discover the art of developing export markets.

Subcontracting should, of course, increase substantially, especially between Egypt and Europe (where it is practically non-existent), and thanks to the cumulation of origin from different sources around the Mediterranean (and even in the Gulf). Agricultural trade, though it will become much less hampered by tariffs and other restrictions, will grow much less, probably more to the advantage of Europe than the other way around, because of increasing difficulties on the Arab side to generate exportable surpluses.

Free trade should by 2015 also extend to the GCC countries and Europe. The completion of the Association Agreement between Egypt and the EU will give a boost in that direction. The inclusion of the Gulf countries (Iraq) into this network will substantially strengthen European Arab relations, both in a vertical and a horizontal sense.

The question must also be asked what impact will the outflow of capital have on the Mediterranean area as economic and financial policies become more liberal? Will the free flow of capital result in a situation where the rich become richer and the poor become poorer?

It is thus essential that the Mediterranean countries must work towards creating an economic and financial institutional design that will generate wealth. At the end of the twentieth century the label "emerging markets" is actually regarded by some as being synonymous with weak economies. The international economic crisis that began in the Asia-Pacific and later spread to Russia and more recently Latin America has cast a darker shadow on developing countries.

If international economic organisations, such as the European Investment Bank (EIB), are serious about assisting the Mediterranean countries they should adopt more proactive strategies towards this area. This should include offering developing states credit guarantees and introducing measures to address the serious debt burden several countries in the region are coping with.

In the short to medium term it also appears essential that some type of a compensation fund be created for those sectors of the population in the least developed countries of the Mediterranean that will suffer most of the socio-economic brunt that free trade could bring with it. Such political action will also give credence to the EU claim that its main interest is to ameliorate socio-economic living conditions throughout the Mediterranean area.

During the past three years the EU has reiterated that one of the central goals of the EMP is the creation of a free trade area by the year 2010. This is to be systematically realised by implementing the second chapter of the Barcelona Declaration that is dedicated towards the establishment of an economic and financial partnership between the twenty-seven countries with the ultimate aim of creating an area of shared prosperity. [16]

Now that a period of time has lapsed since the launching of the Barcelona process the following questions should be addressed:
- How realistic and feasible are such goals given the enormous socio-economic disparities which exist across the Euro-Mediterranean area?
- What can one expect to emerge in the run up to the new millennium in respect to this dimension of the Euro-Mediterranean partnership process?
- Should a more flexible integration model and timeframe be considered given the heterogeneous nature of the Partner countries?
- What should a post-free trade area strategy consist of?

A prerequisite to spurring the existing low levels of intra-regional economic relations in the Mediterranean to a free trade or common market level of integration is the maintenance of cooperative relations between the countries in the Euro-Mediterranean process, particularly those located along the southern and eastern shores of the basin.

The volatile nature of relations between Israel and the Palestinian Authority, Syria and Lebanon's indifference to the peace process in general, the escalation of tension between Greece and Turkey, the failure to negotiate a settlement to the Cypriot stalemate, and European concerns on the increase of violence in Algeria, are just some of the examples which one can mention to illustrate the fragility of peaceful relations in the area.

Light has been further shed on the plethora of obstacles that one has to overcome before the concept of partnership building can take root in the economic sector by the Middle East-North Africa (MENA) economic process. Only after four summits in Casablanca,

Amman, Cairo and Doha in 1994, 1995, 1996, and 1997 respectively, was significant headway registered in the direction of setting up a Middle East development bank.[17] It therefore comes as little surprise that the concept of establishing a Euro-Mediterranean development bank is something for the distant future.

The majority of Mediterranean countries are aware that an economic restructuring phase is necessary but it is a bitter pill they would rather refrain from swallowing. International economic institutions have to date failed to communicate the message that unless such a transition exercise takes place in the near future, the Mediterranean will run the risk of being relegated to the doldrums of the globalisation process that is currently underway.

The shocks that both the MENA and the EMP processes have experienced in the last twelve months reflect the basic fact that the Mediterranean countries have not succeeded in adapting rapidly enough to the globalisation process.

There is therefore an urgent need for more of a self-help attitude to be adopted by the Mediterranean countries themselves. Littoral countries need to identify productive niche areas and start to dedicate research and development budgets to developing such areas of production. Specialising in areas that complement one another will enable Mediterranean countries to adopt a cooperative trade strategy with their counterparts in the region and avoid duplicating development efforts. This will in turn facilitate the task of spurring intra-regional trade since an increase in economic diversity will enable Mediterranean countries to enhance the level of trade with one another.

As mentioned earlier, investment funds to the Mediterranean currently stand at less than 2 per cent of total international financial flows. Although the Mediterranean area has not been directly affected by the regional economic crisis during the last two years, this is not due to the region's economic policies. It is rather the result of the fact that the Mediterranean has not yet successfully integrated into the international political economy. Mediterranean countries must also be aware that the economic crisis that seriously struck Asian tiger countries will make those countries that are able to introduce the necessary reforms even more competitive now that the price of their exports has dropped.

Unless the Mediterranean is able to improve its economic diplomacy track record by introducing the necessary measures to attract the attention of international investors, the latter are much more likely to be attracted to other developing regions. Both Central and Eastern Europe (CEFTA), and the southern cone of Latin America (Mercosur), have already demonstrated an ability to integrate with one another and are therefore better positioned to reap the benefits of globalisation.

As stated earlier, at a bilateral level, the European Union has already signed Association Agreements with Morocco, Tunisia, Israel, the Palestinian Authority, and Jordan and is currently negotiating similar agreements with all its Mediterranean Partners. The EU regards this as a natural progression towards creating a Free Trade Area in about twelve years. The EU is however concerned that a stalemate in the Middle East peace process may slow down further progress in this area. Negotiations with Lebanon remain blocked. Those with Egypt have run into agricultural problems, and although the Commission has a brief to negotiate with Syria it is not clear how the negotiations will develop. Implementation of the agreement with the Palestinian Authority has been delayed due to Israel.[18]

In recent years the EU Commission has stressed that a concerted effort needs to take place to assist the Mediterranean Partners in their effort to replicate aspects of the European single market within their own countries. This would include adopting similar competition law, systems for norms and standardisation and the harmonisation of customs procedures. Only such a strategy would enable them to become more competitive at an international level, and ensure that Mediterranean countries would gain more access to European and international markets.[19]

An increase in private flows of capital to the Mediterranean will only result if the countries concerned move away from dependency upon the energy sector and the low margin ends of the textile and tourism markets towards high value-added industries such as specialised tourism and garment and component production. There is also a necessity to diversify in investment instruments, so that larger flows of portfolio investments bolster the performance of Mediterranean stock markets.[20]

Prospects for the Future

The progressive establishment of Euro-Mediterranean free trade in the coming 15 years will have far-reaching consequences for Mediterranean societies and economies:

•   It will vastly enhance the volume of trade within that gigantic trade area. One may expect that by 2015 the participating 40 odd countries will do 50-60% of all their trade within the zone.

•   It will have a positive impact on the amount of foreign direct investment in the Mediterranean countries: with assured market access and an improved overall political and economic environment, European, American and Asian investors will find it much more attractive to invest.

•   It will accelerate the pace of social and political reforms, the business community will want to have a say in political matters, whether these concern the tax regime, the level of education, the functioning of the judiciary, social security etc.

But this being said, free trade is no panacea to inadequacies of economic policies or of social injustice. Nor will it introduce Western democracy quasi overnight. Free trade may act as a powerful agent of social and economic change, as we have seen in Europe for the last 40 years, but only if many other conditions even more difficult to achieve are fulfilled. This can only done by each country on its own, according to its specific requirements and possibilities. Europe can serve as an example, even as a precedent. But it cannot do the reform work for others. The hard work of learning must always be done by those directly concerned, be they individuals or societies.

As the great French historian Fernand Braudel reminds us the Mediterranean was an economic unity long before Europe. During the sixteenth and seventeenth centuries while very little transcontinental trade took place across Europe, the Mediterranean Sea served as an open area for commercial and cultural trade. The Euro-Mediterranean process offers both Europe and the Mediterranean an opportunity to lay the foundations upon which a free trade area can be established early in the twenty-first century.

The Cultural Dimension

The Mediterranean epitomises many of the problems associated with the North-South debate. These include migration, terrorism, religious intolerance and the lack of human rights. Nurturing cooperative cross-cultural patterns of interaction which address these issues is a prerequisite to improving economic disparities and ethnic divisions in the area.

The eastern Mediterranean is the historic cross-roads for diverse ethnic, cultural, and religious traditions. How can these be safeguarded and respected while at the same time tolerance and understanding are promoted? Can the Barcelona Process' proposals for educational exchanges be turned into concrete and practical programmes?

A concerted effort is required to remove misperceptions and prejudice which continue to exist across the Mediterranean. This is where international cultural activities, such as cultural tourism, may play a strategic role as culture brings about relations based on trust. Tangible proposals that actually initiate cross-cultural ventures of cooperation and seek to further the principles of respect and understanding that are still lacking are long overdue.

Common socio-economic concerns might be one point of embarkation in this respect. It should be mentioned that Euro-Mediterranean networks of economic cooperation have already been created in a number of areas and include Chambers of Commerce, Federations of Industry, commercial fairs, export promotion bodies, and banking associations. These networks aim at establishing permanent links that will enable the exchange of information and projects that will facilitate agreement on respective policies and better implementation.

The third chapter of the EMP termed "Partnership in Social and Human Affairs: Promoting Exchanges between Civil Societies" promotes the idea that the countries concerned should work to encourage the participation of civil society in the EMP. This is to involve joint efforts in education and training, social development, policies designed to reduce migratory pressures, the fight against drug trafficking, terrorism and international crime, judicial cooperation, the fight against racism and xenophobia, and a campaign against corruption.

Further ideas that have been proposed include joint efforts with regard to culture and media, health policy, the promotion of exchanges and development of contact among young people in the framework of a decentralised cooperation programme. Throughout there has been an emphasis on the importance of dialogue between cultures, and exchanges at human, scientific and technological level, deemed as an essential factor in bringing people closer, promoting understanding between them and improving their perception of one another.

But, whereas the political and security and the economic and financial chapters of the EMP have been handled in a "fast-track" manner by different parties participating in the Barcelona Process, the social and cultural chapter has been the subject of long debates and discussions. This is largely due to the fact that the Arab and European views differ sharply on issues such as human rights, immigration, terrorism, the right of political asylum and the role of civil society.

The Barcelona Declaration acknowledges the essential role civil society must play in the EMP. The Euro-Med Civil Forum, which took place in November 1995, was the first formal consolidation of civil society as a partner within the process. It gathered 1,200 experts from very diverse fields, representing civil society in countries from the northern, eastern and southern shores of the Mediterranean. The second Euro-Med Civil Forum took place in Naples in December 1997. Even if one points to the various cultural aspects that have been tackled in these meetings and the numerous projects that were approved in the field of cultural heritage, progress has been slow and difficult. Few tangible results have emanated from the ministerial meetings that have taken place. [21]

The Third Euro-Mediterranean Ministerial in Stuttgart nevertheless reaffirmed the importance of the Civil Forum underlining that regional and local authorities should be more closely associated, as should the business community and the non-governmental organisations. Several Civil Fora were also held in parallel with the Stuttgart conference and these gatherings made recommendations for future activities concerning human rights, the environment and the setting up of a Euro-Med Forum of Trade Unions. It remains to be seen whether the positive remarks regarding the Civil Fora that are included in the Stuttgart Conclusions will eventually assist in strengthening the dialogue between governments and civil society.

Three and a half years into the Euro-Mediterranean Process it is clear that civil fora must play a more direct role in the implementation phase of the Process if this multilateral initiative is to be strengthened and sustainable. It is only through the direct participation of non-governmental organisations that a more grass roots type of Euro-Mediterranean community will be nurtured.

But before significant steps can be taken in this direction the EU must itself decide what policy positions it is prepared to adopt in this sector of the Partnership. For example, should the EU turn a blind eye to regimes whose respect for human rights and democratic principles are widely criticised throughout the Mediterranean? If not, how can Europe's concerns be turned into actions that receive widespread popular support in the region? What can be done to further strengthen the role of civil society?

Suggestions that should be considered:

• Promote dialogue between the civilisations in the Mediterranean.

• Aim at a more objective portrayal of cultural characteristics found in the Mediterranean in the European and international media.

• Encourage the development of civil society and non-governmental organisations. This would assist in nurturing a sense of national unity and stem the threat of rising ethnic, religious and social conflicts.

• Establish a Euro-Mediterranean Institute for Democracy and entrust it with the implementation of a democracy building programme similar to what has been undertaken in the countries of Eastern Europe and the former Soviet Union.

Steps taken in this direction will immediately positively impact upon the contribution civil fora are making to regional stability across the Euro-Mediterranean area. A more integrated civil fora will also ensure that coordination in this field of cooperation is further enhanced.

Lessons to be Drawn from the Euro-Mediterranean Process

Throughout its twenty-six years of direct engagement in the Mediterranean the European Union has failed to contain, let alone reverse, economic disparities between the northern and southern countries of the basin. It is also quite clear that little progress has been registered in removing the misperceptions and prejudice that currently exist in the region or in promoting further the principles of respect and understanding. A concerted effort in implementing the goals set out in the third chapter of the Barcelona Declaration is certainly the most effective way to start tackling such problems.

It is fundamentally clear that the EMP offers a unique opportunity to strengthen political, economic and cultural ties across the Euro-Mediterranean area. But such progress will only be registered if the twenty-seven partner countries direct their actions at the causes rather than the symptoms of contemporary security risks. This is not to say that humanitarian and development assistance is not essential, but this should not become a substitute for efforts that are geared towards increasing higher levels of cooperation between the countries of the Mediterranean.

A cost/benefit analysis of the EMP to date reveals a large number of lessons that can be taken note of about the partnership exercise itself.

Euro-Mediterranean ministerial meetings have shed light on the fact that the objectives spelt out in the Barcelona Declaration will not become attainable without a focused in-depth series of work plans that are more short-term oriented in nature. In technical terms, one should not expect vertical integration to proceed at a rapid speed without a complementary effort occurring at the horizontal level.

Given the state of international relations in the Mediterranean, the Euro-Mediterranean process is probably the most adequate type of multilateral forum that can further cooperative security in the area. The process is to be credited for committing the Europeans to cooperate with their Mediterranean neighbours in a much more comprehensive sense than previously the case.

One should not overlook the fact that the EMP is the only regional institutional arrangement that brings together such a large number of Mediterranean countries. To date, no other trans-Mediterranean security arrangement has been able to move beyond the theoretical stage of development.

Malta must be credited for providing the environment where such cooperative types of interaction could take place. The ability to offer the diplomatic means that are essential to the peaceful settlement of disputes and include that of providing good offices is certainly to be welcomed. Facilitating dialogue between parties to an international dispute and seeking to bring about an amicable solution of existing disputes is the only way the Mediterranean will avoid becoming a conflict based region.

The Malta and Palermo Euro-Mediterranean meetings must also be credited for injecting a dosage of realism into the process. The partnership framework launched in Barcelona must consistently be adapted to the constantly evolving geo-strategic area it is seeking to function within if it is to remain functional and sustainable. It is a valuable lesson to take note of, particularly at such an early stage into the process.

The Third Euro-Mediterranean foreign ministerial meeting in Stuttgart in April 1999 also highlighted a number of other lessons that should be taken note of if the EMP is to become a more effective process. First, the EMP continues to lack visibility. It has not had enough of a direct positive impact on the Euro-Mediterranean citizens it is supposed to be addressing. This can be overcome by directing more of future Euro-Mediterranean programmes to the civil societal level.

Second, the Euro-Mediterranean partnership runs the serious risk of being downgraded on the European Union international agenda. The launching of the EURO, the enlargement process towards Central and Eastern Europe and the increase in interest to develop a post-Kosovo EU/Balkan strategic relationship, could gradually lead to a marginalisation of the Mediterranean. The Mediterranean Partner countries would therefore do well to adopt a more progressive and constructive attitude towards Brussels in order to avoid such an attitude of indifference settling in.

Third, more attention needs to be given to the third pillar of the EMP, that dealing with social, cultural, and human affairs. This *volet* has to date been rather neglected. Closer cross-cultural cooperation can only be achieved if a more concerted effort is made to seek a convergence on the basic values that are part and parcel of the civilisations surrounding the Mediterranean area.

At the same time, an analysis of the ability of international organisations to influence regional relations reveals that while they are often capable of having an impact on the regional patterns of relations they are unable to alter the basic pattern of regional alignment and conflict within such international regions. Contemporary EU involvement in the Mediterranean is a good example of an international organisation's limited ability to influence regional dynamics. In reality, the EU's Mediterranean policy is best seen as a boundary management exercise, rather than a boundary transformation one. Its principal aim is to safeguard the process of regional integration in Western Europe from that of fragmentation that is active throughout the Middle East.

The success or failure of the EMP will actually determine whether the Mediterranean becomes a crossroads of tension, outright conflict and an economic wasteland, or whether it becomes a cooperative zone of peace, prosperity and tolerance. Three and a half years since its launching, the process still holds a great deal of potential, but only if it is adapted to the ever changing regional security dynamics it is attempting to stabilise.

On the eve of the twenty-first century, the Mediterranean is more akin to a fault-line between the prosperous North (the haves), and an impoverished South, (the have-nots). The key development to watch in the Mediterranean in the next decade will be to see whether the phase of cooperative competition that has dominated post-Cold War relations to date is eventually superseded by an era of conflictual competition. If this age of indifference scenario does take hold, disorder will dominate Mediterranean relations and as resources are depleted, the region will become an economic wasteland.

In the post-Cold War world that has emerged, the patterns of relations in the Mediterranean have already moved away from a cooperative security dominant framework to a more competitive security based model. If trends continue as they have been, the Mediterranean is destined to become a geo-strategic zone of indifference. Soft security risks will multiply, demographic growth will exacerbate economic problems, and the developed world will adopt a selective engagement approach towards the area. (See Appendix One).

Rather than undermine or diminish the significance of the EMP, the quasi-conflictual pattern of relations in several pockets of the Mediterranean underlines further the significance of the Euro-Mediterranean process, the only multilateral process of its kind in the area.

Appendix I

INTEGRATION	CO-OPERATIVE SECURITY	COMPETITIVE SECURITY	INDIFFERENCE	FRAGMENTATION
Renaissance	Flexible relations	Gradual Growth	Fault-lines Intensify	War
Mediterranean Region	Core/Periphery	Status Quo	Subregional Instability	Apocalypse
Prosperity	Stability	Boundary Management	Marginalisation	Clash of Civilisations
Transnational dominant	Haves/Have Nots	North-South divide	Wasteland (resource depletion)	
Pax Mediterranea 10%	CSCM 20%	Euro-Med Partnership 25%	Euro-Med Collapse 35%	Meltdown 10%

Appendix II

EU Trade Surplus With Mediterranean Hits 13.7 BN ECU

Exports up sharply by 10%

The EU's trade surplus with the 13 Mediterranean countries[1] rose to a "remarkable" 13.7 bn ECU in 1995, according to a report[2] today from Eurostat, the Statistical Office of the European Communities in Luxembourg. In 1994 the surplus was 10.4 bn.

The report says trade relations with the Mediterranean are of major importance to the EU, although their share of total EU external trade has shrunk somewhat in recent years. In 1995 their share of all EU exports and imports amounted to 9.3% and 7.2% respectively.

In 1995, EU imports from the Mediterranean countries rose by 4% over 1994. Exports were up sharply by 10% after a slight fall of 0.5% the previous year.

Turkey most important supplier

Petroleum products, clothing, textile yarns and fabrics, and fruits and vegetables were the most important imports in 1995. Together they made up 60% of all EU imports from these countries.

EU exports to the area were concentrated mainly in machinery and transports equipment - 38% of the total - and miscellaneous manufactured goods (32%).

Germany, France and Italy accounted for more than 60% of both exports to and imports from the Mediterranean basin. On the other side Turkey (26%), Israel (16%) and Algeria (12%) accounted for more than half of the EU's total trade flows with the region.

Turkey also stands out as the most important EU supplier: in 1995 it was the source of some 24% (9.2 bn ECU) of all the Union's imports from the region. It was followed by Algeria and Libya (both 15% or around 6 bn ECU).

Malta, Lebanon and Israel recorded the highest levels of intra-industry trade[3] with the EU. Trade with Syria, Libya and Algeria was restricted largely to inter-sectoral exchanges.

Positive balances for all except Portugal

France and Germany recorded the largest surpluses: 3.7 bn and 2.7 bn ECU respectively. All Member States had positive balances - except Portugal with a small deficit of around 0.2 bn.

Finland and Sweden showed the most dynamic export growth in 1995: 27% and 24% respectively. Ireland recorded the highest percentage change in imports - a rise of 31%.

Appendix Notes

1. Malta, Cyprus, Turkey, Morocco, Algeria, Tunisia, Libya, Egypt, Jordan, Syria, Lebanon, Israel and Gaza-Jericho.

2. EUROSTAT Statistics in focus, External trade no 13/96, EU trade with the Mediterranean countries, results for 1995.

3. Intra-industry trade means that bilateral trade flows (exports and imports) are concentrated in the same industries.

EUROSTAT No. 7/97 28 January 1997

Notes

1. *International Herald Tribune*, 'Arab States Recommend Sanctions on Israel', April 1 1997, p. 1.

2. Joffé, George, (1994): 'The European Union and the Maghreb', in Gillespie, Richard, (ed.), *Mediterranean Politics*, Vol. 1, Pinter Publishers, pp. 22-45. See also Camier, Alice (1991): *The Countries of the Greater Arab Maghreb and the European Community*, Commission of the European Communities, DE 68, Jan.

3. *International Herald Tribune*, 'Greece Rejects Call By Turkey to Talk', February 13 1998, p. 6.

4. *Economist*, 27 March 1999, pp. 15-16 and 29-30.

5. Aliboni, Roberto (1997): 'Confidence Building, Conflict Prevention and Arms Control in the Euro-Mediterranean Partnership, *Perceptions*, Dec. 1997 - Feb. 1998, pp. 73- 86; see also Tanner, Fred, (1997): 'The Euro-Med Partnership: Prospects for Arms Limitations and Confidence Building after Malta', *International Spectator*, xxxii/2, pp. 3-25.

6. *EUROMED Special Feature*, European Commission DG1BA, 19 March 1999.

7. Calleya, Stephen C., (1997a): 'The Euro-Mediterranean Partnership Process After Malta: What Prospects?, *Mediterranean Politics*, 2/2, pp.1-22.

8. Calleya, Stephen C., (1998): 'Crosscultural Currents in the Mediterranean', *Mediterranean Quarterly*, 9/3, pp. 41-60.

9. Thanks to Bjørn Møller for sharing his insight during the 'World Visions' conference at the University of Aarhus, Denmark, December 1997.

10. *Eurostat*, 'EU Trade Surplus with Mediterranean Hits 13.7 Billion ECU', 7/97.

11. Rhein, Eberhard, (1998), 'Euro-Mediterranean Free Trade Area For 2010: Whom Will It Benefit?' *Friedrich Ebert Stiftung*, pp.129-142.

12. See Special Report on Cairo Summit, *MEED*, 15 November 1996, pp. 9-18. See also *MEED*, 22 November 1996, p. 6.

13. *Agence Europe*, 'EU/Mediterranean', 6 February 1998, p.2.

14. Marin, Manuel, (1997): 'Partners in Progress', *Euro-Mediterranean Partnership*, Vol. 2, London, pp. 7-8.

15. Calleya, Stephen, (1997), op.cit., p. 186.

16. A special thanks to Eberhard Rhein of the European Policy Centre in Brussels, without whose help this analysis could not have been compiled.

17. Marks, Jon, (1996): 'High Hopes and Low Motives: The New Euro-Mediterranean Partnership Initiative', *Mediterranean Politics*, 1/1, pp. 17-19. See also Calleya, Stephen C., (1997): *Navigating Regional Dynamics in the Post-Cold War World, Patterns of Relations in the Mediterranean Area*, Dartmouth, pp. 205-210.

18. Carter, Philip, 'Self help – Mediterranean Style', *Project & Trade Finance*, March 1997, p. 28.

19. *Agence Europe*, 'EU/Mediterranean', 6 February 1998, p.2.

20. Marin, Manuel, (1997): 'Partners in Progress', *Euro-Mediterranean Partnership*, Vol. 2, London, pp. 7-8.

21. James N. Rosenau, Rountable on "Is International Studies an Anachronism?", International Studies Association Annual Convention, March 20 1998, Minn., Minnesota. See also Rosenau, *Along the Domestic-Foreign Frontier, Exploring Governance in a Turbulent World*, Cambridge University Press, 1997.

References

Agence Europe, 'EU/Mediterranean', 6 February 1998, p.2.

Aliboni, Roberto (1997): 'Confidence Building, Conflict Prevention and Arms Control in the Euro-Mediterranean Partnership', *Perceptions*, Dec. 1997 - Feb. 1998, pp. 73- 86.

Associated Press, 'Greece-Turkey agree to Meetings' June 30ᵗʰ 1999.

Barbé, Esther (1996): 'The Barcelona Conference: Launching Pad of a Process', *Mediterranean Politics*, 1/1, pp. 25-42.

'Barcelona Declaration adopted at the Euro-Mediterranean Conference' (27 and 28 Nov. 1995).

Calleya, Stephen (1997a): *Navigating Regional Dynamics in the Post-Cold War World, Patterns of Relations in the Mediterranean Area*, Dartmouth, pp. 131-140.

Calleya, Stephen, (1997b): 'The Euro-Mediterranean Process After Malta: What Prospects?', *Mediterranean Politics*, Vol. 2, No. 2, Autumn 1997, pp. 1-22.

Calleya, Stephen, (1999), '*Is The Barcelona Process Working? EU Policy in the Mediterranean*', ZEI Discussion Paper Series.

Camier, Alice (1991): The Countries of the Greater Arab Maghreb and the European Community, Commission of the European Communities, DE 68, Jan.

Coufoudakis, Van, (1996): 'Greek Foreign Policy in the Post-Cold War Era: Issues and Challenges', *Mediterranean Quarterly*, 7/3, pp. 26-41.

EuroMesco Joint Report, April 1997, pp.29-36.

Eurostat, 'EU Trade Surplus with Mediterranean Hits 13.7 Billion ECU', 7/97.

International Herald Tribune, 'Arab States Recommend Sanctions on Israel', April 1 1997, p. 1.

International Herald Tribune, 'Turk-Israeli Exercise: An Alliance Building Steam', December 20-21 1997, p.1 and p.4.

Joffé, George, (1994): 'The European Union and the Maghreb', in Gillespie, Richard, (ed.), Mediterranean Politics, Vol. 1, Printer Publishers.

Makram-Ebeid, Mona, (1997), 'Prospects For Euro-Mediterranean Relations', *Intercultural Dialogue in the Mediterranean*, Foundation for International Studies, pp. 38-53.

'Malta Declaration adopted at Senior Officials meeting, Brussels, (May 1997).

Marin, Manuel, (1997): 'Partners in Progress', *Euro-Mediterranean Partnership*, Vol. 2, London, pp. 7-8.

Marks, Jon, (1996): 'High Hopes and Low Motives: The New Euro-Mediterranean Partnership Initiative', *Mediterranean Politics*, 1/1, pp. 17-19.

MEED, 'Special Report on Cairo Summit', 40/46, 15 November 1996, pp. 9-18.

MEED, 'Cairo Summit', 40/47, 22 November 1996, p. 6.

Roque, Maria Angels, (1997), 'Position Paper on the Role of Civil Society', *Intercultural Dialogue in the Mediterranean*, Foundation for International Studies, pp. 18-23.

Rosenau, James N., Rountable on "Is International Studies an Anachronism?", International Studies Association Annual Convention, March 20 1998, Minn., Minnesota. See also Rosenau, Along the Domestic-Foreign Frontier, Exploring Governance in a Turbulent World, Cambridge University Press, 1997.

Stuttgart Conference, *Chairman's Formal Conclusions*, Third Euro-Mediterranean Conference of Foreign Ministers, Stuttgart, April 15th-16th 1999.

Tanner, Fred, (1997): 'The Euro-Med Partnership: Prospects for Arms Limitations and Confidence Building after Malta', *International Spectator*, xxxii/2, pp. 3-25.

Time International, 'Who Really Won?, June 21st 1999, pp. 20-23.

Wall Street Journal Europe, 'Reform Efforts Pave the Way for Foreign Investment', 3 December 1997.

Wriggins, W.H. et al. (1992): *The Dynamics of Regional Politics: Four Systems on the Indian Ocean Rim*, Columbia University Press, New York, pp. 293-294.

7. Towards the FTAA: Challenges, Limits and Possibilities of Inter-American Regionalism*

Vilma E. Petrash

This paper is aimed at ascertaining the challenges, limits and possibilities of achieving the long-standing but elusive goal of Inter-Americas economic regionalism through the constitution of a *Free Trade Area of the Americas* (the FTM). With such purpose in mind, some previous considerations will be made on the trend and strategy of regionalism as manifested in the post-Cold War era, and on the economic and political/ideological circumstances that promoted the emergence of the so-called "new regionalism" in Latin America and the Caribbean since the early 1980s. Once this is done, the issue of a Western Hemispheric economic integration area will be examined in terms of (a) its origins, evolution and perspectives, (b) the impact upon it of the two major subregional economic areas of the Americas (e.g. NAFTA and MERCOSUR), and (c) the more feasible paths at hand for the arousal of the FTAA.

*Paper presented at the Panel "Regionalisation and the Devise of the FTM," Joint Conference of the *International Studies Association* and the *Mexican Association of International Studies,* Manzanillo, Colima (Mexico), December 11 - 13, 1997.

An earlier version of this paper was presented at the 38th Annual Convention of the *International Studies Association* (Toronto, March 18-27, 1997) in the panel "The Concept of Regionalism, under the title "From Subregionalism to Inter-American Regionalism: NAFTA, MERCOSUR and the Spirit of Miami."

1. Preliminary Remarks. The Strengthening of Regionalism: A Major Post-Cold War Trend

If there is a characteristic feature of the post-Cold War world it is the remarkable and deep trend towards regionalism and the strengthening of regional cooperation. As treated in this paper, "regionalism" refers to the proneness of the governments of a grouping of two or more states-societies to establish voluntary associations and bring together a pool of knowledge, skills and certainly, desires and expectations, in order to develop functional and structural institutional arrangements (either formal or soft, ad hoc or informal) likely to forge between (or among) them the bonds of a distinct economic, social and prospectively, political entity, and/or increase their negotiating power vis-a-vis the rest of the world. However, for regionalism to exist certain conditions should be met.

Stubbes and Underhill mention three specific dimensions allowing to identify/define this phenomenon: the first concerns the extent to which countries in a certain geographic area shared similar historical experiences and are coping with similar general problems. The second dimension points to the degree to which countries located in the same geographical area have established economic, sociocultural and/or political linkages that render them distinguishable from the rest of the global community of countries. The third dimension emphasizes the extent to which certain groupings of countries have established organisations for the handling of significant aspects of their collective affairs.[1] But even if these three dimensions are found it is still worth keeping in mind that "just as with nations, regions are 'imagined communities', whose identities are artificially constructed and promoted for a specific set of political ends. There are no 'natural' regions, any more than there are 'natural' nations..."[2]

The latter reminder notwithstanding, a fact remains: that in the current post-Cold War and post-bipolar environment, the tendency towards the widening and deepening of "imagined" regional communities has been to a large degree stimulated by the overcoming of intra and inter-regional interaction patterns and schemes motivated and influenced to a large degree, by the ideologically distorting lens of the Cold War bipolarism through which intra and inter-regional relationships were interpreted. Overall, these ideological "blinders" vis-a-vis regional dynamics served for several decades - following Keohane and Goldstein[3] -- both as "road maps" and "focal points" in the making and implementation of policies aimed at obstructing the creation and growth of trade and investment flows among regional neighbours. Yet, as it has been suggested by Andrew (1994), at present worldwide manifestations of active and expanding forms of regionalism signals something else: the opening of spaces for the development of regional power systems in Europe, Asia and, to a more qualified extent, the Americas/the Caribbean. Opening propelled, to a large extent, by the relative "hegemonic decline" and therefore, reduced capacity and/or willingness of the United States -- the territorial center of the "triumphal" global political-economic process of "capitalist democratisation"-- to continue playing the pivotal political and economic role it played throughout the Cold War-bipolar era, and its concomitant attempts to rebuild, at both regional and global levels, its contested hegemony upon more consensual foundations. Among these consensual foundations presently sought by the U.S. there are: the sharing of liberal internationalist values (hence the strategy of enlarging the community of market democracies); the creation and re-creation of international regimes and institutions based upon more solid liberal norms and rules (e.g. UN reform attempts; the backing of the "New OAS" explicitly charged with implementing the Miami Summit hemispheric agenda); and third, the provisions of benefits to weaker partners (e.g. the possibility [or promise] of granting market access to U.S. hemispheric partners through bilateral or regional FTAs).

The latter might well be the primary reason why in the last two decades but even more so in the present one, we have witnessed an outstanding and steady movement, although in no ways exempt from risks and costs, towards the creation, deepening and/or widening of regional spaces of socio-economic integration and of great political cooperation and concertation with strong integrationist possibilities.

Certainly, what has been said hitherto has a general applicability. However, it becomes particularly significant regarding the Western Hemisphere, where even before the downfall of the Berlin Wall, there were evident "value convergences" (and certainly convergences in terms of desires and expectations) in the conduct of economic policies and in development strategies -- mostly observed among its less capitalist-developed members: Latin American and Caribbean countries -- which evolved into both shared criteria and approaches and an increasing interest in establishing or reactivating close linkages and in the development of cooperative relationships: more productive and efficient among them but also, and most importantly, more pragmatically productive and positive with the hemispheric colossus, the United States. At this point it is worth remembering that the free market values undergirding this environment in Latin America at large were at the core of Washington's articulation of a global post-Cold War strategy. This "coincidence" of U.S. post-1989 strategic objectives with the new value orientations of most Latin American government and business elites obviously reveals that after subordinating economic policy for four decades to Western strategic imperatives, a harshly competitive globalised economy in the 1990s forced the U.S. to the reordering of its priorities. In the absence of a global ideological context, this need for reordering was what was left of the policy conceptualisation of the 1980s.[4]

At this juncture, it seems necessary to provide a brief explanation of what has been consensually seen as the central cause of this political coincidence and resulting regional consensus in Latin America and the Caribbean -- political coincidence and regional consensus, in turn, characterised by qualified sources on both regions as a paradigm shift-- namely: the disastrous and strenuous economic and social experience of regional states-societies during the so-called lost decade of the 1980s. An experience of such deep proportions and pervasive consequences in Latin America at large that contributed significantly to expand and/or deepen intra-Latin American economic, political and socio-cultural linkages, and to the creation or reactivation of regional and subregional economic and political institutions for furthering common goals and solving common problems. In this very respect, Latin America events in the last and current decades can be fully equated with the three dimensions that in Stubbes and Underhill's words characterize the phenomenon of regionalism.

2. The "New Regionalism" in Latin America and the Caribbean: A Paradigm Shift

As has been widely mentioned in several studies on the region, during the 1980s Latin American governments increasingly lost faith in the inwardly oriented development policies and the schemes of self-reliance and autonomy that characterised "Third World" thinking since the 1950s. In effect, the levels of inflation, severe external indebtedness for some, a net outward transfer of financial and other resources for many, deep fiscal unbalances and, in short, the economic chaos that affected regional economies during the last decade reflected the irreversible failure and collapse of the hitherto-dominant Cepalist model of inward-looking growth. Briefly speaking, it was a model which assigned a large role to State intervention in the economy, mainly through import substitution industrialisation (ISI) policies, wide-ranging subsidy programs and extensive protection of the domestic markets from external competition through high tariffs. In this sense, and in spite of the well-reported direct pressure exerted by multilateral financial institutions and governments of developed countries and their conditionality of economic assistance to the adoption of liberal economic and political reforms in Latin America, it was essentially a crisis with significant domestic causes. The most overarching of them was, no doubt, the fiscal, political and institutional "terminal crisis" of the "Estado Planificador" ("planning State"), that is, of the image of the State's role in the political and socio-economic realms which began to pervade the thinking of Latin American political and economic elites during the thirties and assumed full expression in regional politics and economic development during the fifties and sixties (right in the midst of the distorting and all-encompassing rhetoric of the Cold War). But it must be added that the 1980s economic and political crisis of the statist-ISI model, long and widely embraced by Latin American and Caribbean nations, had likewise undeniable external causes, e.g.: sea changes in technology; in communications; in the functioning and operation of global markets and in the growth of global systems of productions and distribution, and the deeply eroding impact of those changes on nationally based industries and nationally based and autonomous technological development.

   In summary, the resulting desperate circumstances of economic ungovernability that underwent Latin American/Caribbean economies/societies allowed the emergence of the intra-Latin American political consensus and will (but in several cases only deeply and fully achieved among certain sectors of the political and economic elites) required for the relaunching of the age-old idea of regional economic integration. An idea that was implemented during the sixties at regional (with the Latin American Free Trade Association and the Caribbean Free Trade Association) and sub-regional levels (e.g. the Central American Common Market and the Andean Pact), but not for free trade purposes but rather to protect infant industries behind high tariff walls.

As previously suggested, this commendable but illusory goal was fully abandoned after the "lost decade" and the resulting "latinsclerosis" which pervaded regional/subregional integration projects. Since the late 1980s the primary goal of economic integration would no longer be the protection of member states' production and markets for developmental purposes, but rather the enlargement of national markets into regional ones so as to promote/empower the efficient and fair participation of such integrated enlarged markets into the world economy. This meant revitalising and readjusting prevailing trade and integration arrangements (e.g. the Andean Pact) and creating new ones, both bilateral and multilateral and with different degrees of institutional development (e.g. MERCOSUR and the Group of Three, a "new generation" free Trade Area among Colombia, Mexico and Venezuela), aimed at reinserting both regions in the world economy under parameters of systemic competitiveness and at supporting and "locking in" the domestic strategies of growth and economic and political reforms of Latin American/Caribbean countries, into wider and highly complex networks of "open regionalism". It should be added, however, that the revival of Latin American and Caribbean integration goals was also a reaction to the perceived consolidation of trade blocs in other regions of the World (overall the European Community), perception which called attention to the potential benefits of freer trade with existing partners.

The above explains the recent Latin American/Caribbean propensity to follow somewhat "open" but surely diverse subregional paths -- at times implying multiple articulations -- which may well lead these states-societies in two different but seemingly compatible directions: on the one hand, the progressive building of hemispheric regionalism, e.g., the Inter-American Free Trade Zone unilaterally envisaged and announced by President Bush in his "Enterprise for the Americas Initiative" in June 1990, and openly debated and widely endorsed four and a half years later by 34 hemispheric Head of States in the Summit of the Americas, held in Miami; on the other, the setting up of a regional Latin American/Caribbean integration framework allowing the American nations not directly involved in, and perhaps marginalised from, the North American, European and Japanese-Asian processes of commercial-financial integration, to regionalise their needs and interests and become valid spokesmen before the pre-eminent world triad of economic power.

In the forthcoming parts of this paper I will focus on the first of these two alternatives: the possibilities, limits, and challenges of attaining hemispheric integration by establishing a Free Trade Area of the Americas (FTM). For this purpose, three major points will be addressed: first, the origins, current situation and perspectives of the proposed formation of a Westem Hemispheric integration Area. Second, the two integration schemes of the hemisphere which by virtue of their economic weight and impact on the hemispheric gross domestic Product (GDP) and trade, show the greater chance of becoming either "building blocks" or "stumbling blocs" in the continental integrationist process, namely: NAFTA and MERCOSUR. This will be done by analysing the origins of both sub-regional arrangements; their areas of similarity and differences; the challenges, limits, and possibilities faced by each in contributing to the rise of an FTM, and last but not least, the degree to which both regionalisms are promoting Inter-American macro-regional integration or rather, mutually exclusive geoeconomic blocs. As a third and final point, I will identify and analyse the most likely paths towards the establishment of the FTAA by the year 2005.

3. Free Trade in the Americas: Origins, Current Situation and Perspectives

As any issue involving different countries or groups of countries, it is understandable that for the concerned parties the establishment of such a broad free trade area as a continental one, may mean different things and attracts different interests. As expected, questions, differences and divergent expectations are likely to arise regarding the great variety of economic sizes, and the degree of foreign trade dependence, either at the sub-regional level or in relation to the major macro-regional power (the US). However, a possible common ground of parties' expectations and interests would be the goal of achieving with such large process of "complex" integration, the expansion of the intra-regional flows of trade and investments for the majority of the countries of the Americas.

No doubt, in the case of the Latin American/Caribbean nations, the attraction exerted by the U.S. market, clearly and by far the most relevant market of the region - taken as a whole, about 40 per cent of hemispheric merchandise exports are sold in the U.S. markets [5]-- is a primary motivating force in preserving a "leap of faith" - despite the myriad of ambiguous and even contradictory signals from the U.S. -- on the possibilities of a more open hemispheric trade and investment area. After all, what is so anxiously expected is a huge Free Trade Area which will make the Western Hemisphere the largest trading region in the world, covering 39 million square kilometers, with a combined GDP of more than US $9 trillion and a market of 765 million people. [6]

Nonetheless, the intensity of this "faith" and the subsequent activism to see the Inter-American trade and investment integration crystallised, are largely conditioned by the size of the specific economy or groups of economies and/or, --and most importantly -- by its own geographical proximity to the U.S. market. In other words, trade and investment figures between the U.S. and other American nations unambiguously reveal that the closer the state to the U.S., the higher its trade dependence to the latter's enormous market. This explains why Canada and Mexico show a very similar high proportion of trade/ investment concentration with a single partner: more than three quarters of their goods and services transactions are with the U.S. In turn, for the other nations located North of Latin America (the Caribbean Basin nations), the proportion of merchandise export with the U.S. drops off, but still remains high, generally exceeding 50 per cent and rarely falling below 30 per cent. Certainly for the southern part of the hemisphere, no country's reliance on the U.S. market exceeds 30 per cent.[7] In any case, even for the Southern Latin American countries, the U.S., when taken as a single country, remains the major trading partner, although in composite terms Western Europe is the area which dominates the MERCOSUR and Bolivian markets.

3.1. The Enterprise for the Americas Initiative

The previous data explain why the Enterprise for the Americas Initiative (EAI) announced by former U.S. President George Bush in a major policy address in Washington on June 27, 1990, was so warmly and enthusiastically welcomed in most Latin American and the Caribbean countries. And even more so, because such announcement was seen as a "historic opportunity": the opportunity to establish an entirely new, more reciprocal economic relationship between the U.S. and the other nations of the Western Hemisphere. That is, a relationship based not on the age-old and traumatic patterns and habits of domination but on unprecedented and innovative criteria of partnership. It did not matter too much whether the U.S. conceived the EAI unilaterally and without any consultation. It was a contradictory signal that many regional governments and business communities were willing to overlook as long as the U.S.-proposed sweeping revision of the inter-American economic landscape in line with its trade, investment, and debt pillars could be fulfilled. Besides, it was interpreted as an outright and far-sighted backing by the overwhelming continental power to the painful but presumably "revolutionary" process of economic and political reforms that Latin American and Caribbean nations were undergoing. Of utmost significance was the EAI-included sub-proposal of a Western Hemispheric Free Trade Area (WHFTA), which in spite of President Bush's emphasis on the requirement of a decade or more for its realisation, stimulated a widespread wave of expectations and even fears (e.g. by Brazil, the Southern hemispheric colossus) that gave further and more vigorous impulse to a broad variety of regional and subregional (plurilateral and bilateral) integrationist efforts.

An important consequence of the EAI was the signing of trade and investment agreements between the U.S. and all the countries of the Hemisphere except Cuba, Haiti and Surinam. By establishing trade and investment councils, these agreements promoted an intensive and constructive dialogue and the exchange of information on trade and investment issues hindering economic relations between the U.S. and the other American countries. Another no less relevant consequence of the EAI was that it assured support and granted attention to the negotiating process of the NAFTA. After all, this latter process not only entailed an unprecedented negotiation, both in the Americas and world-wide, between the developed North (the U.S. and Canada) and the developing South (Mexico), but was also sold with considerable success to the Latin American audiences as the first step toward the WHFTA.[8] Unfortunately, the Latin American and Caribbean expectations and hopes regarding the EAI and the possible emergence of a WHFTA were soon frustrated by certain "hard facts":

• The too ambitious objectives of the EAI which, along with the lip-service support paid by the Bush administration to the EAI, may well explain the reduced coordination shown by the U.S. government agencies entrusted with its implementation.

• The prolonged uncertainty that surrounded NAFTA's ratification by the U.S. Congress, the granting of which only occurred after a hard public campaign nationwide and a great lobbying effort by the U.S. President himself'.

• Latin American's growing awareness of the special and complex interdependent relationship existing between Mexico and the U.S. (which explains Mexico's inclusion in a U.S.-dominated North American integration scheme). As such, this "special relationship" was seen as unique and in no ways replicable by the other American countries (with the possible exception, *mutatis mutandi,* of Canada, Cuba and Haiti).

• Latin American and Caribbean countries' second thoughts regarding the obligations entailed for them in an agreement as comprehensive as NAFTA (indeed a GATT WTO plus accord), and their widespread regional uncertainty about the U.S. political conviction to proceed with its promised expansion.

• The deep social and political crisis that hit Mexico on the very same day in which NAFTA entered into effect and which badly worsened during 1994. This crisis, apart from revealing the fallacy of Mexico's First World conversion, served to further convince the protectionist and isolationist sectors of the U.S. society of the undesirability of concluding future FTAs with "other Mexicos".

3.2. The Summit of the Americas and the FTAA

These hard facts and turbulent signals from a regional "role model" like Mexico notwithstanding, did not prevent the Latin American leaders from endorsing VicePresident Al Gore's proposal -- made in Mexico City in December 1993 - to celebrate a "summit of democratically elected leaders in order to discuss the prospect of hemispheric free trade". This summit -- better known as the Summit of the Americas - was formally convoked by President Clinton on March 11, 1993, and was held in December 9-11, 1996 in Miami, the most Hispanic-Caribbean city of the United States. It was undoubtedly a historical reunion, the first of this kind to be held after the one convened 27 years earlier in the Uruguayan City of Punta del Este, and the largest ever in the continent's history insofar as it counted on the participation of the Heads of State and Government of 34 American countries.

Whatever the regional frustrations and apprehensions with, and failed expectations aroused by, the Miami Summit's predecessor, the EAI, it should be remembered that this initiative was based on actual and long-standing inter-American unrealised goals: ensuring that markets in Latin America and the Caribbean would remain open to U.S. goods and services and vice versa, and bringing sustained growth and prosperity to the Americas so that the positive aspects of interdependence could be strengthened and the negative ones substantially reduced. As a result, the same goals strongly motivated the governments attending the Americas' Summit. This was particularly true in the Clinton Administration's case which -- despite its domestic struggle against the strident and vocal anti-NAFTA and anti-GATT WTO forces so influential in the U.S. Congress -- had become allegedly convinced of the fundamental role of improved trading and investment ties within the Americas' republics for the achievement of its foreign and national security strategy of "enlarging the community of market democracies" in the hemisphere and worldwide. By accepting the imperious need of achieving the dual goal of "democracy-free market enlargement" in the Americas, the U.S. government was clearly departing from a well-founded perception of threat and vulnerability vis-a-vis the spill-over effects of Latin American and Caribbean political and economic sustained instability in the increasingly porous U.S. society and economy. It was a perception driven, to a large extent, by the breakdown of a clear division between international and domestic policies, which as such has made it increasingly difficult but even more necessary to formulate and advance a long-term global vision. A global vision that in the Western Hemisphere implied (at least rhetorically) the liberal-internationalist attempt to convert it into the great "Zone of Peace" stretching from Anchorage to Tierra del Fuego, first announced in the EAI and more fully articulated in the Miami Summit.

Of course, other than Wilsonianism, there were good economic reasons underlying the pursuit of a Hemispheric-wide "Zone of Peace": Since the outset of the current decade, the emerging economies of Latin America/the Caribbean had become the second fastest growing market for U.S. exports and investments, after East Asia. This data becomes particularly salient when one takes into consideration two trends in the composition of the US's GDP alluded by U.S. Trade Representative, Charlene Barshefsky, during her testimony in June 10, 1997, before the House of Representatives' Committee on International Relations: first, that exports as a share of such country's GDP grew by 39 per cent between 1986 and 1993, accounting for nearly 50 per cent of its economic growth, and second, that total U.S. trade in 1997 (that is, trade in goods and services plus earnings on foreign investment) will be equivalent to 30 per cent of the U.S. GDP, compared to barely 13 per cent in 1970.[9] Likewise, according to 1994 GATT estimates, North American exports had almost tripled in ten years, growing from a value of 28 billion dollars to a value of 80.7 billion in 1993. Finally, NAFTA was the largest trading partner of most trading groups and most individual countries of the Western Hemisphere, representing around 87 per cent of the hemispheric output. In any case, it should be clarified that the response to the "Spirit of Miami" was hardly uniform regarding the prospects of "reciprocal" and increased hemispheric trade and investment opportunities. As a matter of fact, the smaller and weaker economies of the wider Caribbean region were highly aware of their limited capacity and readiness to be full partners in this proposed continental free trade zone.[10] Most importantly -- and as it will be explained in more detail in the last section of this paper --, Brazil favoured at Miami a more incremental or gradualist approach to the FTAA, based on the interlocking of separate trade groupings until the achievement of a free trade network encompassing the entire continent.

At this point, it should be remembered that at the Summit of the Americas, government leaders in the hemisphere committed themselves, in a collective "Declaration of Principles", to promote and strengthen democratic governance, prosperity through economic integration and free trade, the eradication of poverty and discrimination, and sustainable development. [11]

As expected --and certainly mostly due to the Latin American governments' pressures to see the promise of hemispheric free trade fulfilled -- the centerpiece of the cited Declaration was, no doubt, the long-desired, far-reaching but elusive goal of continental prosperity and trade liberalisation. A process for which it set a target date no later than 2005 for completing negotiations, stating its immediate start with steps oriented to the gradual elimination of barriers to goods and services and with agreements on trade-related measures such as subsidies, investment, intellectual property and rules of origin. With such goals in mind, a 23-point Plan of Action was adopted -- and attached to the Declaration --, containing the specific measures the leaders agree to use to achieve the policy envisaged in the Declaration, and particularly the FTM. In this specific regard, the Plan stated that the FTM would be constructed in a manner consistent with the GATT/WTO and accordingly would not raise new barriers to trade, but it also asserted that the scope of trade agreements would be comprehensive, including a list of areas to be covered, from tariffs on goods to services to agriculture to intellectual property, aimed at attaining a "WTO plus" liberalisation, that is, at improving the WTO rules and disciplines by negotiating areas not sufficiently consolidated or included in the multilateral trading system. Yet, such specific concerns as the need to make trade and environmental policies mutually supportive and the observance and promotion of workers rights were likewise included. As an "immediate action agenda", the Plan of Action entailed a work program for the next 15 months to be coordinately conducted at existing hemispheric fora (the OAS and the IADB with the support of the ECLAC). In this last respect, it should be noticed that the Declaration of Principles and the Action Plan both explicitly called on the OAS and the IADB to take responsibility for following up the Summit's decisions, drawing up the programme of meetings and coordinating the many regional trade pacts already in existence.

From this cooperative institutional effort, reports were to be prepared to serve as the basis for discussion of OAS Special Committee on Trade meetings, which in turn would be entrusted to prepare reports to the Trade Ministerial Meetings between OAS governments in charge of maintaining the momentum and considering progress towards the FTAA. In the inter-governmental ministerial meetings sixteen working groups were to be formed in order to consider such subjects as customs unions, tariffs, human rights, working conditions, and environmental protection. The purpose of these groups was two-fold: firstly, creating a common language and the technical specifications pertaining the major negotiating issues; secondly, identifying the areas of agreement and discord among the various negotiating issues. Other matters mentioned for possible discussion in the Action Plan were efforts to attain governments' accountability, and the need for cooperative and coordinated hemispheric initiatives to deal with such fundamental issues as sustainable development, science and technology, crime prevention, drug trafficking and money laundering.

Up to now, a major report of the OAS Trade Unit (duly supported by research inputs from the IADB and the ECLAC, as established in the Miami's Declaration of principles) has been prepared in which an extensive overview is provided encompassing valuable data on regional, subregional and country trade and investment trends; on recent trade and economic integration developments in the Americas, and the challenges faced by smaller developing countries; on the likely areas of commonality and divergence among such trade arrangements; and on the significance of specific issues (tariff structures, rules of origin and regional-subregional pacts' compatibility with the WTO) to the rise of a continental Free Trade Area. Furthermore, three trade Ministers' meetings have been held, the first and the second in Denver, Colorado (June-July 1995) and Cartagena de Indias, Colombia (March 1996) respectively, from which a total of eleven working groups have been formed whose coordination has been assigned to different countries of the Americas; and the third, in Belo Horizonte, Brazil (May 14-16, 1997), in which after arduous discussions and three previous meetings of the Ministers of Trade, consensus was reached -- based on a complex formula -- that the launching of the FTM negotiations should be initiated at the highest political level at the 11 Americas Summit to meet in Santiago de Chile in March (later changed to April) 1998, once the approaches, structure and location of negotiations were decided, one month before, in San Jose de Costa Rica.[12]

4. Underlying Factors Promoting Or Impairing Inter-American Economic Integration

There are two primary underlying factors that may contribute to enable or delay the emergence of a wider and deeper economic integration in the Western Hemisphere: increased and complex "integration from below" and asymmetry.

4.1. Increasing and Complex(ing) Integration

If for analytical purposes the countries of our Hemisphere are split in two major sub-regionalisations: North America and Latin American/ Caribbean, it is possible to observe important intra-regional dynamics toward economic complex integration, although much deeper in the first case, due to the infrastructural-communicational advantages of that macro-zone vis-a-vis its less developed neighbouring regions.

4.1.1. North American "Integration from Below"

In the North American case, the phenomenon of integration suggests -- as it has been rightly asserted by Jeffrey Garten, former U.S. Under Secretary of Commerce for International Trade (1994) -- a process qualitatively different than merely denser networks of trade, the latter being more noticeable in the Latin American-Caribbean case. On the contrary, North American integration is based on progressively and steadily deepening complex cross-border corporate coproduction, distribution and sourcing networks -- most of which take place in just a handful of industries -- and on increasingly tight linkages in infrastructure.[13] As a matter of fact, these profound and pervasive transterritorial interactions make it difficult to describe the Canada-U.S. and U.S.-Mexico economic relationship in traditional international trade-investment terms. In this sense it is obvious that the huge economic attraction of the U.S. market as well as sub-regional socio-cultural dynamics have played a sine qua non role in the "integration from below" that has been occurring in the northern hemispheric region: it is no wonder that this de facto integration had ended up in a politically-governmentally formalised process of integration, or "integration from above" between the U.S. and Canada in 1988 (the CUSFTA), and between these two countries and Mexico in 1994 (the NAFTA). Again, as explained by Jeffrey Garten, there are some regional parameters of trade and investment relationships which may serve to illustrate this deep and complex macro-regional integration, even if such data suggest fictitious boundaries in some instances.

a. Investment

Foreign Direct Investment (FDI) among the three NAFTA members has doubled in the last decade, reaching more than 120 billion U.S. dollars in 1992. Each North American country is principal investor in each other's market. Certainly, the U.S. is the largest foreign investor in Canada and Mexico, contributing around 65 per cent of total FDI in both Mexico and Canada. Total U.S. FDI to its North American neighbours is 16 per cent, a disproportionate share if one considers Canada's and Mexico's share of the World's GDP. But this share is just a reflection of a historical trend that has been developing in the direction of U.S. intra-regional (and world) investment and which has been largely propelled by Canada and Mexico's past import substitution policies. In turn, the U.S. is the most popular destination for Canadian and Mexican FDI. Specifically, Canada is the fourth largest foreign direct investor in the U.S.

In relation to portfolio investment within North America, it should be said that until the Mexican 1994 financial crisis it grew much faster than FDI, doubling during the 1980s and climbing from US $142 billion to US $175 billion between 1989 and 1992. Given that Mexico was a preferred destination of this type of short-term investment inflows, it seems that this country's 1994-1995 financial crisis sent major alert signs both in North America and worldwide regarding its volatility and hypersensitivity to the instability signs of financial markets, particularly emerging ones. Overall, this unfortunate event unambiguously revealed that, unlike direct investment, portfolio investment can depart for perceived greener pastures with the speed of light. To be sure, a relevant lesson to be reamed from Mexico's late 1994 devaluation debacle and its resulting "tequila effect" on world financial markets is that the source of capital inflows to a developing country may be as important as their magnitude. In one sense - as has been reminded by Jared Hazleton, a Business and Finance expert from Texas A&M University -- Mexico was victimised by its own success in reforming its economy and opening its markets. These actions enabled it to attract an inflow of volatile portfolio capital to finance long-term development needs. But they also made Mexico more vulnerable to disruption when investor expectations changed.[14]

b. Trade

A more remarkable performance in regional economic integration is verified in North American trade relations. To be sure, between 1980 and 1993, intra-North American trade expanded by 170 per cent, 50 per cent faster than the region's trade with the rest of the World. Of particular relevance in this sense has been the growth of intraregional exports which have done so twice as fast as North American exports to the rest of the world.

4.1.2. Latin American "New Integration": An "Integration from Above"Building "Integration from Below"

In the Latin America and the Caribbean's case, the "new integration" that reportedly started at the closing of the last decade -- and was so decisively pushed from above, due to its high priority in national policies around the region-- has had a fundamental effect in increasing "integration from below". In effect, regional trade is being experiencing significant transformations since the late 1980s to the point of showing unprecedented changes in the nature of Latin American and Caribbean external trade. This is strongly visible in the intra-regional trade boom which has kept its growing tendency regardless of such factors as: the interdependent volatility of regional capital markets which was evidenced since the Mexican peso crisis; the unilateral trade openings to all the partners of the region practiced by several countries, or the trade diversion effect that the initiation of the process of hemispheric integration could have. As has been reported by the Latin American Economic System (SELA),[15] intraregional trade is expanding at a faster rate than trade with the rest of the world, jumping from 13.1 per cent of total regional trade in 1990 to 20 per cent in 1995. At the same time, intra-regional trade has become an important element in the foreign trade of many Latin American countries, representing 59 per cent for Paraguayan exports, 52 per cent of Uruguay's, 46 per cent of Argentina's, and more than 20 per cent for Brazil, Colombia and Chile.

An important common feature of both the North American and Latin American/Caribbean integration processes is the growth of intra-scheme trade. Put simply, this means that countries belonging to the same trade agreement are trading more with their partners, although it is clear that the intensity of the relationship varies from one country to another and from one group to another. Thus, NAFTA countries are not only the ones that trade most with each other (over 40 per cent of their total trade) - although trade flows are mostly directed to and from the U.S. market -- but they are likewise the ones whose trade have soared more (17 per cent just in 1994).[16] The above notwithstanding, inter-scheme trading in Latin America and the Caribbean have also increased sensibly from 1990 to 1994: 2.9 times within MERCOSUR, 2.6 times in the Andean Groups' case, and 1.9 times in the Central American Common Market.[17] In turn, inter-scheme trade has been grossly in NAFTA's favour which remains the largest partner of most trading groups and most countries in the continent, accounting for 48.8 per cent of CACM's trade, 48.9 per cent for the Caribbean, 65 per cent of the Group of Three, and 46.1 per cent for the Andean Community. A glaring exception from this trend is MERCOSUR for which the European Union is the largest trading partner (27 per cent of MERCOSUR exports), followed by South America (almost 27 per cent), and NAFTA (which remained at 21 per cent).[18]

4.2. Asymmetry

The other inescapable factor underlying inter-regional and intra-regional dynamics in the Americas which may promote or inhibit hemispheric integration is the asymmetry existing between North America and Latin America/the Caribbean and within each of these two major sub-regions of the Americas.

In the North American case, it is rather obvious that asymmetry has been a predominant feature of both the Canada-U.S. and the Mexico-U.S. relationship, but is also present in the Canada-Mexico relationship. To be sure, these countries do not operate as a threesome, but -- as suggested before -- operate two by two, by what has been described as a process of "dual asymmetry."[19] This latter term allows us to distinguish between two kinds of asymmetries: on the one hand, the "North-North" asymmetrical relationship between Canada and the U.S., in which there are significant differences in terms of economic size and differential economic, social and political institutions but channeled within a framework of mostly cooperative interactions; and on the other hand, a "North-South" asymmetrical relationship in which to Mexico's much smaller economic size than that of the U.S. and the former's "institutional deficit" to deal with the challenges of domestic economic and political reforms and relate with its overwhelmingly powerful neighbour, is being increasingly added the less intense but also significant differences along the same mentioned dimensions existing between this Latin-North American country and Canada, the other developed and more northern country of the region.

In any case, for both Canada and Mexico -- regardless of their differences and own asymmetrical relationship -- a substantial part of their trade takes place with the United States: an impressive 86 per cent for Canada, showing around a 10 per cent increase in trade concentration vis-a-vis the U.S. since the decision to negotiate the CUSFTA, and more than 75 per cent in the Mexican case. Interestingly, and in spite of large asymmetries between the North-American de facto "hub" and its neighbouring "spokes", these two countries are the first (Canada) and the third largest (Mexico) U.S. trading partners, representing more than 20 per cent and almost 10 per cent of U.S. total trade, and around 58 per cent and 24 per cent of U.S. trade in the Americas.[20]

Asymmetries are also readily verified in the economic relations both between North American countries and their counterparts of Latin American and the Caribbean countries and among the latter themselves. In effect, and as has been said elsewhere, due to the centripetal impact of the interplay of geography and economic size and strength, in composite terms NAFTA is the largest partner of most trading plurilateral arrangements and most countries in the Americas: it represents 87 per cent of the overall hemispheric GDP and 83 per cent of its foreign trade,[21] 48.8 per cent of CACM's trade, 48.4 per cent of the Caribbean, 65 per cent for the Group of Three, and 46.1 per cent for the Andean Community. In turn, the United States is plainly the major trading pattern in the Western Hemisphere, accounting for 69 per cent of the whole region's GDP. By contrast, Latin America/Caribbean's share in the GDP of the entire Hemisphere amounts to 24 per cent, of which 11 per cent corresponds to MERCOSUR, 4 per cent to the Group of Three, 0.76 per cent to the Andean Community and 0.35 per cent to Central America and

Caricom.[22]

From the above it is possible to deduct that hemispheric-wise there are also great disparities in economic size. Thus, the most important hemispheric plurilateral trading arrangement after NAFTA is undoubtedly MERCOSUR, a custom Union created in 1991 and established as such from January 1, 1995, of which are members two of the largest countries of the Americas: Brazil and Argentina, together with Uruguay and Paraguay, and to which are formally associated Chile and Bolivia through bilateral FTAs signed in June and November 1996 respectively. Yet, the four MERCOSUR countries together account for only 8 per cent of the FTAA's total output. Aside from the obvious MERCOSUR's asymmetry vis-a-vis NAFTA, there is also a major intra-MERCOSUR asymmetry to be highlighted: within this major subregional trading group, Brazil accounts for almost two thirds of its economic activity, thus being the natural "hub" of this plurilateral integration scheme. In addition, Brazil commands the largest, most dynamic economy in Latin America as a whole -- eleven times that of Chile, for example -- reason for which it has the greater capacity -- along with the declared hegemonic aspiration and political will -- to create a South American Free Trade Area (SAFTA) centered around itself.[23] The Brazilian government, and its political and economic elites seem well aware of the cited facts and opportunities, particularly of the possibility that a Brazil-centred MERCOSUR become the pole linking the eventual inter-fusion of the myriad of freer trade integration alternatives underway in Latin America/the Caribbean, as it became evident in 1993 when former Brazilian President's Itamar Franco openly proposed the creation of a SAFTA.

5. NAFTA and MERCOSUR

At this point is should be crystal-clear that NAFTA and MERCOSUR are the primary integration arrangements in the Western Hemisphere: on the one hand, because both of them account for the bulk of the continental GDP and trade, and on the other, because unlike the other trading arrangements existing in the Americas, only these two large plurilateral economic groupings actually approach their basic purposes.[24] Furthermore, the importance of both arrangements goes well beyond the Americas, since NAFTA and MERCOSUR are also two of the world's largest integrated markets - being NAFTA the first and MERCOSUR increasingly mentioned as the fourth. Therefore, an agreement between these two groupings - either by MERCOSUR's countries accession to NAFTA or by interlocking both plurilateral schemes through an FTA -- would certainly be an essential step toward an FTAA. In particular, since it would set up inescapable pressures for other countries in the Hemisphere to put their affairs in order so they could join the emerging Inter-American trading Area. But also, the NAFTA-MERCOSUR formal economic approachment would mean a development of major global significance: the undebatable preponderance of the U.S.-hegemonised Western Hemisphere in the world's geoeconomic structure of power.

Given Brazil's leadership in MERCOSUR and its emergence as a leading market force in Latin America, and the United States' dominant role both in NAFTA and in the Hemisphere as a whole, it is a truism to argue that there can be no FTAA without the consent of any of them. Yet, insofar as both countries seem to be holding different views regarding the best path to achieve such a major continental goal, it looks pertinent at this point to provide brief background information on NAFTA and MERCOSUR, as well as to establish comparisons in both countries' pivotal weights on their respective economic integration scheme. Once this is done, the preferred options of the U.S. and Brazil vis-a-vis Inter-American integration, as well as the possibilities and limits of bringing the two major trading agreements they command into a single FTM will be ascertained.

5.1. Origins and Conceptualisation of the Two Major Integration of Poles of the Americas

5.1.1. The NAFTA

The North American Free trade Agreement between the U.S., Canada and Mexico, better known by the acronym NAFTA, has 7 per cent of the world's population and produce 28 per cent of the world's output, having a regional GDP of US$ 7.2 trillion. It is, no doubt, a gigantic trade liberalisation and integration agreement whose emergence can be traced back to a number of factors: first, the already successful negotiation of a FTA between the U.S. and Canada, that is, between the partners of the single most dynamic and largest bilateral commercial and financial relationship in the world. It was a bilateral FTA that covered goods, services and investment but dealt superficially with the issue of intellectual property. For its part, Mexico had gradually become the U.S. third trading partner, and had undertaken economic and trade reforms during the de la Madrid and Salinas Administrations. Lastly, the three North American countries had converged -- although due to diverging factors[25] -- on the belief that the widespread and profound trade and economic ties in the region called for a comprehensive FTA designed to fit this widely interdependent but asymmetrical reality: the NAFTA. In that very sense, with the incorporation of Mexico, the NAFTA allowed to extend to a developing country the modality of preferential trade agreements between developed countries in the continent which had been established in the 1989 Canada-U.S. FTA -- and which, in turn, had fully departed from previous U.S.-Canada's reliance on multilateral mechanisms to act in international markets.[26]

Briefly speaking, the NAFTA negotiations were started in Toronto, Canada in June 1991, and were concluded fourteen months later, on August 12, 1992 in Washington, D.C. Even though the agreement was signed on December 17, 1992, President Clinton, in fulfilment of its electoral promise of not signing legislation implementing NAFTA until the reaching of "additional agreements to protect America's vital interests" proposed to supplement the original negotiated text with two "side agreements" on labour protection and environment cooperation and safeguards. These agreements were bilaterally negotiated and concluded in August 1993, thus paving the way to NAFTA's legislative approval, process which, it is worth remembering, still required a major public and inside-the-Hill campaign from the Clinton Administration in order to gain the necessary congressional votes for its passing in mid-December 1993. Just after that breath-taking and stressful campaign in the U.S., NAFTA and its side agreements came into effect on January 1, 1994.

NAFTA is thus a comprehensive free trade agreement which aside from establishing a five to ten-year schedule for abolishing tariff barriers on most goods (and a fifteen-year transition period for some sensitive agricultural products, e.g.: corn and dry beans for Mexico, orange juice and sugar for the U.S.), also entails free trade in services, protection for investment and intellectual property, the applying of rules to government procurement and the operation of government enterprises, and contains highly developed systems for trade dispute settlement. In addition, the agreement grants market access conditions for sectors such as transportation, telecommunications, and financial services, considered critical to the steady development of North America's infrastructure.[27] Innovative features such as a broader scope, complex and detailed provisions regarding competition, and a more selective process for broadening the market than the one included in traditional (or "first generation") Free trade Areas, may well explain why NAFTA is called a "new generation" Free Trade Area in a recent document released by the Permanent Secretariat of SELA.[28]

A major feature of the agreement is the inclusion of a Canadian-proposed accession clause (and improved by Mexico's supplementary proposal to extend its provisions to all countries in the world meeting the required conditions), which is allowing accession negotiations with the government of Chile which were launched on June 1995 in Toronto, Ontario, and while suspended by the anti-NAFTA and anti-Free Trade atmosphere surrounding U.S. Presidential campaign, are showing certain although still weak reactivating signs, together with the "Miami Spirit", in the second Clinton Presidency.

5.1.2. The MERCOSUR

The Mercado Comun del Sur, known commonly as MERCOSUR, has been termed the "most vibrant example of South-South regional trade integration currently available... [and] the only major customs union outside the European Union."[29] This Southern integration scheme has a combined population of close to 200 million - equivalent to 44 per cent of Latin America's population --, and a combined GDP in 1994 of nearly US$ 800 billion, with US$ 61.5 billion in exports and US$ 56 billion in imports. Its territory covers nearly 12 million sq. km. (4.6 million sq. mi.), thus comprising 59 per cent and 70 per cent of the total land of Latin America and South America respectively, and including some of the world's most important agricultural and mineral resources.[30]

MERCOSUR's origins can be traced back to the opening up of the Brasilia Buenos Aires axis, a political framework with obvious economic and trade consequences.[31] As several specialised sources have asserted, some of the political motivation for this agreement came from the transition to civilian rule in both Argentina and Brazil. Back then, it was widely perceived to be in the interest of these two countries to improve relations, to diffuse mutual suspicions and fears, and to remove the justification for greater military expenditures that came from poor relations between these two major South American countries. A fact worth mentioning here is that the motivation for closer and deeper bilateral economic linkages came from above, from the Samey and Alfonsin's governments themselves. Indeed, in the specific case of Brazil, there was scant support from either the corporate community or, for that matter, Brazilian academics, who were not particularly interested or involved in early discussions. On such more positive political grounds of democracy and military detente, the governments of Brazil and Argentina signed the Act of Iguazu in 1985 and established a joint committee to study the regional economic integration between these two countries. In July 1986, the Act of Argentina-Brazil Integration was signed, which created the *Economic Integration and Cooperation Programme* (PICE), providing for the creation of a common economic space with incentives for complementary economic sectors based upon the principles of gradualism, flexibility, and balance. As reflected from the formerly said, the MERCOSUR process seems to have been conceived from its very onset as an endeavor to conform a joint economic space by means of the complementation of key productive sectors and cooperation so as to promote an atmosphere suitable for development under democratic institutions.[32]

Certainly, at that time (1985-86) the afore-mentioned initiatives were considered particularly innovative. In fact, the eventual establishment of a common market between the two countries was one of the most relevant new regional integrationist projects in existence. Likewise, it was a process highly coincidental with similar events occurring in the Northern part of the Western Hemisphere where the governments of two more developed countries of the Americas, the U.S. and Canada, had formally launched in October 1985 negotiations aimed at concluding a comprehensive bilateral FTA (the CUSFTA). Such coincidence extended even further, since by the time Brazil and Argentina concluded the Treaty of Integration, Cooperation and Development (November 28, 1988), Canada and the U. S. had already signed the CUSFTA (January 2, 1988), and it had just been ratified by the U.S. Congress (November 21,1988). By July 1990, the Act of Buenos Aires was signed, which became a major step toward the eventual emergence of MERCOSUR, insofar as it mentioned the end of 1994 as the date for the definitive constitution of the Binational Common Market. A month later, Paraguay and Uruguay would join as observers in the negotiation process, allowing another year for their full incorporation in the Argentinean-Brazilian integration scheme.[33] In March 26, 1991 the MERCOSUR would be created through the Treaty of Asuncion, signed by the Presidents of Argentina, Brazil, Paraguay and Uruguay, which exhorted the signatories to establish a full common market arrangement among its members by January 1, 1995.

In brief, the MERCOSUR agreement calls for a gradual elimination of all tariffs on goods originating in and traded among the member states and the formation of a Common External Tariff (CET). It operates within the context and terms of larger groupings, including ALADI and GATT, of which it is a part. During the transition period that ended December 31, 1994, tariffs were reduced automatically, with a sharp initial cut and progressing in linear increments until all tariffs were eliminated. In December 1994 Argentina, Brazil, Paraguay, and Uruguay signed the Protocol of Ouro Preto, implementing the Southern Common Market. As of the inauguration of the customs union on January 1, 1995, -- exactly one year after NAFTA has taken effect approximately 80 per cent of all products traded -- about 8,000 categories of goods began to be traded duty-free within the bloc. Exceptions include textiles, steel, automobiles, and petrochemicals, which will remain protected by domestic tariffs for a period of four years. Subsequently, in June 1996, Chile and Bolivia agreed to join MERCOSUR, extending the frontiers of this South American major trading area. Chile's participation took effect on October 1, 1996, and Bolivia's formal association with MERCOSUR began on January 1, 1997.

At present, MERCOSUR is far from being a true common market. In fact, it is still not yet a full free trade zone and its "common market" label is more an aspiration than a reality. Even so, this is the world's most ambitious scheme of regional integration since the birth of the European Economic Community in 1957. Accordingly, its members have managed to approach a customs union stage and continue negotiations aimed at full common market status by 2006. As a would-be common market, MERCOSUR is supposed to do more than reduce and harmonise tariffs. It should also coordinate the economic, legislative, environmental, and infrastructure and technology policies of the various member countries. Members are expected to harmonise their standards, establish a supranational bureaucracy with considerable power to affect the policymaking decisions of each country's government, and implement fully a common external tariff structure. To achieve these goals, they have a long way to go and certainly major disagreements will have to be overcome, for instance regarding the establishment of supranational institutions, to which Brazil is the most reluctant.[34] Nevertheless, trade among MERCOSUR countries has already increased fourfold from US$ 4 billion, intra-MERCOSUR trade more than tripled to US$ 14.5 billion by 1995, and with Brazil alone MERCOSUR trade amounted to US$ 10.5 billion a year earlier — since the initial agreement was signed in anticipation of even greater cohesion. More importantly, MERCOSUR has helped to lock in the economic liberalising changes already made by its members during the past few years. A momentum toward such change has been created that may well prove difficult to halt or reverse.

As it should be obvious by now, MERCOSUR represents a very significant hemispheric and worldwide achievement by historical standards. Indeed, following Masaaki Kotabe, an International Business Professor of the University of Texas at Austin, it is possible to assert that this Southern integrationist scheme is overall a socioeconomic experiment in rapid evolutionary change. An experiment whose overarching goal is to incorporate all South American countries into a regional common market by 2005.[35] Yet, if it is to keep progressing, it would probably have to confront greater and tougher challenges than those it has surmounted so far. First and foremost, it will have to maintain macroeconomic stability, open trading regimes and economic growth in Brazil and Argentina. This is a sine qua non condition not just for MERCOSUR's sustained prosperity but also for the economic prospects of Latin America at large given that both Brazil and Argentina together account for 97 per cent of MERCOSUR's GDP and more than half of Latin America's GDP. Another no less important challenge facing MERCOSUR is to make an integrated market a reality by improving transport links and customs procedures, standardising or simply eliminating a mountain of rules and regulations, and finding the right balance between the nation state and common market institutions.[36]

5.2. United States and Brazil:
The Regionalisation of two Global Traders and the
Roots of Sub-Regional Economic Interdependence

No doubt both NAFTA and MERCOSUR have been path-breaking events in the geoeconomic, geo-social, and surely, geopolitical dynamics of the Western Hemisphere. More specifically, these two integration schemes represented fuming points in the trade and investment policies of the two leading countries in the Americas: for the U.S. political leadership, NAFTA meant continuing the formal shift towards regionalism it had overtly taken with the 1989 FTA with Canada, as well as its somewhat reluctant recognition of the inescapable forces of regionalisation at work in the North American region. For Brazil, the awakening colossus of the South, MERCOSUR symbolised the acceptance of the regional card as a viable alternative to preserve and expand its hemispheric and global economic position, which it sensed strongly threatened -- even at risk of outright exclusion -- by the increasingly regionalised power spaces that were leading the world economy: Germany-EU, Japan-East Asia, and U.S.-North America. Certainly, neither the U.S. nor Brazil seemed to have perceived the active support of regional initiatives or a commitment to a regional project, as contradicting long-pursued goals of multilateral liberalisation through GATT WTO, given both countries' strong global or extra-regional commercial interests and linkages, or even (and much more glaringly in the U.S. case) undermining the possible resort to unilateralism or managed trade mechanisms, e.g.: raising tariffs or excluding "temporarily" certain items from agreed liberalisation schedules (in the case of Brazil), or imposing trade sanctions as a tool to protect trade interest affected by "unfair competition" and "unfair trade practices" or to gain "market access" (in the case of the U.S.).

An aspect prone to comparison between NAFTA and MERCOSUR is the fact that at the heart of both integration arrangements are two genuine global traders: the U.S. and Brazil, although obviously one of them (the U.S.) has been during most of this agonising century fully engaged and strongly responsible for the flow of the global movement of goods and services worldwide. For instance in 1994, 40% of U.S. merchandise exports went to the Western Hemisphere,[37] 29 per cent to the Asia and Pacific Rim, 24 per cent to Europe and 7 per cent to the rest of the World. The markets for Brazil's exports were also widely spread: in 1995, 27 per cent went to the EU, 21 per cent to NAFTA and around 18 per cent to Asia.[38] On the other hand, whereas the U.S. economy is still individually the world's largest national market for consumer and industrial products and services, representing around 20 per cent of the world's GDP and around 70 per cent of NAFTA output, (an output which, in turn, accounts for 80 per cent of the Western Hemisphere's output0;[39] by itself, Brazil accounts for 68 per cent of the non-NAFTA continental market, and close to 75 per cent of the MERCOSUR intra-regional trade. This simply means that Brazil commands the largest, most dynamic economy of Latin America.[40]

Another aspect suitable to comparison between the two leaders of the major regional economic spaces in the hemisphere is the fact that both continent-states chose to follow regional paths due to the strong pressures and dynamics of regional "complex interdependence".[41] Although, it must be clarified, in the U.S.-NAFTA case such interdependence is much deeper and denser, following along North-North and North-South lines, while in the Brazil-MERCOSUR case, it solely encompasses still limited but clearly expanding South-South linkages. Another glaring difference is that while for the U.S. intra-NAFTA trade links are of utmost significance, both within the Western Hemisphere (representing around three quarters of U.S. trade with the Americas) and worldwide (accounting for near 30 per cent of U.S. total trade), Brazil's trade with its MERCOSUR partners made up only 15 per cent of its total trade in the first half of 1996. The equivalent figure for Argentina was 28 per cent. Percentage which assumes an even bigger proportion in Argentinean total trade figures when one considers that at present the Brazilian state of Sao Paulo has displaced the United States as the largest single outlet for Argentina's exports.[42]

In the specific case of NAFTA, the process of dense and complex interdependence is not a new phenomenon. Rather, it has been evolving for more than a century, creating strong, though obviously asymmetrical economic, cultural and political ties between the U.S. and its two bordering neighbours: Canada and Mexico. Nonetheless, in this trilateral relationship (more definable as such after the NAFTA, since before then, the North American "networks of interdependence" strongly developed along a "hub-and-spoke" configuration, which placed the U.S. at the centre of the underlying structure of production, trade, and investment patterns connecting the three economies) it is obvious that the Canada-U.S. relationship was the long-standing core upon which the North American integration process was built. To be sure, the so called "pressures for continental harmonisation" between these two North American nations have been felt well into the 19th century, and have manifested in an extensive history of transborder and other bilateral irritants but also in many instances of deep-seated binational cooperation along a wide range of "domestic" policies: water management, pollution control, immigration, energy, the environment, boundaries, and of course, trade.

No doubt, commercial ties between both North American states were crucial ever since the time the British adopted free trade and its North American colonies (British North America or today's Canada) lost their imperial advantages to the point of having promoted the first trade agreement (the 1854 reciprocity treaty) between the U.S. and BNA, agreement whose termination during the U.S. Civil War helped enormously to drive the movement for Canadian Confederation in 1867 and ultimately to Canadian National Strategy in 1879, a policy of import substitution which introduced high Canadian Tariffs, leading foreign firms, and particularly U.S. firms to establish branch plants in Canada to serve the local market. As expected, trade and investment issues have since that time been of foremost significance in this bilateral relationship, but even more so since the end of the second World War when the U.S. replaced Britain as Canada's main trading partner and the U.S. became its major source of foreign investment. No wonder, as both countries entered the 1980s, they had not just become each other's first trading partner, but had likewise developed the largest bilateral trade-investment relationship in the world, with 80 billion US dollars in two-way trade, and a combined 55 billion US dollars in foreign investment in these two economies.[43] It was precisely the magnitude and nature of trade and investment flows between Canada and the U.S. that primarily convinced Prime Minister Mulroney to propose an FTA to President Reagan in 1985. Yet, since by almost any measure (but geography) the U.S. is ten times larger than Canada, and given the absolute size of the Canadian and U.S. markets, and the relative importance of each economy to the other, it is clear that these deep harmonisation pressures were more strongly felt in Canada than in the U.S.

The above in no ways means that the history of cooperation on the U.S.Mexican side was of no intra-regional relevance. Conversely, it also gravitated along the border on such harsh issues as water boundaries (arising from the alteration in the Colorado and Tijuana Rivers and in the Rio Grande) and legal and illegal immigration. Still, formal bilateral economic cooperation accelerated and intensified much later. Just since the late seventies, concrete steps toward freer trade between the U.S. and its Southern neighbour were taken. These integration moves included: a tariff reduction agreement reached in 1979, a subsidies code in 1985, and a trade and Investment Facilitation Agreement in 1987. Still, the actual road to regional free trade was to be encouraged with Mexico's accession to the GATT in 1986 and its unilateral economic reforms: that is, the series of policies adopted to promote domestic economic growth by reducing tariffs, opening the economy to international competition, loosening investment restrictions, and selling a number of state-owned enterprises.

In the MERCOSUR case, the cooperation required for a more formal integration is a much more recent development. The reason for this is that throughout the 19th Century -- practically since the Southern Cone states attained independence --, and a great part of the 20th century, a pattern of rivalry and mutual distrust, if not outright conflict, prevailed among the so-called ABC countries (Argentina, Brazil, and Chile). A case in point is that of Chile and Argentina, countries with a long history of bilateral territorial disputes which almost caused them to go to war as recently as 1978. A more relevant case for the analysis of MERCOSUR's origins is that of Argentina and Brazil, countries which have been rivals throughout a good part of their history as independent nations because of competing geopolitical and geoeconomic interests. This could well explain why, up to the late 1950s, trade and other economic links were almost absent.

This situation began to change when the idea of preferential trade relations was introduced, leading to the establishment of the Latin American Free Trade Area in 1960. Even though LAFTA was conceived as to include all South American nations and Mexico, trade relations tended to concentrate in the ABC countries. LAFTA's practical results were therefore quite limited, and of course it never achieved its formal goal of a region-wide free trade zone, mostly because it was incompatible with the Import Substitution Industrialisation (ISI) policies which were then applying the governments of its member states with the full endorsement of their private sectors. A sort of consensual realism regarding the scarce chances of regional economic integration under the prevailing developmental-protectionist mood of the Latin American governments and entrepreneurs led to LAFTA's transformation into the Latin American Integration Association (LAIA/ALADI) in 1980. With a much less ambitious and hence more attainable mandate, LAIA became a broad collective discipline framework for their member states in the conclusion of partial preferential agreements which were usually confined to a smaller group of Latin American countries. It was precisely within the LAIA/ALADI framework that Southem Cone countries experienced significant progress in building the political confidence and economic relationship necessary for a deeper and more formal economic integration. A first fuming point in this respect was, no doubt, the 1979 tripartite agreement among Brazil, Argentina and Paraguay -- the Tripartite Corpus-ltaipu Agreement -- concerning the use of the Parana river for energy purposes.[44] The second one was the 1984 Argentina-Chile Peace and Friendship Treaty. These two agreements set the basis for a new pattern of political and economic relations within the region.

But, as pointed out before, these favorable events would have hardly been possible without a more solid subregional foundation, i.e.: the return of democratic institutions and the opening of economies to international trade and investment. This was particularly certain regarding the two primary "regional powers" of South America: Brazil and Argentina, whose economic relationship was to represent the largest part of the Southern Cone economic activity, and whose own political willingness to cooperate made possible the creation of MERCOSUR. Put otherwise, just as the Canadian-U.S. deep social, economic, and certainly political relationship played a crucial part in the economic integration of North America, so too the Brazilian-Argentine political rapprochement and the lifting of the artificial barriers that until the mid-eighties had restrained the development of cooperative ties, frequent contacts and certainly commerce between these two otherwise "natural" political and economic partners were the primary forces leading to the forming and continuing expansion of MERCOSUR. Before then, aside from a few border encounters, only three Brazilian presidents had ever visited Argentina, and only two Argentine rulers had made the trip the other way. Hence, the historical significance of the Act of Iguazu, a document signed in 1985 between Argentina and Brazil -- at times when both countries were just commencing with their democratisation processes -- with the specific purpose of bilaterally increasing trade relations, industrial complementarily and technological cooperation.

It was precisely in line with this first rapprochement initiative, that the governments of Argentinean President Raul Alfonsin and of his Brazilian colleague Jose Samey, at their meeting in Buenos Aires on July 29th, 1986, entered an agreement for the establishment of a Program of Integration and Economic Cooperation between both their countries, as well as the twelve protocols that would constitute said program's first phase. As expected, these agreements raised great interest and expectation at both the binational level, and the sub-regional and extraregional ones. After all, this was a rapprochement between two traditional rivals whose power elites had put to practice since the 19th century a sub-regional balance of power logic, which led during a good part of the current century to a wide and fluent shaping of geopolitical thinking. But other than the return of democratic ruling, it is evident that the already alluded boisterous exhaustion of the import substitution and economic intervention development model, that had been adversely influenced by the debt crisis and by deep macroeconomic imbalances, together with the new democratic governments' awareness of the need to undertake the revision of the interventionist-developmental-protectionist model and the third worldist multilateralism that hitherto had guided their foreign policies, were both factors of great impulse for the innovative cooperation/integration agreements of the mid-eighties between the two most important countries of South America. It must be cleared out, however, that even back then there were attempts by both Southern governments to revive ill and yet protectionist economies through selective bilateral trade preferences, in the form of sectorial agreements, while maintaining restrictions on imports from other countries.[45]

In any case, at present MERCOSUR is starting to promote, though slowly, a firmer basis for growing "integration from below". Evidences of this is mentioned in *The Economist Survey on MERCOSUR*, which reports that in southern Brazil, universities, chambers of commerce and agricultural cooperatives are all forging close links with their counterparts in north-eastern Argentina. Also, according to this same survey, even in Brazil's north-east, Chilean fruit farmers have been invited to bring their know-how in quality control and marketing, and textile factories are sending T-shirts to Argentina. Petrochemical plants in the north-eastern state of Bahia are busily swapping products with distant partners.[46] This merely attests to an undeniable fact: that in the new market-based model of integration, it is business that is starting to turn integration projects "from above" like MERCOSUR into a reality. However for that to happen, major political decisions have to be made and implemented, in as much as they will serve as "road maps" (or as a minimum "common ground") and/or provide the "focal points" necessary to remove the fictitious barriers and certainly build the actual roads and transportation systems and establish better organised and more efficient border procedures that have withheld Southern Cone states-societies from taking their "natural" (geographical, economic and social) course, whether regional or global.

6. Hemispheric Integration: NAFTA and MERCOSUR, Building Blocs or Stumbling Blocs?

The arguments presented here suggest that the U.S.-proposed Inter-American free trade concept and the actual possibilities of its fulfilment do not depend so much on the convergence of the various multilateral subregional arrangements and the host of bilateral and plurilateral agreements which exist in the hemisphere, but overall on finding a common ground in both NAFTA and MERCOSUR's diverging views and preferred options for achieving hemispheric free trade. This simply means that the evolution of NAFTA and MERCOSUR are at the heart of the Miami Summit's goals of hemispheric free trade, and that, as such, both arrangements will most probably be the main pillars of a continental regime of free trade and investment.

At this juncture, it is worth pointing out that until the Miami Summit the U.S. government seemed locked on its traditional mode of policy development, based on a partial view from Washington, for the pursuit of a hemispheric agenda centered on NAFTA. All this changed after the Miami Summit, the end result of which brought some reality to the position of the United States. Thereafter, it had to recognise that accession to NAFTA was only one possible path toward the Free trade Area in the Americas, and not necessarily the first choice in Latin America, and especially, in the Southern Cone. As a matter of fact, rather than aiming at making NAFTA the centerpiece of hemispheric trade liberalisation (U.S. privileged option to the FTM), South American countries, and above all Brazil, were strongly inclined during the Miami Summit to favour the conclusion of agreements between separate groupings until there was a free-trade network covering all countries of the Hemisphere. Particularly, since this approach promised to keep intact and allow the consolidation of its own subregional arrangement, the MERCOSUR, by then already viewed continentally and worldwide as the second most relevant economic integration grouping in the Americas.

The undeniable presence of these two diverging options may well be the reason why in the ministerial discussions which followed the Summit, Latin American and Caribbean governments agreed on the following principles for the establishment of an FTAA by the year 2005:

1) to maximise and consolidate existing trade liberalisation

initiatives while not imposing commercial barriers with other nations outside the hemisphere;

    2) to make the FTAA fully compatible with the WTO agreements;

    3) to seek to build on existing regional and subregional trade and investment agreements;

    4) to reach a balanced and comprehensive agreement so as to integrate all mutual rights and obligations.[47]

6.1. Brazil's Independent Stance Vis-A-Vis Hemispheric Integration: Evidence and Rationale

The Brazilian opposition to a NAFTA-centered FTAA was predictable since the time the EAI was announced. After all, as has been reminded by Brazilian Political Scientist Jose Guilhon, the Brazilian government was the only one in Latin America - with the clear exception of Haiti and expectedly Cuba - who never responded affirmatively to the U.S. invitation to conform a Western Hemisphere Free Trade Area. Likewise, when the countries of MERCOSUR were negotiating the framework agreement envisaged by the EAI, the Brazilian government was the one pressing the most for a MERCOSUR-U.S. agreement - under a "4+1" formula - instead of bilateral ones between MERCOSUR members and the U.S. Interestingly, while the U.S. government accepted to sign an agreement in July 1991 with a barely existing entity (the Asuncion Treaty had been signed just three months before), Brazil, in exchange for achieving such an agreement, was compelled to make more concessions than it had made in a bilateral accord. Its reward, however, was the containment of the strong integrationist impulse of MERCOSUR members toward the most attractive market of the planet.

    By the same token, even the consolidation of Brazilian-Argentinean cooperation and the own decision to create MERCOSUR has been interpreted, at least partially, as a defensive reaction to the prospective creation of NAFTA.[48] The basis for the latter interpretation might well be grounded in certain facts: from a geoeconomic perspective, Brazil is, of the MERCOSUR members, the country which shares the most similarities with Mexico in terms of trade with the U.S. In effect, 47 per cent of the products sold by Brazil to the U.S. market are also exported by Mexico. Also, Brazil is a competitor with the U.S. in regard to 219 products it sells to Mexico.[49] Therefore, it seems quite logical that NAFTA had been seen as a means to weaken Latin America's collective power, and that its formation and consolidation had threatened countries like Brazil with pressing economic costs, e.g. Mexican competition in the U.S. market, U.S. competition in the Latin American markets; and in the absence of the advantages of proximity and zero tariffs, a significant diversion of foreign investment to Mexico.

Brazil would display a somewhat stronger attitude of resistance in response to the invitation to the Summit of the Americas. After all, by then Brazilian President Itamar Franco had already announced the goal of working towards the rise of a SAFTA, centered on MERCOSUR, by the year 2006. Thus, it is hardly surprising that practically until the summit's eve, Brazilian government officials were publicly criticising the political agenda proposed by Washington and expressing their skepticism regarding the U.S. interest in discussing trade, and even more around its willingness to commit itself to the short or long-term building of a continental Free Trade Area.

The Brazilian disposition to maintain an independent stance not only in regards to the region's free trade process but most importantly regarding the United States' preferred course of action, has been attributed to several factors.

The primary factor is, according to Guilhon, ideologically-rooted. In the first place, the decades of resentment accumulated after the U.S. government, as a result of the start of the Cold War, frustrated the Brazilian government's expectations of remaining as a privileged ally of the "Big Brother of the North". From that time onwards, the Brazilian elite began to foster the perception, regardless of particular ideological preferences, that Brazilian development was grossly incompatible with U.S. interests and vice versa. A perception that was strongly reinforced as increasingly acrimonious trade and investment disputes began to dominate the Brazil-U.S. agenda. This perceived bilateral incompatibility could thus be summarised in a phrase: whatever was thought to be good for Brazil was surely bad for the U.S., and whatever was seen as good for the U.S. was certainly bad for Brazil. Secondly, most of the diplomats, academics and politicians that are currently occupying positions of power and influence in Brazil, are individuals whose formative period occurred during the so-called nationalpopulist era, in which exploiting anti-American feelings was an important instrument of political mobilisation. In the specific case of Itamaraty, many officials reached maturity at a time when the survival of a national project of development and modernisation seemed highly conditioned to the country's capabilities to find alternatives to the political subordination and economic dependence to the U.S.[50]

The second factor has a sociological nature, and entails a certain insecurity regarding the objectives or goals of economic diplomacy. The acceptance of market rules as a given, in both the domestic and international economic realms, along with the uncertainty elicited by such a recent acceptance, provide good grounds for such a generalised cautiousness. As a result, Brazilian negotiators rather than making of negotiations an instrument for achieving pre-established goals, precisely for lacking the required clarity about them, tend to conduct themselves as if their objective were to obtain an intermediate position between Brazilian objectives and those of their counterparts.[51]

All the above notwithstanding, it is obvious that for Brazil the MERCOSUR and, in general, South American economic regionalism, is both a relevant geoeconomic option given the fact that South America is its third trading partner,[52] and an essential geopolitical option, given the objective of the Brazilian government - fully articulated since the beginning of the Cardoso Administration - to transform Brazil into a worldclass actor/player at the world stage in the next ten or twenty years, recognised as such by Washington itself. Specifically, from a geopolitical standpoint the Cardoso government seems to have put aside Brazil's previously critical/revisionist international stance in order to embrace a global strategic orientation centered on a "qualified" or "conditional" endorsement of the U.S.-led "democratic-capitalist" path. This re-directing of Brazilian foreign policy is said to be part of Cardoso's plan of causing a fundamental shift in Brazilian history. A former Brazilian Foreign Minister, Rubens Ricupero summarises this diplomatic repositioning as follows:

"In the current complex world, which does not fit in any of the past schemes, there is space for new actors, especially for those who have engaged in efforts for achieving a certain regional configuration. In an atmosphere of systemic convergence (productive globalisation), there is room for Argentina, Brazil, Uruguay and Paraguay's joint efforts and for a more important presence for them than the one they had when they were advancing purely national projects."[53]

In this expanding subregionalist strategy towards Latin American and eventually hemispheric regionalism, Brazil is being accompanied, albeit cautiously and for independent reasons, by Argentina, which from the very beginning of the first Menem's Presidency showed its eagerness and readiness to establish a much closer relationship with the U.S., --a foreign policy shift deemed as an unprecedented and nearly "automated alignment" -- as a means to obtain political and economic benefits in the domestic front, where it was (and still is) implementing risky political and economic reforms, as well as in the hemispheric and global political and economic power fronts. In this very sense, the so-called Argentinean alignment with the U.S. has had a plain instrumental character. However, given that for Argentina, closer relations with the U.S., not only economic but also political and military, are of higher importance than for Brazil, Argentina has been much more willing than Brazil to accept the NAFTA-bandwagoning alternative to the FTAA. Some analysts even assert that Argentina, had it been promised a trade deal by the United States, might at one time have left MERCOSUR.

Brazil, in the meantime, has shown little inclination to join NAFTA, thus rejecting the Mexican model for establishing free trade agreements, and arguing that FTAs should be developed under the umbrella of ALADI. For that purpose, the Brazilian government has proposed, with the acquiescence of its MERCOSUR partners, the conclusion of a South American Free-Trade Area (SAFTA), both as a potential counterweight to NAFTA, and as a way to strengthen the South American region's bargaining chips in the forthcoming negotiations aimed at the emergence of a continental free trade area. In summary, it is Brazil's stance, currently backed by other MERCOSUR members, that hemispheric integration must be attained through the strengthening and convergence of sub-regional agreements, and not through the adoption of new compromises which supersede those priorly endorsed at the subregional and WTO levels.[54] Otherwise, Brazil argues, South American countries may resort, if given the opportunity, to the signing of bilateral FTAs with Mexico or the U.S., the end result of which would be the weakening of the region's negotiating position. In this context, and as part of the path toward SAFTA, Brazil has purposively sought MERCOSUR's broadening (instead of its deepening, which is more Argentina's objective) through the promotion of associations between other schemes/countries and MERCOSUR. This latter goal, which has been fully encouraged by Brazil, is already being achieved with Chile and Bolivia's formal associations through FTAs to this subregional arrangement, and may well lead to a SAFTA with the eventual interscheme association between MERCOSUR and the Andean Community (formerly the Andean Pact), a possibility that is being currently negotiated. To be sure, if the negotiations between the Andean Community and MERCOSUR reach a successful conclusion, this joint group could become the liaison point in the trade and investment integration between the north and the south of Latin America.[55]

Fortunately for Brazil and its geoeconomic/geopolitical MERCOSUR-SAFTA project, since the hard-won approval of the NAFTA agreement by the U.S. Congress, the Clinton Administration's commitment to NAFTA expansion "beyond Mexico", a first step of which would be Chile's accession, likely to be followed by that of Argentina seemed to have been substantially eroded. Other regional concerns pertaining to Haiti's unlikely "democratisation" and Cuba's crumbling economy and the fears of further refugee flows from the Caribbean, together with more long-standing regional issues as illegal immigration from its southern neighbour, and more so in light of the social and political crisis facing post-NAFTA/post-Chiapas Mexico, and NAFTA's impact on U.S. jobs were getting most of the U.S. government's attention. This was even reflected in the U.S.-proposed Summit of the Americas agenda, in which in spite of endless repetitions that trade was the "centerpiece" of the U.S. hemispheric strategy, the wording of the U.S. initial agenda hardly emphasised its leading edge role in the U.S. interaction with other countries of the Americas. Such an agenda, as promoted, was thus perceived as diffuse; trade yes, but also democratic governance and sustainable development, with no clear sense of priorities. As Fauriol and Weintraub assert:

"It was as though the U.S. framers of the original agenda had not grasped the profound transformation undergone in South American countries during the 1980s away from the insistence on import-substituting industrialisation in favor of export-promoting development."[56]

Certainly an important end result of the Summit was the U.S. formal acquiescence to the establishment of an FTAA, although putting off the date to the year 2005. Nevertheless, the Clinton Administration's attempt to relaunch the idea of hemispheric trade suffered a major setback with the Mexican financial meltdown that broke out right after the Miami Summit. Henceforth, the U.S. government's commitment even to Chile's admission to NAFTA became very uncertain. This uncertainty would deepen and along with it, Clinton's negotiating position to create the FTM, owing to the U.S. electorate's rejection of the Clinton leadership in the November 1994 midterm elections. A direct consequence of such electoral defeat was that political power in the United States largely shifted from the Executive to the Congress, thus reducing substantially the President's capacity to further its vision of U.S. strategic political and economic interests in the Western hemisphere and worldwide. Predictably, throughout 1995, 1996 and 1997 the U.S. government was to confront several frictions and difficulties with both its NAFTA partners and other Latin American countries over such unilateral and interventionist Congress-made foreign policy initiatives as the Helms Burton legislation and the decertification U policy so harshly applied to Colombia. At the same time, there was hard evidence of the predominance of isolationist tendencies in the U.S. government. On the one hand, the passage in mid-1996 and the Presidential Approval in September of the *Illegal Immigration Reform and Immigrant Responsibility Act*, which aside from its emphasis on enhancing INS punitive capabilities to control illegal immigration, placed considerable discretion power on INS officials. A power, in turn, likely to elicit human rights violations against any alien entering U.S. territory, regardless of its legal or illegal status. On the other hand, the flagrant failure of the Clinton Administration to get a favourable Congressional vote on the Bill to renew the Executive's "fast track" negotiating authority and its decision to postpone such voting until early 1998, before the 11 Americas Summit.

Blows against the Clinton Administration's FTM strategy -whether NAFTA-centered or not, as the ones just mentioned, have helped to reinforce the MERCOSUR-centered option to South American and eventually, hemispheric regionalism advocated and led by Brazil. And even more so, since its January 1995 inauguration as a Custom Union. Also, MERCOSUR's coming into effect and subsequent progress would greatly contribute to Argentina's realisation of the U.S. government inability to negotiate a NAFTA extension on a firm ground, due to the lack of Congressional granting of the required "fast track" negotiating authority. In effect, until numerous issues started to erode Clinton's commitment to the FTM, President Menem had been strongly interested in a NAFTA connection to counter's Brazil's influence. After all, with the approaching of the Custom Union inauguration, he had become aware of potential intra-regional imbalances resulting from MERCOSUR's implementation and expansion, and of the risk that

Argentinean industry could be heavily substituted by Brazilian products. However, by September 1994 the Argentinean government had already acknowledged that seeking admission to NAFTA was no longer a feasible option. It would have to choose, as it did, the MERCOSUR Custom Union, a form of economic integration that calls for a common external tariff (CET), rather than the NAFTA free trade approach and accept the cost of not being able to accede to NAFTA individually because this would violate MERCOSUR's CET.[57]

6.2. Significance of the FTAA and Paths Towards its Emergence

6.2.1. Significance of the FTAA

As has been pointed out in a recent SELA document, the FTM is neither a joint development effort nor an exercise in cooperation. Rather it is an attempt to regularise and regulate the markets at a continental level so as to prepare the economies of the Americas for a multilateral system of trade with a world scope. In that respect, its is strongly different from, and even much less ambitious in its integrationist goals than the subregional integration schemes and the proposals for a common market currently at work in Latin America and the Caribbean. Even so, since the transition between the setting up of the hemisphere free trade zone and the full functioning of world trade liberalisation may be long, the FTM is likely to act as a "zone of influence" as regards to both the trade among its members and the own world regulations. As a result, it is unlikely that the FTAA promoters will limit themselves to apply WTO regulations, but rather that they will probably engage in the development and adoption of WTO-plus disciplines. [58]

Regarding the FTM relevance for the subregional and regional trade and investment flows in the Americas, several "hard facts" can be mentioned. North American economies represent 87 per cent of the continent's total output, whereas the U.S. provides 78 per cent of the regional GDP, accounts for a dominant share of foreign trade, and is the primary export market and the main source of foreign investment and technology for many LAC countries. As expected, an inter-American trade and investment liberalising regime as the one envisioned through the FTM would certainly fulfill two of the major interests of most regional economies vis-a-vis the formation of the FTM:

a) A more secure access to the North American market, and particularly the U.S. market; and

b) a predictable (i.e. rules-based) access to the afore market by formalising and regularising it, so as to protect LAC economies from U.S. neo-protectionist practices in the technical, legal and political fields and from the lack of generally accepted regulations respected by all parties, regardless of their economic size.

Likewise, there are important advantages attached to the conformation of the FTM:

a) It will allow the affiliation of all American countries to the United States, by far the most important market of the entire region;

b) its rise will ensure the consolidation of trade flows which are important to all its member countries;

c) since the FTAA does not call for deeper levels of integration, it will allow each member to preserve, under WTO provisions, its own tariff as well as its own trade policy toward non-member states.

In relation to the FTM possible drawbacks, two can be mentioned:

a) The overwhelming presence and resulting dominance of the most developed countries, especially the U.S., a situation which may render the differences of development decisive;

b) The uncertainty regarding the continental FTA impact on the eventual constitution of a LAC common market.

6.2.2. Paths Towards the FTAA

Prior to the Belo Horizonte Trade Ministers' meeting there were extensive speculations and discussions on possible paths to the FTAA. For instance, in a study for the Washington-based Centre for Strategic and International Studies author Richard L. Bemal, Jamaica's Ambassador in the U.S., identified five non-exclusive options to the FTAA:

a) NAFTA as the core or the NAFTA accession option to the FTM;

b) MERCOSUR as an ogle, both for the creation of a SAFTA and the eventual amalgamation with NAFTA;

c) Bipolar amalgamation or NAFTA-MERCOSUR inter-bloc discussions aimed at some type of agreement pertaining to the FTAA;

d) Convergence of Regional Trade Groups or regional trading

groups' agreements as building blocks for the FTAA; and

e) <u>Hemispheric negotiations</u> or the forging of a single agreement on "WTO plus" standards towards which all countries in the hemisphere would move according to a designated schedule.[59]

Among such possible FTAA paths, it must be said that the first one, that of forming the FTM through the extension of the NAFTA with the gradual incorporation of the LAC countries, was initially very strong. Several advantages were thought to be implied by this option. Advantages which as such, given the continental weight of the North American economy, resemble those already mentioned regarding the FTM itself: first and foremost, the affiliation of all countries to the United States; secondly, simplified trading practices, in particular of rules of origin; third, and given that NAFTA was a free trade area, the preservation of each member capacity to keep under the WTO provisions, its own tariff and trade policy toward non member states. Still, the proliferation of "anti-globalist forces" in the U.S. domestic front after the "Tequilazo". The sustained and strident labour and environmental criticism on the negative effects of the NAFTA implementation on the U.S. economy and quality of life, and the resulting inability to expand the membership of the North American bloc, soon convinced the governments and enthusiastic pro-NAFTA technocratic and business sectors of the region including those of Chile, of the unfeasibility of this option as a reliable path to the FTAA. Moreover, regional studies of the LAC integration "Think Tank", the SELA, contributed to deligitimise this option as they ascertained that the NAFTA accession road to inter-American free trade negotiations was to cause prior subordination to the NAFTA regulations, the resulting fragmentation of Latin America/Caribbean integration schemes and agreements, and by implying hard to implement successive access to this FTA, a strong competitive disadvantage, if not outright exclusion, for some LAC countries.[60]

In any case, after the joint Ministerial Declaration at Belo Horizonte, some convergence areas were set forth which reasserted principles and decisions that had been formerly embraced within the framework of the FTAA process. Such principles and decisions were the following:

· *Consensus:* decisions were to be achieved by consensus;

· *Single undertaking:* the FTM negotiating process would result in "a single comprehensive commitment incorporating mutually agreed

commitments and obligations";
· *Coexistence and WTO congruence:* the FTAA could coexist with bilateral and regional agreements and would be congruent with the WTO agreements;
· *Recognition of asymmetries:* special attention should be granted to the needs, economic conditions and opportunities of smaller economies to allow their full participation in the FTM process;
· *Preparatory committee:* a Preparatory Committee composed of the 34 Vice Ministers of Trade was formed in order to conduct, evaluate, and coordinate the tasks of the eleven Working Groups;
· *Dispute settlement:* a twelfth Working Group in charge of Dispute settlement was established.

Therefore, from the Belo Horizonte meeting a predominant path towards hemispheric free trade has aroused: the "single undertaking" and comprehensive option.

6.2.3. The "Single Undertaking Option" to the FTAA

As suggested by Richard Bemal, several major advantages come to mind regarding the adoption of the 'single path' principle to hemispheric free trade negotiations articulated at the Belo Horizonte trade ministerial meeting, namely:

1) Avoiding the confusion, duplication efforts and delays which could result from the coexistence of different paths.
2) The enhanced commitments of governments to the FTAA in light of a focused FTAA process with a clear end in sight.
3) Full and direct participation by all countries, thus offering transparency and equanimity and fostering the level of attention required for the successful conclusion of the FTM negotiations.
4) A relatively simple and more familiar process to the governments of the Americas, given their exposure to it in the preparatory rounds held in various organisations between 1995 and mid-1997.
5) By being a "single undertaking", this path allows trade-offs among countries hence facilitating the emergence of consensus.
6) Greater legitimacy and agreements extending beyond the negotiations, thus allowing the stability basis necessary for the implementation and endurance of the final agreement.[61]

Yet, the primary obstacle for the advancement of the FTM "single path" option is that still it is far from clear whether the United States, and specially Congress, is actually prepared and willing to consider free trade arrangements with all the countries of the Americas. After all, the legislative branch remains strongly dominated by the isolationist-nativist-populists impulses that have been pervading the political attitudes of the U.S. population from the end of the Cold War. To be sure, since 1993 the main obstacle to the extension of the new negotiating authority has been the intense disagreement over labour rights and the environment. Unlike trade policy, which *per se* has been a comparatively non partisan matter, labour and environmental issues have caused partisan conflicts for decades. While Republicans have refused to link such matters to trade, many Democrats have insisted that any new trade agreements must include the NAFTA provisions increasing protections for the environment and workers. As expected, controversies over these issues have been likewise responsible for the U.S. Congress' inability to put together the required votes for the passage of the fast track legislation.[62] Nevertheless, given the disproportionate weight of the U.S. on the hemispheric GDP, Latin American and Caribbean governments are well aware, from previous trade negotiations involving the U.S., that without fast track legislation, the FTM will strongly lose force and credibility.

7. Concluding Comments

Certainly, since the Miami Summit important technical progress aimed at the conclusion of an FTAA has been made. For instance, the FTAA-aspiring nations have forged an agreement on the core principles of this fundamental endeavor and the eleven working groups formed hitherto have begun moving toward the first concrete actions for the hemispheric free trade area, which are likely to involve procedures dealing with mutual acceptance of product standards and electronic customs filing. As a matter of fact, these working groups are generating highly valuable information on tariffs, investments, trade and other national practices previously unavailable at the continental level.[63] However, after the Belo Horizonte meeting of Trade Ministers, the general principles of the FTAA negotiation process were laid down along with a recommended place and time for its beginning: the Summit of the Americas to be held in Santiago de Chile in 1998. Nonetheless, as had been rightly asserted by Luis Felipe Lampreia, Brazilian Minister of Foreign Affairs, for such a continental process to be successful, prior agreement must be reached on such essential issues as the scope of the agreement (an issue that may well be the heart of the entire process), and the objectives, structure, focus and venue of the negotiations as was discussed at the San Jose Ministerial Meeting held in February 1998.[64]

In as much as the FTAA conversations have now acquired a formal nature, the dimension and significance of this trade area is posing a fundamental problem regarding the relationship between Latin American/Caribbean and hemispheric integration and, hence, the articulation between both, and between each one of them and the already established plurilateral and bilateral subregional integration arrangements. Pertaining the possibility of negotiating with and adhering to the FTM individually or as a member of a subregional subgroup, it is worth pointing out that the "coexistence" principle endorsed at Belo Horizonte states that the FTM can coexist with bilateral and subregional agreements, as long as their rights and obligations do not exceed those of the FTAA. This principle, though, has a significant flaw: for instance, it has already allowed the U.S. government to announce that it will negotiate and join the FTM individually (thus reflecting its long-standing habit and propensity to favour unilateral courses of action). However, for Latin American countries like the MERCOSUR members, so eager to expand, through the widening of the membership of that subregional scheme, their collective negotiating capacity vis-a-vis the hemispheric trade liberalisation process, the coexistence principle has led them to formally agree on acting as a single unit in the successive hemispheric trade negotiations. Such joint negotiating position has been reinforced from the XII MERCOSUR meeting held in Asuncion in June 1997, with the adding of Chile and Bolivia.

In turn, since the deadline for the conclusion of the FTAA negotiations is "no later than the year 2005", and due to the progress achieved and likely to be achieved towards the emergence of a SAFTA, it is possible that such subregional integration regime becomes an unavoidable point of reference for the FTAA negotiations. Likewise, a joint LAC integration effort such as the one sought through the SAFTA, may well serve the countries of the region to overcome the evident disadvantages they would have in such areas as infrastructure, telecommunications, transport, financial services, proximity of the biggest markets, and human resources.

An important fact that has been highlighted throughout this paper is that since both NAFTA and MERCOSUR account for the bulk of hemispheric gross domestic product (GDP) and trade, agreements between these two groupings with the goal of deepening and harmonising trade disciplines and, perhaps, identifying a common ground for coping with the economic asymmetries pervading the continent, seems not only necessary but a sine qua non condition for the rise of an FTAA. In fact, the approach and eventual coordinated efforts of both subregional integration groups in the forthcoming FTAA negotiations would surely pave the way towards their successful conclusion, and even pose pressures for other countries in the Western Hemisphere to put their affairs in order so they can join the emerging inter-American integration regime. This, after all, was the basis of the compromise at the Miami Summit. The above also means that there can be no viable FTAA without the consent of both the United States and Brazil.

In any case, it is crystal-clear that as long as the Clinton Administration is not granted fast-track authority, widely acknowledged as a fundamental precondition for successful trading negotiations, the U.S. credibility vis-a-vis other FTAA participants will remain badly hurt. Without such procedure in hand, the current U.S. Administration cannot simply enter into serious trade negotiations with Chile or any other country, and Latin American/ Caribbean governments know it. Accordingly, none of them will invest the human and financial resources or the time in negotiating with the U.S. if the latter's negotiators are unable to guarantee that any accord reached will not be mutilated beyond recognition by the U.S. Congress.

Therefore, the primary challenge faced by the second Clinton Administration is to find viable ways to rebuild U.S. political consensus for the FTAA negotiations, so as to secure fast-track negotiating procedures. Something that it will have to do while other Western Hemisphere countries, at the heart of which is predictably Brazil, continue to make trade agreements with each other, though, usually accepting lower standards on services, investment, and intellectual property protection than expected and pursued by the U.S. and even by Canada and Mexico in an FTM. In the process, the Brazil's envisaged SAFTA, so likely to be formed if the

MERCOSUR-Andean Community negotiations conclude successfully, may not only arise but also become the most important cornerstone of the hemispheric free trade area. Whether SAFTA will become a building or rather a stumbling block to the FTM will unquestionably depend on the U.S. In effect, by getting fast track authority, Washington would possibly be signaling seriousness about opening trade and a real prospect of progress. Such a positive signal from the U.S. government would send Latin America a powerful message: that the Northern giant has re-engaged in the FTM process.

Otherwise, if the Clinton Administration is unable to get fast track procedures, it will deepen the already pervasive image of the U.S. as a reluctant partner, a partner that remains ambivalent about expanding NAFTA, even to the "standard for market reform" and "first in line" in the NAFTA waiting list as Chile. Under such circumstances there is the danger that the Hemisphere could solidify into two exclusionary free trade areas, one in the North and the other in South America. This will mean a fundamental setback and perhaps, a difficult to reverse sense of defeat and betrayal to the prospects of Inter-American regionalism. And even more so, because a defeat in the economic issue-area, an area so overwhelmingly prioritised at present by most Latin American and Caribbean countries, apart from intensifying the trend towards a U.S.excluded subregional integration (thereby affecting U.S. geoeconomic dominance continent-wise), would surely reverberate in the Hemisphere's political and security agenda, which so ostensibly concerns the U.S. e.g. combating the drugs trade, dealing with organised crime and terrorism, slowing illegal immigration, encouraging environmental protection, and shaping regional institutions. The latter, of course, would be the worst of all possible outcomes since it would diffuse, maybe for a long time, the chances of developing the effective cooperative inter-American framework required to build or rebuild Latin American/Caribbean sustained governance and prosperity.

Notes

1. Stubbs, Richard and Geoffrey R.D. Underhill, "Introduction: Global Issues in Historical Perspective." In: Richard Stubbs and Geoffrey R.D. Underhill, eds., *Political Economy and the Changing Global Order* (Toronto, Ontario: McClelland and Stewart Inc., the Canadian Publishers, 1994), p. 331.

2. Hurrell, Andrew, "Regionalism in the Americas." In: Abraham F. Lowenthal and Gregory F. Treverton, eds., *Latin America in a New World Order* (Boulder, Col.: Westview Press, 1994), p. 177.

3. Goldstein, Judith and Robert O. Keohane, *Ideas and Foreign Policy. Beliefs. Institutions. and Political Change* (Ithaca and London: Cornell University Press, 1993).

4. Fauriol, Georges and Sidney Weintraub, "U.S. Policy, Brazil, and the Southern Cone," *The Washington Quarterly*, Vol. 18, N° 3 (Summer 1995), p. 126.

5. Weintraub, Sidney, "Getting to Hemispheric Trade". http://info.lanic.utexas.edu/cswhV TIP3/html

6. *Integration Bulletin for Latin America and the Caribbean* N 0 4, May 1977; http://www.sela.org/ en-integra/engint4.htm

7. Fauriol Georqes and Sidney Weintraub, "U.S. Policy, Brazil, and the Southern Cone",. p. 130.

8. Petrash, Vilma E., "El Espiritu de Miami: De Donde Viene?, Donde Esta?, Hacia Donde Va?" *Venezuela Analitica*, N° 10, January 1997 ; http:/www.analitica.com/

9. Reported by U.S. Trade Representative Charlene Barshefsky in her Testimony before the Committee on International Relations, U.S. House of Representatives, 105th Congress, 1st Session, June 1997. Information quoted by Sweeney, John, "Myths and Realities of the Fast-Track Debate", *The Heritage Foundation Backgrounder*, October 22, 1997. p. 6.

10. Rodriguez, Luis A. "Free Trade Area of the Americas by 2005: The New Dimension," *Capitulos SELA*, Special Edition 1996. http://www.lanic.utexas.edu/~sela/capitulos/rcapin5.htm, p. 1.

11. "Cumbre de las Americas. Declaracion de Principios. Pacto Para el Desarrollo y la Prosperidad: Democracia, Libre Comercio y Desarrollo Sostenible en las Americas". http://americas.fiu.edu/summiV Agreements/zdops.txt

12. "Belo Horizonte: The Complexities of the FTM, *Integration Bulletin for Latin America and the Caribbean*, N° 4, May 1997. http://www.sela.ora/eng_integra/angnt4.htm

13. Garter, Jeffrey E., "The Changing Face of North America in the Global Economy." Speech before the Americas Society and the Council of the Americas, New York City, May 17, 1994.

http://www.aiea.ualr.edu/depts/econ.rsh/econtalk/intl/may1794.html

14. Hazleton, Jarel E., "The Peso Devaluation in Retrospect".
http://info.lanic.utexas.edu/cswhV TIP2b.html

15. SELA Permanent Secretariat, "X-RAYING Latin American and Caribbean Trade Policy," Capitulos *SELA*, Special Edition 1996.
http://lanic. utexas.edu/-sela/capitulos/rcapin 13. html

16. OAS Trade Unit, "Report for the discussions of the Special Committee on Trade at its second meeting held in Montevideo, Uruguay on June 14-15, 1995".
http:/hvww.oas.org/EN/PROG/ TRADE/free1 e.htm

17. SELA Permanent Secretariat, "X-RAYING Latin American and Caribbean Trade Policy," op. cit.
    Thorstensen, Vera, ''Desenvolvimento da cooperac:ao economica e das relaciones comerciais entre a UE e o MERCOSUR: intereses comuns e desafios, *Politica Extema* Vol. 5, N° 1 (June-July-August 1996), p. 41.

18. Brunelle, Dorval and Christian Deblock, "Economic Blocs and the Challenge of the North American Free Trade Agreement," *North America Without Borders? Integrating Canada, the United States, and Mexico.* (Calgary, Alberta: University of Calgary Press, 1992) p. 124.

19. Ibid. pp. 124-125; and OAS trade Unit Report "Chapter 1: Merchandise Trade in the Americas". http://www.oas.org/EN/PROG/TRADE/free3e.htm

20. "Belo Horizonte: The Complexities of the FTM." *International Bulletin for Latin America and the Caribbean*, op. cit.

21. OAS Trade Unit Report, "Trade in North America".
http://www.oas.org/..../free32e.htm

22."Belo Horizonte: The Complexities of the FTM,n op. cit., and "Latin American and Caribbean Integration Trends and Options," SP/CLOO(111.0/Di No. 8.
http:/www.sela.org/eng_consejo/ documents/spcl23di81 .htm

23. Weintraub, Sidney, "Getting to Hemispheric Trade," op. cit.

24. The factors leading the U.S., Canada and Mexico to start negotiations in June 1991 aimed at concluding a comprehensive and far-reaching trilateral free trade agreement were glaringly different, albeit plainly and for understandable reasons, Mexican and Canadian motivations were less strategically-driven than those of the U.S. and Canada, for example, which was at that time already in the midst of adjusting to the CUSFTA, was at first afraid of facing a second round of adjustment with a new, low-cost Mexican partner. Indeed, Canada neither wanted nor encouraged Mexico to approach the United States to open trade talks. However, as this possibility became more certain, it decided, somewhat reluctantly, to participate in the negotiations to protect the recent advantages it had hard-gained in the U.S. market. In this last

sense, the Canadian government, which vacillated for some time before asking for a seat at the negotiation table, recognised it had to be a party to discussions which will shape the trade and investment rules in North America. Mexico's preferred FTA option was a bilateral FTA with the U.S. At first, the possibility of a trilateral agreement was mostly seen as disadvantageous for Mexico, given the chance that the U.S. and Canada could jointly request concessions from the smallest and poorest partner and the own limited trade and investment linkages between Canada and Mexico, and the greater complexity that trilateralisation could add to the negotiating agenda. However, the Mexican government also perceived certain advantages in Canada's participation: the potential market opening that Canada may provide, and the possibility of increased Canadian FDI; the possibility that a NAFTA strengthened the competitiveness of North American firms; and last but not least, the common experiences of Mexico and Canada in dealing with the U.S. and the expertise of Canadian negotiators in the CUSFTA, factors which were seen as means of improving the bargaining leverage of Mexico in its negotiations with the United States.

In contrast, hegemonic concerns led the United States to adopt, at the beginning of the 1980s, a more realistic international policy framework and to strengthen economic ties with its closest neighbours. Such concerns, in short, were germane to the questioning of its leadership and influence in the world economy as a result of the severe economic crisis it faced since the early seventies. This realism implied the promotion of American values and the defense of American commercial interests, the pursuit of the postwar ideal of one undivided world, and the drive towards trade liberalisation to eliminate the obstacles of state interventionism based on nationalism and keynesianism. Such realist approach was thus applied in three fronts: at the international level, by advancing the GATT multilateral trade negotiations, renewing efforts to revitalise international institutions and, more recently, promoting a new world order; at the bilateral/regional level, by using a fast-track procedure to negotiate reciprocal market accessibility and to gain a preferential treatment for U.S. goods and investments; and at the domestic level, by sanctioning protectionist legislation at both the Federal and state levels. It is in the interplay of the international-bilateral-domestic contexts, that the analysis of U.S. foreign economic policy endeavors which gave rise to NAFTA as well as to the EAI proposal is to be focused. Even so, it must be acknowledged that there were two specific U.S. foreign policy domestic factors which provided special impetus to NAFTA: (1) the U.S. desire to ensure an economically strong Mexico as a model to the hemisphere and especially the heavily indebted and/or politically unstable South and Central American countries; and (2) helping halt Mexican immigration across the border and enlarging the growth prospects in U.S. states such as California, Florida, New Mexico and Texas. See: Ostry, Sylvia "The NAFTA: Its International Economic background," p. 27; Eden, Lorraine and Maureen Appel Molot, "The View from the Spokes: Canada and Mexico Face the United States," pp. 73-74, 77, and Brunelle, Dorval and Christian Deblock, "Economic Blocs and the Challenge of the North American Free Trade Agreement," pp. 128-130. In: Stephen J. Randall, Hemman Konrad and Sheldom Silvemman, eds., *North America Without Borders? International Canada, the United States, and Mexico* op. cit.

25. Latin American and Caribbean Integration Trends and Options,. SP/CL/)O(111.0/ Di No. 8. http:/hvww.sela.org/eng_consejo/documents/spc1 23di83. htm

26. OAS Trade Unit Report, "Free Trade Agreements".
http://www.oas.org/.../free43e.htm

27. SELA Permanent Secretariat "Toward the Convergence of the Regional Integration Processes," Caoitulos *SELA,* Special Edition 1996.
http://lanic.utexas.edu/.../rcapin9.htm

28."South-South Economic Cooperation: Regional Trade Agreements among Developing Countries as a Basis for Development.
http://www.undp.orgAcdc/kotsch.htm

29. See: "Mercosur and other Trade Agreements" http://invertir.com/07/trade.html> and Chaloult, Yves, The Southern Common Market (Mercosur) and the Latin American Intearation." In: Nicole Lacasse and Louis Perret, eds., *Le Libre-Echanae dans les Amerioues (Une Perspective Continentale). Free Trade in the Americas (An Hemispheric Perspective)* (Montreal: Wilson & Lsafleur Itee, 1994) p. 437.

30. Coes, Donald V., "NAFTA and Brazil's Trade Policy Options." In: A. R. Riggs and Tom Velk, eds. *Bevond NAFTA: An Economic, Political and Sociological Perspective* (Vancouver, B.C.: The Fraser Institute, 1993), p. 192.

31. "Latin American and Caribbean Integration Trends and Options," SP/CLD(X111.0/Di No. 8.
http://www.sela.org/eng_consejo/documents/spc123di82.htm

32. Arcagni, Jose Carlos, "Mercosur: Bilan de l'Etape de Transition et Perspectives de Realisation," and Chaloult, Yves, "The Southem Common Market (Mercosur) and the Latin America Integration." In: Nicole Lacasse and Louis Perret, eds., op. cit., pp. 438.

33. While Brazil is naturally opposed to ceding sovereignty to smaller countries like Paraguay and Uruguay, Argentina often cites the EU as a model for MERCOSUR's future. Grossly speaking, Brazil insists that MERCOSUR should be a union of states, with a minimum of supranational institutions, and decisions made by consensus. In a way this explains why, up to now, MERCOSUR merely has a small permanent secretariat in Montevideo, Uruguay's capital, but decision-making power rests with an inter-governmental Common Market Council, made up of the member countries' foreign and finance ministers, and in practice more often with the national presidents, at their twice-yearly meetings. Beneath the council, the groundwork is done by a group of civil servants from half-a-dozen ministries, and the central banks, in each country. But these individuals are not permanently seconded to the group. In other words, there is no Mercosureaucracy, no southern-hemisphere Brussels (in spite of Uruguay's aspiration in this regard), no parliament (and, because the group speaks only two, fairly similar, languages, no permanent group of interpreters or pile of translated documents). Brazilians diplomats estimate that this minimalist approach to institution building is a realistic if not pragmatic way to deal with the realities of transborder trade and investment flows, while also avoiding the repetition of past mistakes, in which the excessive erecting complex structures unrelated to the real needs of the actual people involved in trading, contributed to the flagrant failure of

earlier Latin American integration efforts. See: *The Economist Survey of MERCOSUR* - 12/10/96. http:/hvww.demon.co.uk/ltamaraty/mercosusrO3.html

34. Kotabe, Masaaki, "MERCOSUR and Beyond: The Imminent Emergence of the South American Markets". http://info. Ianic. utexas.edu/cswhUkotabe.html

35. *The Economist Survey on MERCOSUR* - 12/10/96. http://www.demon.co.uk/ltamaraty/ mercosurO1 .html

36. Regarding U.S. merchandise exports to the Westem Hemisphere, in 1994, 55.7% went to Canada, 24.7% to Mexico, 6.7% to MERCOSUR and 5.3% to the Andean countries. Source: Report of the OAS Trade Unit. Chapter l: Merchandise Trade in the Americas". http://www.oas.org/EN/PROG/TRADE/ free32e.htm

37. *The Economist Survey on MERCOSUR* - 12/10/96. http://www.Demon.co.uk/.../ mercosurO3.html

38. See: The Canadian American Trade Site, ' Canada, The United States, and Intemational Trade", (http://web.badm.sc.edu/canus.htm) and Stewart, John B., and James F. Kelleher, "Free Trade in the Americas. Interim Report," p. 32.

39. Guilhon Alburquerque, Jose A., "Relagoes Brasil-EUA e integragao continental," *Politica Externa*, Vol. 5, N° 1 (June - July - August 1996), pp. 6 and 33.

40. As used in this paper, the term "complex interdependence" has the meaning assigned by Canadian scholar David Leyton-Brown, namely, a "policy relationship" with two basic features: first, that (domestic) policy actions by one government inevitably have effects in the other country, whether intended or not; and second, that one government is unable to achieve, on many issues, its (domestic) policy objectives unilaterally without the cooperation of the other(s). See: Leyton-Brown, David, Canada-U.S. Relations and the Quandary of Interdependence". http:/www.csfc.dnd.ca/strath/strath1f.html

41. *The Economist Survev on MERCOSUR* -12/10/96. http:/www.Demon.co.uk/ltamaraty/ mercosurO3.html

42. Garter, Jeffrey E., "The Changing Face of North America in the Global Economy," op. cit.

43. Di Filippo, Ammando, "MERCOSUR: Evaluation and Perspectives,. *CaDitulos del SELA* N° 49, January- March 1997. http://www.sela.org/eng_capitulos/rcapin493.htm

44. *The Economist Survey on Mercosur* - 12/10/96. http://www.demon.co.uk.ltamaraty/ mercosurO1.html

45. *The Economist Survey on Mercosur* - 12/10/96. http://www.demon.co.uk.ltamaraty/ mercosurO3.html

46. Rodriguez, Luis Alberto, "Free Trade in the Americas by 2005..."

http://lanic.utexas.edu/ .../rcapin5.html

47. Hurrell, Andrew, "Regionalism in the Americas," op. cit., p. 172.

48. Ricupero, Rubens, "Regional Agreements and the Future of the World Trade System: Stumbling Blocs or Building Blocs." In: Rod Dobell and Michael Neufeld, ed. *Bevond NAFTA: The Westem HemisDhere Interface.* (Lantzvil e, B.C.: Oolichan Books, 1993), p. 62.

49. Gilhon Alburquerque, Jose Augusto, "Rel. 5:oes Brasil-Estados Unidos e a integragao continental," op. cit., pp. 11-12.

50. Ibid., p. 12.

51. For Brazil, MERCOSUR is a platform from which to increase its trade with South America.. A Goal which it considers of foremost significance for two reasons: first, because the ten ALADI members represent nearly 24 % of Brazilian exports and 18% of its imports; and second, because the Brazilian government firmly believes that the regional integrationist process is leading to a free trade area with the rest countries of the region and/or the entire hemisphere. See: Tachinardi, Maria Helena, NMELCOSUL: Desafios e Oportunidades.R *Politica Externa,* Vol. 3, N° 4 (March 1995), p. 85.

52. Castro, Jorge, "Brasil, Argentina e EAU. *Politica Externa,* Vol. 3, N° 4 (March - April - May, 1995), p. 38.

53. Di Filippo, Ammando, "MERCOSUR: Evaluation and Perspectives," op. cit.

54. "Latin American and Caribbean Integration Trends and Options." http://www.sela.org/ eng_consejo/documents/spc123di83.htm op. cit.

55. Fauriol, Georges, and Sydney Weintraub, "U.S. Policy, Brazil, and the Southem Cone," op. cit., p. 130.

56. Wilkie, James W. And Olga M. Lazin, "Free Trade and the Challenge of MERCOSUR. http:/www.meiico.com/mexworldNol1/Art2/Freetrde.html

57. "Latin American and Caribbean Integration Trends and Options." SP/CLDOt111.0/Di No. 8. http://www.sela.org/eng_consejo/documents/spcl23di85.htm

58. Bernal, Richard L., "Path to the Free Trade Area of the Americas," *Capitulos del SELA* N° 49, January-March 1997. http://www.sela.org/eng_capitulos/rcapin498.htm

59. See for instance: "Latin American and Caribbean Integration Trends,n SP/CL/)(X111.0/Di No. 8. http://sela.org/eng_consejo/documents/spc123di83.htm

60. Bernal, Richard L., Path to the Free Trade Area of the Americas." op. cit.

61. Van Grasstek, Craig, "Latin America, The United States and Congress." *Capitulos del SELA* N° 50, April-June 1997
http://www.sela.org/eng_capitulos/rcapin506.htm

62. Stewart, John, and James F. Kelleher. "Free Trade in the Americas," op. cit., p. 32; "Towards a Free Trade Area of the Americas: The Moment of Truth.. *Capitulos del SELA,* N° 50, April-June 1997. http://sela org/eng_capitulos/rcapin5010.htm

63."Towards the FTM: Steps Forward and the Future Agenda." <http:/ hvww.sela.org/ eng_docs/spdredi161.htm>; and Lampreia, Luis Felipe, "The FTAA as a Tool for International Insertion." *Capitulos del SELA* N° 50, April-June 1977. http://www.sela.org/eng_capitulos/ rcapinS010.htm

64."Latin American and Caribbean Integration Options."
http://www.sela.org/.../spc123di83.htm and
http://www.sela.org/.../spc123di85.htms

8. The Caribbean Regional Integration: What Developments?

François Taglioni

At the time of the globalisation of exchanges led by the World Trade Organization (WTO), the increasing formalisation of free trade areas is expected on a regional scale. The paradox is only apparent because the free trade areas constitute as many "areas", of variable size, which will be integrated at the proper time in the multilateral dynamics of the exchanges.

From this prospect, the America-Caribbean sector, also includes many regional organisations with a vocation of economic integration: NAFTA, MERCOSUR, Andean Community, Central American Common Market, Group of Three, CARICOM, OECS as well as the recent Association of Caribbean States (ACS).

The Association of Caribbean States seems a space hinge between the NAFTA and the common markets of Latin America. For this reason, although proceeding from an internal will to the area, the ACS falls under the intention of the United States to create, by the year 2005, a free trade area on the scale of the western hemisphere in its totality, "from Terra del Fuego to Alaska": the Free Trade Area of the Americas (FTAA).

The Association of Caribbean States, which will be at the centre point of this analysis, remains currently heteroclite perhaps even baroque gathering of States and territories. Its operational budget is quite modest with regards the ambitions it displays. Does it have to be considered so much as an additional association in the concert of the regional organisations orchestrated in increasing spheres in the Caribbean? On the contrary, is it not likely to cooperate or integrate traditionally isolated countries like the Dominican Republic, the

Republic of Haiti, Panama and especially Cuba? Does it not offer a real insertion opportunity for the French Departments of America (FDA) which were always excluded from the local organisations? In this case, which role can France play through its FDA in the Caribbean-Latin American area?

The Caribbean Basin: An area Historically Turned Towards The Regional Cooperation

Surely the geographical fragmentation of the Caribbean area is doubled by a dispersion of the political and economic forces. The small size of the Caribbean market, national interests as well as the similarity of the structures of production and thus a lack of complementarity, reinforce the logic of competitiveness between islands. In addition the exiguity of the territory, constitutes a severe handicap to economic integration. In fact, the prospects for intra-regional trade cooperation are truly restricted and do not constitute a real alternative to the economic development. North-American and European markets remain for the time being, vital outlets to exports of the islands of the area. As far as trade is concerned, the only immediate advantage of a larger regional consultation is the setting up of pressure groups, powerful enough, to maintain some privileges on the foreign markets, sugar and especially banana production are obvious examples. Though, the WTO decision for banana production seems irrevocable. Besides, the various Spanish, English, French, Dutch speaking groups have their own social, political, administrative, academic and indeed linguistics structures. This recess by "colonial" entity causes problem when regional cooperation on the scale of the Caribbean is to be dealt with. Thus, these groups are unequally members of the existing regional organisations (Table 1).

In spite of what has been previously stated, the progress carried out in the regional cooperation is noticeable and will continue in the future. Indeed, the Caribbean does not avoid the heavy world tendency of regrouping States and territories of a same geographical area. This purpose of economic integration goes beyond the cultural and political requirements. Generally, the secular dependence has constrained the micro-States to be integrated or joined within the framework of inter-official organisations of cooperation (Blerald, 1986: 30). In the case of the Caribbean, aiming at regional integration will last but experience which has been gained over centuries is beneficial. From this point of view, the Association of Caribbean States gathers, on paper, all countries of the Caribbean basin.

To seize the potential content of the Association of Caribbean States, some elements on the past experiments of cooperation and federation should be pointed out. The methods and the objectives of the former regroupings vary according to the groups of countries.

Thus the English, in order to reduce the costs of management and operation of their colonies, tried as early as the XVIIth century to confederate the territories of Caribbean, from British Honduras to Guyana and from Jamaica to the Lesser Antilles. Until the early 60s these attempts at integration were driven by political union. Those unions were the Federation of the Windward (1674-1798), followed of a new Federation of the same islands from 1871 to 1956 then of the Federation of the Leeward and Barbados (1833-1885). The brief Federation of the West Indies from 1958 to 1962 can also be mentioned as well as its alter ego in the small islands: the Federation of the Lesser Antilles (1962-1965).

These experiments at political union were not realistic because too many physical and ideological constraints opposed them. Therefore, it is difficult to make an economically and geographically scattered space coherent.

The accession to independence of the majority of the islands and territories combined with the developmentalists theories of the politicians and the West-Indian economists generated new institutions aiming at economic integration and no longer politics. After various trials, two of them operate nowadays: the OECS since 1981 and the CARICOM since 1973 (Table 1). The latter gathers all English-speaking States except the dependent territories which are variously associated with it.

The French Departments of America (FDA), after a troubled history for several centuries, appear today in the form of a marginal group on the insular scene of the Caribbean. They constitute, since their assimilation with the French metropolis (1946) and the European Union, the most integrated group of territories in a structured system. The corollary of this assimilation without restriction (or almost) was to isolate them from the rest of the Caribbean area in a significant way.

In the federation of the Dutch West Indies, the strong return of particularisms requires even more the existence of a solid economic basis to build a political federation particularly in an insular environment characterised by territorial fragmentation of the various entities making up the group. Thus, since the withdrawal of Aruba (1986), serious economic problems have challenged the legitimacy of its 200 year old political union. In the same way, Curacao and St Maarten seek to pull out because they no longer want to sustain the North islands (Saba, Statia and Bonaire), with economies in deficit.

At last, for the **Spanish-speaking community** of the Caribbean basin (Table 1), things are different because these countries have been independent for a long time. The experiment of regional integration is quite real for the countries of Central America (except for Panama) which have been gathered within the Central American Common Market (CACM) since 1960. The recent constitution (1992) of the Group of Three, which managed geographically the CACM, proves the will of Venezuela and Colombia[1] to turn more to "North" than "South" through the Andean Community.[2] Surely, the potentiality of the North-American market carries at the moment more economic outlets for Venezuela and Colombia than the Andean countries. Thus, these two countries prepare their future insertion in the FTAA or at the very least reinforce their capacity of negotiation for this integration.

In the same way, the Group of Three is moving closer towards the insular Caribbean. This move is in line with a similar point of view although of second importance: to widen their zone of influence, to increase their outlets for trade and to carry out possible investments in the zone and in particular in the Dominican Republic and the Republic of Haiti. Besides, Venezuela, Colombia and Mexico are members of the Caribbean Development Bank (CDB) and observer members of the CARICOM (Venezuela is likely to become adherent shortly). It remains that Cuba, Panama and the Dominican Republic are not, for well known political reasons, integrated or associated with any of the regional organisations including the Spanish-speaking members.

Considering the previous elements, the Caribbean region could reasonably support a role of pivot and a geographical continuum between North America and Latin America. If an economic and political recentring is possible, the Caribbean may take advantage of it by the implementation of the Association of Caribbean States.

Table 1.
States and territories of the Caribbean in the regional cooperation

	Independent States	Dependent Territories*	DOM**
	Economic Organisations of Regional Cooperation		
ACS Association of Caribbean States	• Members of CARICOM • Members of the Group of Three • Members of the Central American Common Market as well as Cuba, Panama Dominican Republic	Anguilla, Bermuda, British Virgin Islands, Cayman Islands, Montserrat Turks and Caicos Islands Puerto Rico US Virgin Islands Netherlands Antilles Aruba	Guadelou Martiniqu French Guiana
CARICOM Caribbean Community and Common Market	Members of OECS as well as Bahamas, Barbados, Belize, Jamaica, Guyana, Republic of Haiti, Surinam, Trinidad & Tobago	Montserrat	Observer Members
OECS Organisation of Eastern Caribbean States	Antigua & Barbuda, Dominica, Grenada, St. Kitts & Nevis, St. Vincent & the Grenadines, St. Lucia	Montserrat	None
Group of Three	Colombia, Mexico, Venezuela	None	None
CACM Central American Common Market	Costa Rica, Guatemala, Honduras, Nicaragua, El Salvador	None	None

* British Antilles; Netherlands Antilles; Aruba; Puerto Rico; US Virgin Islands
** FDA = French Departments of America

The Association of Caribbean States: A New Deal?

The Association of Caribbean States was created in an economical and political environment through fast change for the States and territories of the Caribbean basin: ratification in 1994 of the North-American Free Trade Agreement (NAFTA), so that Mexico, which supplies a workforce five to six times less expensive than the United States, diverts partly the foreign investments and receives the subsidiaries of the transnational companies; implementation since 1995 of the World Trade Organisation (WTO); questioning of the commercial protocols of the Lome Convention for sugar and banana; adhesion of two "heavy duties", the Republic of Haiti and the Dominican Republic, with this convention (Lome IV); enlargement of the European Union and emergence of the Eastern European countries; overall disappointing economic performances within CARICOM whereas at the same time Caribbean Basin Initiative benefits more to the United States exports towards the Caribbean than the other way around; significant regression of the intra-regional trade within the Common Market of Central America and the CARICOM; precarious return of the democracy in the Republic of Haiti; and policy of opening in Cuba.

In this context the West Indian Commission recommended, as early as 1992, the creation of the Association of Caribbean States including the English-speaking and Spanish-speaking elements, as well as the continental States of the Caribbean Sea.

This way, the commission echoes the Enterprise for the Americas Initiative (EAI, ratified in June 1990) of President Bush who in particular proposed "the installation of a free trade commercial area between all the countries of America". Probably aware of the danger which the NAFTA represents right now (Chile, Jamaica and Trinidad-Tobago are candidates there), the conference of the heads of government of the CARICOM adopted as of October 1992 the proposal of the West Indian Commission. The things were specified a few months later, in May 1993, at the time of the second ministerial conference of the CARICOM and the Central America during which the Ministers for the two sub-regions declared in favour of the ACS. The summit of October 1993 including the presidents of the Group of Three, the heads of State and government of the CARICOM and the president of Surinam confirmed the same proposals for the creation of the ACS.

The hesitant CARICOM, in spite of its contradictions and its low economic results, is starting a policy of opening of its community to non English-speaking members to give more economic and political weight to its decisions. This process of enlargement was started by the joining of Surinam in February 1995. It continued with the Republic of Haiti entering in July 1997, with a nation of almost 7 million inhabitants, which doubles the population of the CARICOM. The negotiations for a free trade agreement with the Dominican Republic fall under this same dynamics, although the acknowledged ambition of the Dominican Republic is to establish the link between the CARICOM and the Central American Common Market. Lastly, the CARICOM tends to move towards South America since talks relate to a protocol of free trade with the four countries of the Andean Community,[3] Venezuela being at the top of the list.

This expansionist policy indicates growing concerns of the CARICOM with regards the progress of the implementation of the Free Trade Area of Americas (FTAA, decided in Miami in December 1994 during the summit of the Americas) which is likely to sweep the last trade advantages it granted. Currently the CARICOM and even less the OECS are not in position to influence the methods of the future FTAA. All the more so since the multiplicity of the preparatory meetings penalizes the small States limited in their financial means and human resources. In parallel, the renewal of the Lome Convention, by the year 2000, is also source of negotiations and expenditure.

The Association of Caribbean States potentially gathers 25 countries "full members" and 12 dependent territories "associate members" (refer to table 1 and map 1), i.e. all the States and territories of the Caribbean Sea and Gulf of Mexico to which are added Guyana, Surinam and French Guiana. The United States is not a member of the Association and thus distance their "back-yard" with which they do not obviously share economic or political worries. Accordingly the economic weapon that represents the NAFTA and the future FTAA is far more powerful than the ACS.

Whether they are insular or continental, the members of the Association of Caribbean States differ greatly. The area and the populations vary, from almost 2 million km² for Mexico with a population of 96 million inhabitants to 13 km² and 1 200 inhabitants for the territory of Saba. Between these two extremes, there are large countries (Colombia, Venezuela), intermediate countries (Guyana,

Cuba, Guatemala, Honduras, Nicaragua, Surinam) more or less densely populated and finally small-sized countries with especially the archipelago of the Lesser Antilles which stretches on more than 1,000 km from Puerto Rico to Trinidad.

Ultimately, the ACS fits geographically in a square of approximately 4,000 km by 3,000 km, i.e. approximately 12 million km². It gathered, in 1997, a population of 226 million individuals, which places it at the fourth world rank of the regional economic zones of the world (after the NAFTA, the European Union and the ASEAN; refer to table 2).

Its economic potential situates it at the fifth world rank with a total GNP of 600 billion US dollars in 1997. But here again, the economic situations are not very homogeneous and their evolutions are not steady. For example Bahamas, Martinique or the Cayman Islands are infinitely more developed than the Republic of Haiti, Nicaragua or Honduras.

Table 2.
ACS compared to other economic zones in the world

	Members	Population 1997 Million	Area Km2 Million	Density h/km2	GNP 1997 Billion	GNP $ per capita
Association of Caribbean States	25+12	226	5	45	600	2,655
NAFTA (a)	3	394	20.3	19	8,125	20,625
MERCOSUR (b)	4	204	11.8	17	894	4,385
Group of Three (c)	3	156	3.8	41	458	2,935
Andean Community (d)	5	80	3.3	24	162	2,035
Central American Common Market (e)	5	31	0.4	77	39	1,255
CARICOM (f)	14	13	0.5	26	21	1,615
European Union (g)	15	374	3.1	121	8,025	21,455
Japon	1	126	0.4	315	4,995	39,685
ASEAN (h)	9	490	4	115	663	1,353

Sources: Compilation of the author from INED (Institut National d'Études Démographiques, France), World Bank, Caribbean Development Bank, Inter-American Development Bank, Centraal Bureau voor de Statistiek.

(a) United States, Canada, Mexico

(b) Argentina, Brazil, Paraguay, Uruguay (associate members: Bolivia and Chile)

(c) Colombia, Mexico, Venezuela

(d) Bolivia, Colombia, Ecuador, Venezuela (Peru withdrew in April 1997)

(e) Costa Rica, Guatemala, Honduras, Nicaragua, El Salvador

(f) Antigua & Barbuda, Bahamas, Barbados, Belize, Dominica, Grenada, Guyana, Jamaica, Montserrat, Republic of Haiti, St. Kitts & Nevis, St. Lucia, St. Vincent & the Grenadines, Surinam, Trinidad & Tobago

(g) Austria, Belgium, Denmark, Finland, France, Germany, Greece, Ireland, Italy, Luxembourg, Netherlands, Portugal, Spain, Sweden, United Kingdom

(h) Brunei, Indonesia, Laos, Malaysia, Myanmar, the Philippines, Singapore, Thailand, Vietnam (Cambodia and Papua New Guinea are observer members).

Geographical and economic fragmentation is added to the variety of political and cultural situations. There is a large dominating Spanish-speaking group (96%), an English-speaking group constituted of many countries and territories but numerically low and very minor French-speaking and Dutch-speaking groups. These various sets present a broad range of governmental institutions which goes from the republican presidentialist system to the various status of dependent territories (British Antilles and Netherlands Antilles) as well as the system of Westminster, the parliamentary republics, the military dictatorships and the overseas departments (French West Indies).

Map 1
Independent States members of the ACS

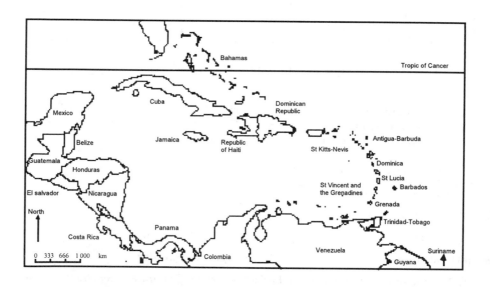

The Objectives of the Association and its Procedures

In spite of these exceptional conditions of heterogeneity, the constitutive convention of the Association of Caribbean States was signed in Cartagena in July 1994. It became effective in August 1995. All the independent States are to this date members of the ACS.[4]

The dependent territories attached to Great Britain, the United States and the Netherlands will be able to obtain, if they wish, the status of associate member. The Netherlands Antilles have applied. France signed the text as an associate member in respect of its departments of America (Guadeloupe, Martinique, French Guiana). The absence of the US Virgin Islands and Puerto Rico at the inaugural summit of the Association, in Port-of-Spain in August 1995, clearly shows that the United States is reluctant to carry out any closer move with Cuba. For the rest, the United States do not seem to be more touched by the creation of the Association which will be used when needed as a take over position for their policy in the Region.

In its preamble and its thirty one articles, the convention that created the ACS states multiple objectives. Here are the major ones:

- to support by economic integration the liberalisation of trade, investment and transportation;

- to reinforce the inter-Caribbean economic exchanges, which currently represent a low share of foreign trade of the countries in the area;

- to allow a better coordination of the national policies by acting on cooperation especially as regards tourism, transportation, natural and environmental protection and development.

Clearly, these good intentions, which seem quite theoretical and sometimes abstract, do not bring currently anything new when considering that the operational budget amounts to only 1.5 million US dollars for one biennial period. Mexico, Venezuela and Colombia, not surprisingly, each support about 15% of the whole budget and Trinidad-Tobago approximately 7%.[5] The Group of Three, in addition to its dominating economic weight in the area, is as previously stated holding the best position to take benefit from the ACS. Its participation to a total value of 45% of the budget and the designation of Mr. Simon Molina Duarte, a Venezuelan national, as secretary general[6] of the ACS confirms this leadership. Through great experience in the CARICOM, Trinidad is politically influent and shelters the Secretariat of the Association in Port-of-Spain.

In addition to the Secretariat, the other permanent organ of the Association of Caribbean States is the Council of Ministers. It includes the representatives of the Member States. Its role is to establish[7] policies and directions of the Association. The Council of Ministers of the ACS will resort, under the terms of the convention of Cartagena, to the procedure of the consensus for the decisions on substantial questions. This procedure should guarantee some flexibility of operation. The second Council of Ministers[8] took place in Havana in December 1996. It highlights the political will of Cuba and President Castro to be involved in the ACS in order to give a new dimension to its foreign policy, to multiply the economic partners and "to legitimate" its government in relation to the United States. Castro is indeed warmly acclaimed at each of his interventions at the ACS. It shows, if needed, that Cuba remains the symbol of resistance against the imperialism of the inescapable American neighbour.

For the concrete operations of cooperation, the Council of Ministers established a special fund aiming at the financing of research and technical cooperation programs. This fund is made up of contributions provided on a purely voluntary basis by States Member, non members and other entities. A call to open contribution is requested from the two last categories of backers and especially from the traditional organisations of development in cooperation in the Caribbean: the European Union and bilateral assistance of its States Member, the USAID and the system of the United Nations. The rules of operation of this Fund were adopted during the Council of Ministers in Havana. The terms and the methods of contributions will be negotiated by the Secretary General.

To this date, the Association of Caribbean States has shown to be particularly active in the field of tourism which remains one of the driving elements of the economic activity of the States and territories of the Caribbean basin. The creation of a regional fund for tourism development in the Caribbean (FORETUR) was also decided in 1995. This fund will have to obtain financing from international organisations or from private companies. It may not receive, for obvious reasons, contributions from the States Member of the ACS. Similarly, a scheme for education and vocational training in the field of tourism was adopted during the Council of Ministers in Havana.

Looking back over the past three years and in the absence of statistical data, it would be difficult to draw up an economic assessment of the Association of Caribbean States. On the other hand, the Association moves the right way, simply because it exists. For "it is unrealistic to believe that small countries can become competitive while remaining inside restrictive systems based on the non reciprocity" (Gonzales, 1997: 72). In fact, the advantages of the Lome Convention and Caribbean Basin Initiative are more and more restricted and will be reduced with the increasing liberalisation of the world trade and the lowering of the advantages of Generalised System of Preferences (GPS). This report is all the more founded since the countries or groups of territories have narrow scale economies.

This applies especially to the French Departments of America (FDA). Since the middle of the Eighties, France has multiplied the conferences, the reports of reflect and the projects of development in order to integrate the FDA in their regional environment by the means of the financing of technical cooperation projects initiated from the three concerned departments. However it seems that the concretisation of the Association of Caribbean States somehow took the French authorities by surprise. France must now lead operations of development and diplomatic actions no longer according to the dimension of the under area of the Lesser Antilles but to the scale of the Caribbean.

FDA in the Association of Caribbean States: A Delicate and Limited Insertion

Usually, speaking about the French Departments of America, the intense economic, social, cultural and political crisis which still affects them can be recalled. Actually, many elements which consolidate the FDA in a serious distress are: the structural reorganisations imposed by European integration and liberalisation of the world trade exchange;[9] the increase in unemployment; growing social conflicts; the identity crisis of young peopole who are more and more marginalised facing the rising globalisation of economy as well as political stagnation. The strategies of development advocated by France and the European Union (in particular the POSEIDOM) have been able to this day to avoid social explosion, at the cost of massive financial transfers. But the multiple archaisms inherited from the past and the drawback from the regional scene do not allow the entrance of the FDA in the modernity within the Caribbean space.

With a population of 870,000 inhabitants, the French Departments of America only represent quite a small share of the 226 million people part of the Association. In addition, trade exchanges of the FDA with their partners in the area are very weak. Besides, French is spoken far too little in the neighbouring States to induce a valid factor of integration. Moreover, for statutory reasons related to their assimilation with the French metropolis, the departments of Guadeloupe, Martinique and French Guiana were always excluded from all the regional (CARICOM, OECS) and extra-regional (CBI, CARIBCAN) organisations. This statutory problem which has been highlighted for a long time to justify the isolation of the FDA, was not however a major obstacle to their taking part in the ACS.

This participation falls under the desire which the FDA have expressed for several years to develop all kinds of exchanges with their West-Indian neighbours. For example, Guadeloupe and Martinique confirmed by multiplying actions in this direction and by organising on these two islands alternate "Europe/Caribbean Contacts" with major topics regarding regional cooperation.

For the time being, although the general census of the possible fields of cooperation between the FDA and the members of the ACS (and more particularly the members of the OECS) were established and financial means were released, many obstacles remain. Some reasons of a structural and cultural nature are related to these obstacles. The structural problems are mainly due to the insufficiency and high cost of transportation as well as administrative procedures, inherited from colonisation, which differ between the French islands and the members of the OECS. The major cultural obstacle is the reciprocal ignorance of languages. In the case of the FDA this ignorance is coupled with a reflex, conditioned by centuries of dependence, and which consists in turning systematically towards the metropolis. Lastly, their economic integration in the European Union excludes them, for the moment, from clauses of economic integration planned by the ACS.

Indeed, the stake of the regional cooperation for the FDA is significant because while turning too resolutely to Europe, they are likely to let go the opportunity of their insertion in the Caribbean which is, essentially, their natural framework of opening up.

From this prospect, France has shown for about fifteen years a renewed interest in the Caribbean region. Its actions are based on a diplomatic device of fourteen embassies of France,[10] several consulates, Alliance françaises, commercial, financial and defense consultants, as well as the two missions of cooperation in St Lucia (since 1984) and the Republic of Haiti (since 1973). France takes part in some regional organisations: it is observer member of the OECS and member of the Caribbean Development Bank (CDB).[11]

It appears however that the Official Development Assistance (ODA)[12] emanating from the ministries for the Cooperation, the Foreign Affairs and National Education for the Lesser Antilles and the Republic of Haiti has shown a significant drop (French Direction of the Treasury, 1996) since 1990 in particular for the Lesser Antilles.

Similarly, the interministerial conference on the regional cooperation[13] had allowed the appointment of an interdepartmental delegate for the development of the regional cooperation in the Caribbean. This delegate managed the Interministerial Fund of Cooperation (IFC)[14] provided with 15 million francs. However, since 1994 the Funds has been lowered to 7 million francs. The interministerial mission was dissolved in 1996 and with it the position of the delegate which, because of his exteriority to the region, was not too well accepted in the FDA. Currently the Prefect of Guadeloupe manages the fund. The role of Mrs. Michaux-Chevry, former Secretary of State for the Human Action and President of the regional council of Guadeloupe, is not irrelevant to her nomination.

Apparently, France seems to have lost, in spite of financial and diplomatic efforts, the individual initiative in the implementation of the processes of regional cooperation in the Caribbean. However it scored by centring its action of Official Development Assistance through multilateral organisations. France obviously prefers working in relation with these organisations and in particular the Lome Convention of the European Union. Unlike Great Britain and Germany whose main concerns are savings and management, and have therefore decreased their participation in the European Development Fund (EDF), France is involved for a total value of 25% of the 8th EDF (1996-2000). This position of leader among the fifteen countries part of the European Union which finance the EDF, provides France with a political weight and credibility in the authorities of the Association of Caribbean States. The instruments of the Lome Convention are truly the first factors of exogenous development in the insular Caribbean[15] of which all the States are members except Cuba. More specifically, financial resources of the EDF allocated to the regional cooperation in the Caribbean have quickly increased for the past twenty years. To strengthen its position, France deals with 10% of the total budget of the ACS, which makes it the second financial backer, in relative value, after Colombia, Venezuela and Mexico.

France, after a difficult start, thus appears now well appreciated by the members of the Association of Caribbean States. Signatory in the capacity of "associate member in respect of Guadeloupe, French Guiana and Martinique", it concluded the agreement of association to the ACS. This text was signed on May 24, 1996 in Mexico City by the minister, Mr. Herve de Charette and by his Mexican counterpart, Mr. Angel Gurria. The presence of the French minister stresses the importance given by France in taking part within the Association. Besides, the Secretary General of the ACS, Mr. Duarte, visited France in June 1996 and was received by the French Minister for the Overseas Departments and Territories and various persons in charge of qualified technical administrations as regards maritime and air transport, environmental protection and natural disaster preparedness and relief.

However, to point out its will to leave them room for manoeuvre and initiative in the perspective of their insertion in the Caribbean area, France decided to entrust control of its delegations, to persons in charge of the French Departments of America. France also took into account the will of the three presidents of the region as to appoint one of them to supervise their delegation[16] during the Councils of Ministers of the ACS. Similarly, France appoints consultants on site in the FDA, to attend meetings of the special committees, opened to any member of the ACS.

Indeed France succeeded in obtaining for the French language a status identical to English and Spanish, within the framework of the Convention of Cartagena. A project is being studied in Guadeloupe to design a programme of intensive and systematic teaching of French in the Caribbean area. The other possible fields of intervention of the FDA could be articulated around renewable energies, prevention of the natural risks, protection of the environment, specialised trainings and health.

Beyond these few "traditional" possibilities of cooperation, limits of an institutional nature always constitute a barrier to the whole insertion of the FDA in the Association. Thus, the convention of Cartagena stipulates that France takes part in the consensus and the votes, in the Council of Ministers, on the relevant questions but which do not concern the competence of the European Union. Decisions made by the ACS on questions depending on the competence of the European Union, thus do not apply to the FDA. There will be in particular no participation of the FDA in a free trade area as this would go against their membership in the customs area of the European Union.

Conclusion

Success of the Association of Caribbean States will depend on the extent of cooperation and deepening of economic integration that will be reached in the coming years. Aware of the potentiality of the NAFTA and the Free Trade Area of the Americas (FTAA), the project seems ambitious but also hypothetical. Moreover, the world liberalisation of exchanges will produce loss of interest to the possible trade preferences concluded within the ACS. Concerns are all the more legitimate since the Association does not plan in its convention to carry out a monetary union and even less political. It is true that the US dollar has been the dominant "single" currency of the area for a long time. Anyway, the Association is the expression of the will of 25 countries, close to twice as much as the European Union, to manage their future and fight together in the vast arena of the world economy.

Cultural dimension will undoubtedly play a great role in the cohesion of the Association. From this point of view the FDA, already handicapped by their small economy, can hardly count on their influence or the size of their population to facilitate their insertion in an area which is besides quite heteroclite. France remains at the time much more concerned by the completion of European construction and the role that it will play there than by the Caribbean region with limited economic and strategic interests. However, it can hope for an anchoring through its FDA, no matter how minor it is in this vast economic free trade area which will constitute Americas in the next few years. The stake is serious and France would like to take, as a European country, a "dominant" position in the Caribbean by occupying the vacant position left by the old colonial powers: the United Kingdom, the kingdom of the Netherlands and Spain.

References

Blérald, Alain (1986), "Les variations de la souveraineté : de l'intégration à la résistance". *Revue Politique et Parlementaire*, n° 924, Juillet-Août 1986, Paris, pp. 13-46.

Bryan, Anthony, (1997),"The New Clinton Administration and the Caribbean: Trade, Security and Regional Politics". *Journal of Interamerican Studies and World Affairs*, vol. 39, n°1, Miami, pp. 101-120.

Convention créant l'Association des États de la Caraïbe (1994), Office of the Secretary General, Port-of-Spain, p. 32.

Erisman, Michael (1995), "Evolving Cuban-CARICOM Relations: a Comparative Cost/benefit Analysis". *New West Indian Guide*, n°1&2, Leiden, pp. 45-66.

Gonzales, Anthony (1997), "Les liens futurs entre l'UE et les Caraïbes". *Le Courrier ACP-UE*, n° 161, Janvier-Février, Bruxelles, pp. 72-73.

Gonzales, Anthony (1998), "Caribbean-EU Relations in a Post-Lomé World". *Working papers on EU Development Policy*, n°2, Friedrich Ebert Stiftung, Bonn, p.32 .

Harding, Lisa (1996), "Whither CARICOM". *Broad Street Journal*, Monday February 26.

Harker, Trevor (1996), *Small States and The Free Trade Area of the Americas (FTAA)*, Paper presented at the colloquium entitled "Diplomacy After 2000: Small States and Negotiating Space in the New International Trading Environment" Organised by the Institute of International Relations, UWI, Trinidad, 8th-9th October.

Les DOM-TOM dans la politique de défense de la France (1992). Le Nouveau Monde, IRIS/Dunod, Paris, p.192.

Les organisations internationales à vocation régionale (1995). Les Notices, La documentation française, Paris, p.124.

Lorenzo, Tania Garcia (1995), "La Asociacion de Estados Del Caribe. Potencialidades y Desafios". Paper presented at the 1995 annual conference of the Caribbean Studies Association, Curacao, p.20.

Robson, P. (1990), *The Economics of International Integration*. Allen and Unwin, London. Serbin, Andrés (1996), *El ocaso de las islas : el Gran Caribe frente a los desafios globales y regionales*. INVESP/Nueva Sociedad, Caracas, p.120.

Sachwald, Frédérique (1997), La mondialisation comme facteur d'intégration régionale. *Politique Étrangère*. n°2, Paris. pp. 257-264.

Siroen, Jean-Marc (1996), "Régionalisme contre multilatéralisme?". *Cahiers Français*, n° 269, Paris, pp.90-96.

Sachwald, Frédérique (1997), La mondialisation comme facteur d'intégration régionale. *Politique Étrangère.* n°2, Paris. pp. 257-264.

Siroen, Jean-Marc (1996), "Régionalisme contre multilatéralisme?". *Cahiers Français,* n° 269, Paris, pp.90-96.

Taglioni, François (1998). "Essai de comparaison géopolitique entre les États de la Méditerranée eurafricaine et de la Méditerranée américaine" in A-L. Sanguin (dir.). *Mare Nostrum, géopolitique de la Méditerranée et de ses marges.* L'Harmattan. Paris

Taglioni, François (1995), *Géopolitique des Petites Antilles. Influences européenne et nord-américaine.* Éditions Karthala, Paris, p. 324.

Taglioni, François (1993), "European Community Action Concerning British and Dutch Dependent Territories in the Lesser Antilles". *Bulletin of Eastern Caribbean Affairs,* Vol. 18, n° 4, December, Barbados, pp. 13-31.

Watson, Patrick (1995), "CARICOM and the Global Integration Movement: Retrospect and Prospect". *Revue d'Économie Régionale et Urbaine,* n° 2, pp. 249-268.

West Indian Commission. *Towards a Vision of the Future* (1991) ; *Time for Action* (1992), West Indian Commission, Barbados.

Notes

1. Mexico on its own signed in January 1991 an agreement to establish an economic free trade area with the members of the Central American Common Market.

2. The difficulties of operation of the Andean Community but also of the Latino-American Association of Integration (ALADI) and of the Group of Rio corroborate the idea that the impulse for the creation of a free trade area between the Americas comes from "North".

3. Peru withdrew from this organisation in April 1997.

4. In addition, those countries are observer members: Argentina, Brazil, Canada, Chile, Ecuador, Egypt, India, Italy, the kingdom of Netherlands, the kingdom of Morocco, Peru, the Russian Federation and Spain.

5. The participation of the other contributors, classified in four categories corresponding to decreasing percentages, does not exceed 3%.

6. The Secretary General is elected on the basis of rotation for a period of four years. She/He is the administrative person in charge of the Association.

7. With this intention, the Council of Ministers worked out the following special committees: development of trade and foreign relations; protection and preservation of the environment and the Caribbean sea; natural resources; science, technology, health, education and culture; budget and administration. All the special committees have been able to meet until now.

8. The first Council of Ministers was held in December 1995 in Guatemala and the latest was held in November 1997 in Colombia.

9. Considering the requirements of the "Fifteen" and of the WTO, the protocols which protect the markets of banana, sugar, rum as well as the tax relief related in particular to the law of tax exemption will not be continuously extended.

10. Colombia, Costa Rica, Cuba, Guatemala, Republic of Haiti, Honduras, Mexico, Nicaragua, Dominican Republic, El Salvador, Saint Lucia, Surinam, Trinidad and Venezuela. The embassy of Jamaica stopped operating in December 1996.

11. France is a non regional member as well as Canada, Germany, Italy and the United Kingdom.

12. This ODA is mainly supported by the Ministry of Cooperation through the French Assistance and Cooperation Fund (ACF). The ACF finances various projects which range from rural development to health and social facilities as well as teaching and training, institutional development and cultural actions. The budgets of the Ministry for Foreign Affairs and the Ministry of National Education are negligible when taking into consideration the budget of the Ministry of Cooperation.

13. This conference took place in Cayenne (French Guiana) in April 1990. It gathered a broad range of government agencies, high-ranking civil servants and the socio-professionals of the FDA.

14. This Fund aims at promoting the insertion of the FDA in their Caribbean environment by actions definitely involving one FDA and other States or territories of the area.

15. Among the continental countries of the Caribbean only Guyana, Surinam and Belize are members of the Lome Convention. However the European Union carries out action of technical cooperation and assistance to the project with all the countries of Latin America.

16. Indeed the three Presidents of the region have created a delegation of the FDA, chaired alternatively by one of them for two years, responsible for adopting provisions with regard to the ACS.

Closing Remarks

Regional Dynamics in the Post-Cold War World

Stephen C. Calleya

The latter part of the twentieth century has seen a resurgence of regional dynamics in international relations. The process of decolonization coupled with the end of the Cold War has created an environment that is conducive to an increase in regional patterns of interaction. As a result, regionalism is again becoming a major characteristic of the international system.[1]

The increase in regional arrangements since the end of the Cold War is partly due to the fact that great powers and regional powers welcome the opportunity to participate in collective security and co-operative frameworks where the costs of foreign policy actions are shared among several actors. Although common historical links, cultural and linguistic backgrounds plus a common civic culture continue to influence regional constellations, the post-Cold War era has seen an increase in the impact that geo-economic and geo-political factors have on the foreign policy direction that countries decide to adopt.

One can for example draw parallels between the systemic changes taking place between the Caribbean and Central America and the North American Free Trade Area (NAFTA) which embraces the United States, Canada and Mexico and the Mediterranean countries vis-à-vis the European Union.[2]

Theoretically, there are several possible patterns of regional development that can be highlighted. "Regional restabilization" refers to those instances where an external hegemon intervenes in regional affairs to restore order. The intervention of the United States and the European Union in the Balkans during the last decade illustrates this type of regional development. The participation of a hegemonic actor in regional relations also increases the probability of aggravating existing intra-regional tensions and polarization.[3]

Regional fragmentation, peripheralization, and bilateralization of internal and external relations is another form of development. This model has dominated regional relations across Central Africa as states have sought to re-draw boundaries left behind by colonial powers several decades earlier.

A neo-regional alternative model of development is one that implies regional restructuring based on symmetrical and solidarity-oriented patterns of development which would consist of both intergovernmental and transnational patterns of relations. This model of development is manifesting itself across Western Europe as member states of the European Union become more closely integrated with one another.[4]

The end of the Cold War has had a number of geopolitical implications on international relations. First, ten years after the fall of the Berlin Wall the East-West dimension has largely disappeared. Russia's leadership is now largely committed to establishing firmer links with the West. Even the tense situation that developed during the Kosovo crisis did not shake Russia's foreign policy priority of integrating further with the West.

Second, several geographical areas have emerged as "grey areas" which are trying to find their position between traditional cultural backgrounds and the process of "westernization". The countries going through this process of transformation are often labelled "emerging economies" and can be found in Central and Eastern Europe, the Mediterranean, Latin America and south-east Asia.

Third, the United States' policy of selective engagement is having a major impact on patterns of relations in different regions of the world. No other actor in the international system has had the same influence on regional relations as the last superpower. American military, political and economic supremacy are a leading force when it comes to shaping regional dynamics around the world. Patterns of interaction across the Middle East, Central and East Europe, Central Africa, Latin America and south-east Asia have been directly affected by policy decisions taken in Washington.

The collapse of the Soviet Union and the American foreign policy of selective engagement has allowed the European Union (EU) to gradually emerge as an alternative patron in global affairs. The EU enlargement process towards Central and Eastern Europe and the Mediterranean, the Euro-Mediterranean process, the EU-ASEAN summits and the Euro-Latin American Forum are evidence of the increasing ability of the EU to project political and economic power at an international level. The evolution of the EU's common foreign and security policy (CFSP) and its more direct involvement in regional affairs such as its key role in the reconstruction of the Balkans are initial steps that could lead to an upgrade in EU status as an international actor. Such a development would allow the EU to wield more influence at a regional level of affairs as the twenty-first century unfolds.

The post-Cold War international system is thus somewhat more fragmented than it was during the Cold War now that superpower domination has all but disappeared. During the Cold War regional powers either pledged allegiance to one of the superpowers or else opted to remain equidistant between both superpowers by joining the non-aligned movement. Geo-political parameters were firmly established, allowing countries to formulate long-term foreign policy agenda. Once the firm ground of the Cold War and deterrence thinking collapsed, relations became more nebulous and challenging. In the post-Cold War international system that has emerged, the kind of *sancta simplicitas* that the Cold War provided has been replaced by regional relations that are much more fluid, volatile and uncertain than before.

The lack of coherence that exists between the different processes of globalisation, regionalisation and nationalism reflects the *"reality sui generis"* of international society in an era of system transition. The fact that the character and structure of world politics has been radically altered is indisputable. But no one consensus exists as to whether the phase we are now in is a transitory or a permanent one.[5] Some observers claim that the post-Cold War period is a temporary phase that may last for a few decades before the outlines of a new world order emerge. Once this happens it will probably be more by trial and error than by design.[6] Others argue that the uncertain era we are now in is here to stay and that any visions of a world order based on equality and justice are nothing more than wishful thinking.[7]

In emphasising the significance of international regions as an intermediate level of analysis between the nation-state and the global international system this study assists in identifying what changes are taking place in international relations at the end of the twentieth century. Each chapter in this book offers a precise description and analysis of the internal and external attributes of regional development. The continuous diffusion of power to the peripheral members of the international system has resulted in a process of global and regional transformation in which international economic and political transactions take place in a much less organised manner.

This book has helped in focusing on the relationship between increasing regionalism across the international system and the specific role different actors are playing at this level of analysis. Section One was dedicated to providing a comparative analysis of regionalism and contemporary world politics. The tentative conclusions on regionalism in a changing global order shed light on the balance of power shifts that have occurred since the end of the Cold War.

Section Two concentrated on the evolution of regional dynamics at a European level. Although the European Union experiment is the dominant regional model in this catchment area of global politics, the Nordic model of regionalism is another example of a regional co-operative grouping. The concept of a Northern Dimension of regional integration is certain to become more prominent as illustrated by the support given to the idea by the Finnish Presidency of the European Union in the second half of 1999. In contrast, regional tendencies across the Balkans reveal a wide array of different evolutionary patterns unfolding simultaneously.

Section Three mapped out regional developments taking place in different parts of the world. While the concept of regionalism has remained a theoretical aspiration in the Mediterranean, regional co-operation has increased across the Americas with NAFTA being a principal mechanism in this area. As a result there has been an increase in synergies between North and Latin America and between the Americas and other regions of the world.

This study further promotes research into the regional level of analysis. Although there has been an increase in the study of regionalism in recent years, this framework of analysis remains underdeveloped in the discipline of International Relations. This is partly explained by the fact that the study of regions goes against the grain of the Anglo-American analytical tradition in International Relations which developed an insular perspective of international affairs by concentrating on the interaction between reigning great powers. Understanding the impact that the diffusion of power is having on the level of interaction between states in the international system is however essential if the dynamics of the multipolar international system are to be better understood.

The theme of regionalism lends coherence to the history of twentieth century international relations as it draws our attention to a specific pattern of interaction and oscillation between actors in the international system. Since the end of the Cold War regionalism has been carried forward by the most powerful states as a means of preserving their own self-interests. Governments have recognised that regionalism is an effective political vehicle that can assist in the management of domestic and external pressures.[8]

While one can continue to debate the extent to which regional cooperation and regional arrangements can provide the most effective framework for order and stability it is clear that such constellations are certainly having a significant impact on patterns of relations in global affairs.[9]

By providing a reality check of regional developments at the end of the twentieth century this study goes some way towards raising the profile of regional theory and empirical analysis. It is hoped that the schema provided encourages other regionalists to focus more comprehensively on the factors that contribute to regional integration and fragmentation, regional power centres and extra-regional intrusive action.

Further research and theorising is necessary if a better understanding of the relationship between regionalism and world order, the mechanisms of regional integration, the development of inter-regional dialogue and collaboration is to take place. The analysis provided on regional processes in Europe, North America, Latin America and other geographical areas is an important first step towards further elucidating the complex resurgence of regional dynamics in the post-Cold War world. It is hoped that this study will attract a wider arena of research and reflection in the area of comparative theoretical frameworks for analysing regionalism.

Notes

1. Buzan, Barry, et al., (1994), "Regional Security: A Post –Cold War Framework For Analysis", Working Paper, Centre for Peace and Conflict Research, Copenhagen, p.8.

2. Hettne, B. (1994), "The regional factor in the formation of a new world order", in Sakamoto, Y. (ed.), Global Transformation, Challenges to the State System, University Press, Tokyo, p. 146.

3. Acharya, A. (1992), "Regional Military-Security Co-operation in the Third World: A Conceptual Analysis of the Relevance and Limitations of ASEAN", Journal of Peace Research, Vol. 29, No.1, p. 15.

4. Martin, W.G. (1991), The Future of Southern Africa: What Prospects After Majority Rule", Review of African Political Economy, No. 50, pp. 115-134.

5. Rosenau, James, N. (1992), Turbulence in World Politics, Harvester Wheatsheaf, p. 68.

6. Hyland, William G. (1991/1992), "The case for Pragmatism", Foreign Affairs, Vol. 71, No. 1, p. 43.

7. Freedman, Lawrence, (1991/1992), "Order and Disorder in the New World", Foreign Affairs, Vol. 71, No.1, p. 21.

8. Clark, Ian, (1997), Globalization And Fragmentation, Oxford University Press, pp. 197- 202,

9. Fawcett, L. and Hurrell, A. (1995), Regionalism in World Politics, Oxford University Press, pp. 310-327.

Select Bibliography

'Barcelona Declaration adopted at the Euro-Mediterranean Conference' (27 and 28 Nov. 1995).

'Malta Declaration adopted at Senior Officials meeting, Brussels, (May 1997).

Acharya, A. (1992), 'Regional Military-Security Co-operation in the Third World: A Conceptual Analysis of the Relevance and Limitations of ASEAN', *Journal of Peace Research*, vol. 29, no.1.

Adler, Emanuel, (1997), 'Imagined (Security) Communities: Cognitive Regions in International Relations', *Millennium. Journal of International Studies*, vol. 26, no. 2.

Aliboni, Roberto (1997), *'Confidence Building, Conflict Prevention and Arms Control in the Euro-Mediterranean Partnership'*, Perceptions, Dec. 1997 - Feb. 1998.

Anderson, Benedict, (1991), *Imagined Communities. Reflections on the Origins and Spread of Nationalism*, London: Verso.

Andrén, Nils, (1991), 'On the Meaning and Uses of Neutrality', *Co-operation and Conflict*, vol. 26, no. 2 (June 1991).

Ayoob, Mohammed, (1995), *The Third World Security Predicament. State Making, Regional Conflict, and the International System*, Boulder: Lynne Rienner.

Bach, Robert L., (1993), *Changing Relations: Newcomers and Established Residents in U.S. Communities: A Report to the Ford Foundation by the National Board of the Changing Relations Panel*, New York: Ford Foundation.

Bahr, Egon & Dieter S. Lutz (eds.), (1986), *Gemeinsame Sicherheit. Idee und Konzept. Bd. 1: Zu den Ausgangsüberlegungen, Grundlagen und Strukturmerkmalen Gemeinsamer Sicherheit,* Baden-Baden: Nomos Verlag.

Bailes, Alyson, and Cottey, Andrew, (1998), *Regional Co-operation Frameworks,* Macmillan, London, April 1998.

Barbé, Esther (1996), 'The Barcelona Conference: Launching Pad of a Process', *Mediterranean Politics, 1/1.*

Bebler, Anton, (1992), 'The Neutral and Non-Aligned States in the New European Security Architecture', *European Security,* vol. 1, no. 2 (Summer 1992).

Binter, Josef, (1992), 'Neutrality in a Changing World: End or Renaissance of a Concept?', *Bulletin of Peace Proposals,* vol. 23, no. 2 (June 1992).

Bjurner, Anders, (1998), 'European Security at the End of the Twentieth Century: The Subregional Contribution', in Subregional Cooperation in the New Europe: Building Security, Prosperity and Solidarity from the Barents to the Black Sea, Cottey, Andrew (ed.)., Macmillan Press.

Boulding, Elise, (1993), 'States, Boundaries and Environmental Security', in Dennis J.D. Sandole & Hugo van der Merwe (eds.), *Conflict Resolution Theory and Practice. Integration and Application,* Manchester: Manchester University Press.

Brunelle, Dorval and Christian Deblock, (1992), "Economic Blocs and the Challenge of the North American Free Trade Agreement," North America Without Borders? Intearatina Canada, the United States, and Mexico, Calgary, Alberta: University of Calgary Press.

Bull, Hedley, (1995), *The Anarchical Society, A Study of Order in World Politics.* Second Edition, Houndsmills, Basingstoke: Macmillan.

Buzan, Barry, (1991), *People, States and Fear. An Agenda for International Security Studies in the Post-Cold War Era,* Second Edition, Boulder: Lynne Rienner.

Buzan, Barry, et al., (1994), "Regional Security: A Post –Cold War Framework For Analysis", Working Paper, Centre for Peace and Conflict Research, Copenhagen.

Buzan, Barry, Morten Kelstrup, Pierre Lemaitre, Elzbieta Tromer & Ole Wæver, (1990), *The European Security Order Recast. Scenarios for the Post-Cold War Era* London: Pinter.

Buzan, Barry, Ole Wæver & Jaap de Wilde, (1998), *The New Security Studies: A Framework for Analysis*, Boulder: Lynne Rienner.

Calleya, Stephen C., (1997a), *Navigating Regional Dynamics in the Post-Cold War World. Patterns of Relations in the Mediterranean Area*, Aldershot: Dartmouth.

Calleya, Stephen, (1997b), 'The Euro-Mediterranean Process After Malta: What Prospects?', *Mediterranean Politics*, vol. 2, no. 2, Autumn 1997.

Calleya, Stephen, (1999), 'Is The Barcelona Process Working? EU Policy in the Mediterranean', ZEI Discussion Paper Series.

Camier, Alice (1991), The Countries of the Greater Arab Maghreb and the European Community, Commission of the European Communities, DE 68, Jan.

Cantori, Louis J. & Steven L. Spiegel (eds.), (1970), *The International Politics of Regions: A Comparative Approach*, Englewood Cliffs, NJ: Prentice-Hall.

Castaneda, Jorge, (1995), *The Mexican Shock: Its Meaning for the United States*, New York: W.W. Norton.

Charnay, Jean-Paul, (1996), 'Representation stratégique de l'Islam', paper for the *Colloque Prospective des Ménaces*, Paris: Centre d'Étudues et de Prospective.

Clark, Ian, (1997), *Globalization And Fragmentation*, Oxford University Press.

Clarke, Douglas, (1992), 'A Guide to Europe's New Security Architecture', *European Security*, vol. 1, no. 2 (Summer 1992).

Clément, Sophia, (1997), "*L'Europe du sud-est après les élargissements de l'Union européenne et de l'OTAN*", in Les Balkans, deux ans après les Accords de Dayton.

Clément Sophia and Thierry Tardy (eds.) *Relations Internationales et Stratégiques*, Paris, December 1997.

Cornelius, Wayne A., (1995), 'Nafta Costs Mexico More Job Losses Than U.S.' *New York Times*, 17 October 1995.

Coufoudakis, Van, (1996), 'Greek Foreign Policy in the Post-Cold War Era: Issues and Challenges', *Mediterranean Quarterly*, 7/3.

Crone, Donald, (1993), 'Does Hegemony Matter? The Reorganisation of the Pacific Political Economy.' *World Politics*, 45, no. 4 (July).

Daase, Christopher, Susanne Feske, Bernhard Moltmann & Claudia Schmid (eds.), (1993), *Regionalisierung der Sicherheitspolitik. Tendenzen in den internationalen Beziehungen nach dem Ost-West-Konflikt* (Baden-Baden: Nomos Verlag.

DePalma, Anthony, (1995), "For Mexico, Nafta's Promise of Jobs Is Still Just a Promise." *New York Times*, 10 October 1995.

Deutsch, Karl W. *et al.*, (1957), *Political Community and the North Atlantic Area. International Organization in the Light of Historical Experience*, Princeton, N.J.: Princeton University Press.

Economides, Spyros, (1992), *The Balkan Agenda: Security and Regionalism in the New Europe*, London Defence Studies, Center for Defence Studies, Brassey's.

EuroMesco Joint Report, April 1997.

Falk, Richard & Saul H. Mendlovitz (eds.), (1973), *Regional Politics and World Order*, San Francisco: W.H. Freeman and Company.

Fawcett, L. and Hurrell, A. (1995), *Regionalism in World Politics*, Oxford University Press.

Fawcett, Louise & Andrew Hurrell (eds.), (1995), *Regionalism in World Politics*, Oxford: Oxford University Press.

Fischer, Dietrich, (1993), *Nonmilitary Aspects of Security. A Systems Approach*, Aldershot: Dartmouth.

Fishlow, Albert and Stephan Haggard, (1992), *The United States and the Regionalisation of the World Economy*, Paris: Organisation for Economic Cooperation and Development.

Fukuyama, Francis, (1989), "The End of History?" *The National Interest*, 16 (Summer).

Fuller, Graham E. & Ian O. Lesser, (1995), *A Sense of Siege. The Geopolitics of Islam and the West*, Boulder: Westview, 1995.

Gaddis, John Lewis, (1994), 'Rescuing Choice from Circumstance: The Statecraft of Henry Kissinger', in Gordon A. Craig & Francis L. Loewenheim (eds.): *The Diplomats, 1939-1979*, Princeton, NJ: Princeton University Press.

Gaer, Felice D., (1993), 'The United Nations and the CSCE: Co-operation, Competition, Confusion?', in Michael R. Lucas (ed.): *The CSCE in the 1990s: Constructing European Security and Co-operation*, Baden-Baden: Nomos Verlag.

Gligorov, Vladimir, (1997), "Trade in the Balkans", paper prepared for the seminar on "South east Europe after NATO and EU Enlargement: Towards Inclusive Security Structures?", Institute for Security Studies, Western European Union, Paris, 11-12 December 1997.

Goldstein, Judith and Robert O. Keohane, (1993), Ideas and Foreign Policy, Beliefs. Institutions, and Political Change, Ithaca and London: Cornell University Press.

Haas, Ernst B., (1966), *International Political Communities*, New York: Anchor Books.

Haggard, Stephan, (1994), "Thinking about Regionalism: The Politics of Minilateralism in Asia and the Americas." Paper presented at the annual meeting of the American Political Science Association, New York, NY, September.

Harden, Sheila (ed.), (1994), *Neutral States and the European Community*, London: Brassey's, UK.

Harker, Trevor (1996), *Small States and The Free Trade Area of the Americas (FTAA)*, Paper presented at the colloquium entitled "Diplomacy After 2000: Small States and Negotiating Space in the New International Trading Environment" Organised by the Institute of International Relations, UWI, Trinidad, 8th-9th October.

Heisler, Martin O., (1990), 'The Nordic Region: Changing Perspectives in International Relations', *The Annals of the American Academy of Political and Social Science*, vol. 512, London: Sage.

Herz, John M, (1951), *Political Realism and Political Idealism, A Study in Theories and Realities*, Chicago: Chicago University Press.

Hettne, B. (1994), "The regional factor in the formation of a new world order", in Sakamoto, Y. (ed.), Global Transformation, Challenges to the State System, Tokyo:UN University Press.

Higgott, Richard and Richard Stubbs, (1995), "Competing Conceptions of Economic Regionalism: APEC vs. EAEC in the Asia Pacific", *Review of International Political Economy*, vol. 2, no. 3 (Summer).

Holbrooke, Richard, (1995), "America, a European Power." *Foreign Affairs*, vol. 74, no. 2 (March/April).

Holm, Hans-Henrik & Georg Sørensen (eds.), (1995), *Whose World Order? Uneven Globalization and the End of the Cold War*, Boulder: Westview Press.

Huntington, Samuel P., (1993), "The Clash of Civilisations?" *Foreign Affairs*, vol. 72, no. 3 (Summer).

Huntington, Samuel, (1996), *The Clash of Civilizations and the Remaking of World Order*, New York: Simon & Schuster.

Hurrell, Andrew, (1994), 'Regionalism in the Americas', in Abraham F. Lowenthal and Gregory F. Treverton, (eds)., *Latin America in a New World Order*, Boulder, Col.: Westview Press.

Ischinger, Wolfgang (1998), 'Nicht gegen Rubland. Sicherheit und Zussamenarbeit im Ostsee-Raum', Internationale Politik 2/1998.

Jervis, Robert, (1976), *Perception and Misperception in International Politics*, Princeton, N.J.: Princeton University Press.

Jervis, Robert, (1982), 'Security Regimes', *International Organization*, vol. 36, no. 2 (Spring 1982).

Joenniemi, Pertti (ed.), (1993), *Co-operation in the Baltic Sea Region*, London.

Joennini, Pertti, (1989), 'The Underlying Assumptions of Finnish Neutrality', in Joseph Kruzel & Michael H. Haltzel (eds.), *Between the Blocs, Problems and Prospects for Europe's Neutrals and Non-Aligned States*, Cambridge: University Press.

Joffé, George, (1994): 'The European Union and the Maghreb', in Gillespie, Richard, (ed.), *Mediterranean Politics*, vol. 1, Pinter Publishers.

Jones, Charles & Little Richard, (1993), *The Logic of Anarchy, Neorealism to Structural Realism*, New York: Columbia University Press.

Kaiser, Karl, (1986), "The Interaction of Subregional Systems: Some Preliminary Notes of Recurrent Patterns and the Role of the Superpowers", *World Politics*, vol.21, no.1, October 1968.

Keating, Michael & John Loughlin (eds.), (1997), *The Political Economy of Regionalism*, Newbury Park: Frank Cass.

Kissinger, Henry M., (1979), *The White House Years*, London.

Kruzel, Joseph & Michael H. Haltzel, (1989), *Between the Blocs. Problems and Prospects for Europe's Neutrals and Non-Aligned States*, Cambridge: Cambridge University Press.

Lake, David A. & Patrick M. Morgan (eds.), (1997), *Regional Orders. Building Security in a New World*, University Park, Pennsylvania: Pennsylvania State University Press.

Lapid, Yosef & Friedrich Kratochwill (eds.), (1995), *The Return of Culture and Identity in IR Theory*, Boulder: Lynne Rienner.

Lapidoth, Ruth, (1996), *Autonomy. Flexible Solutions to Intrastate Conflicts*, Washington, D.C.: United States Institute of Peace Press.

Lawrence, Robert Z., (1996), *Regionalism, Multilateralism, and Deeper Integration*, Washington, D.C.: The Brookings Institution.

Lisbon Document (1996), Lisbon Summit, 3 December 1996.

Lynn-Jones, Sean M., (1992), 'The Future of International Security Studies', in Desmond Ball & David Horner (eds.): *Strategic Studies in a Changing World: Global, Regional and Australian Perspectives*, Series 'Canberra Papers on Strategy and Defence', vol. 89 (Canberra: Strategic and Defence Studies Centre, Research School of Pacific Studies, ANU, 1992).

Makram-Ebeid, Mona, (1997), 'Prospects For Euro-Mediterranean Relations', *Intercultural Dialogue in the Mediterranean*, Foundation for International Studies.

Marin, Manuel, (1997), 'Partners in Progress', *Euro-Mediterranean Partnership*, vol. 2, London.

Marks, Jon, (1996), 'High Hopes and Low Motives: The New Euro-Mediterranean Partnership Initiative', *Mediterranean Politics*, 1/1.

Martin, W.G. (1991), "The Future of Southern Africa: What Prospects After Majority Rule", *Review of African Political Economy*, no. 50.

Møller, Bjørn, (1994), 'Security Concepts: New Challenges and Risks', in Antonio Marquina & Hans Günter Brauch (eds.): 'Confidence Building and Partnership in the Western Mediterranean. Tasks for Preventive Diplomacy and Conflict Avoidance', *AFES-PRESS Reports*, no. 5, Mosbach: AFES-PRESS.

Mouritzen, Hans, (1995), 'The Nordic Model as a Foreign Policy Instrument: Its Rise and Fall', *Journal of Peace Research*, vol. 32, no. 1 (February 1995).

Mouritzen, Hans, (1997), *External Danger and Democracy. Old Nordic Lessons and New European Challenges*, Aldershot: Dartmouth.

Mouritzen, Hans, (1998), *Finlandization: Towards a General Theory of Adaptive Politics*, Aldershot: Gower.

Neumann, Iver B., (1996), 'Self and Other in International Relations', *European Journal of International Relations*, vol. 2, no. 2 (June 1996).

Nye, Joseph E. & Sean M. Lynn-Jones, (1988), 'International Security Studies: A Report of a Conference on the State of the Field', *International Security*, vol. 12, no. 4 (Spring 1988).

Nye, Joseph S., (1971), *Peace in Parts: Integration and Conflict in Regional Organization*, Boston: Little, Brown & Co.

Nye, Joseph S., (1990), *Bound to Lead: The Changing Nature of American Power*. New York: Basic Books.

Osherenko, Gail & Oran R. Young, (1989), *Age of the Arctic: Hot Conflicts and Cold Realities*, Cambridge: Cambridge University Press.

Palme Commission (1982), (Independent Commission on Disarmament and Security Issues): *Common Security, A Blueprint for Survival, With a Prologue by Cyrus Vance*, New York: Simon & Schuster.

Pasha, Mustapha Kamal and Ahmed I. Samatar, (1996), 'The Resurgence of Islam.' in *Globalisation: Critical Reflections*, (ed.) James H. Mittelman, Boulder: Lynne Rienner.

Perkins, Bradford, (1993), 'The Creation of a Republic Empire, 1776-1865', *Cambridge History of American Foreign Relations*, vol. 1, Cambridge: Cambridge University Press.

Petrash, Vilma E., (1997), "El Espiritu de Miami: De Donde Viene?, Donde Esta?, Hacia Donde Va?" *Venezuela Analitica*, no. 10, January 1997.

Poitras, Guy, (1995), "Regional Trade Strategies: U.S. Policy in North America and toward the Asian Pacific." Paper presented at the annual meeting of the International Studies Association. Chicago, February.

Prins, Gwyn: 'Politics and the Environment', *International Affairs*, vol. 66, no. 4 (1990).

Roberts, Adam, (1976), *Nations in Arms, The Theory and Practice of Territorial Defence*, London: Praeger.

Robinson, William I., (1996), *Promoting Polyarchy: Globalisation, US Intervention, and Hegemony*, Cambridge: Cambridge University Press.

Roque, Maria Angels, *(1997)*, 'Position Paper on the Role of Civil Society', *Intercultural Dialogue in the Mediterranean*, Foundation for International Studies.

Rosenau, James, N. (1992), *Turbulence in World Politics*, Harvester Wheatsheaf.

Rosenau, James, N., (1997), *Along the Domestic-Foreign Frontier, Exploring Governance in a Turbulent World*, Cambridge University Press.

Rotfeld, Adam Daniel, (1996), 'Europe: Towards New Security Arrangements' (with appendices), *SIPRI Yearbook 1996*.

Rother Rizwi *etal., (1986), South Asian Insecurity and the Great Powers*, London: Macmillan.

Russett, Bruce, (1967), *International Regions and the International System*, Chicago: Rand McNally.

Singer, Max & Aaron Wildawsky, (1993), *The Real World Order. Zones of Peace / Zones of Turmoil,* Chatham, NJ: Chatham House Publishers.

Snyder, Glenn H., (1984), 'The Security Dilemma in Alliance Politics', *World Politics,* vol. 36, no. 4.

Stråth, Bo, (1995), 'Scandinavian Identity: A Mythical Reality', in Nils Arne Sørensen (ed.), *European Identities. Cultural Diversity and Integration in Europe since 1700,* Odense: Odense University Press.

Stubbs, Richard and Geoffrey R.D. Underhill, (1994), "Introduction: Global Issues in Historical Perspective." in Richard Stubbs and Geoffrey R.D. Underhill, eds., Political Economy and the Chanaina Global Order, Toronto, Ontario: McClelland and Stewart Inc., the Canadian Publishers.

Stuttgart Conference, Chairman's Formal Conclusions, *Third Euro-Mediterranean Conference of Foreign Ministers, Stuttgart, April 15th-16th 1999.*

Tanner, Fred, *(1997): 'The Euro-Med Partnership: Prospects for Arms Limitations and Confidence Building after Malta',* International Spectator, *xxxii/2.*

Taylor, Paul, (1993), *International Organization in the Modern World. The Regional and the Global Process,* London: Pinter Publishers.

Thomas, Caroline, (1992), *The Environment in International Relations,* London: Royal Institute of International Affairs.

Tow, William T., (1990), *Subregional Security Co-operation in the Third World,* Boulder, Col.: Lynne Rienner.

Väyrynen, Raimo (ed.), (1985), *Policies for Common Security,* London: Taylor & Francis/SIPRI, 1985.

Väyrynen, Raimo, (1987), 'Adaptation of a Small Power to International Tensions: The Case of Finland', in Bengt Sundelius (ed.), *The Neutral Democracies and the New Cold War,* Boulder: Westview.

Wæver, Ole, (1993), 'Identities', in Judit Balázs & Håkan Wiberg (eds.): *Peace Research for the 1990s,* Budapest: Akadémiai Kiadó.

Wæver, Ole, (1996), 'Europe's Three Empires: A Watsonian Interpretation of Post-Wall European Security', in Rick Fawn & Jeremy Larkins (eds.), *International Society after the Cold War, Anarchy and Order Reconsidered,* Houndsmills, Basingstoke: Macmillan.

Wæver, Ole, (1997), 'Imperial Metaphors: Emerging European Analogies to Pre-Nation-State Imperial Systems', in Ola Tunander, Pavel Baev & Victoria Einagel (eds.): *Geopolitics in Post-Wall Europe,* London: Sage.

Wallerstein, Immanuel, (1992), *Geopolitics and Geoculture. Essays on the Changing World-System,* Cambridge: Cambridge University Press.

Waltz, Kenneth N., (1979), *Theory of International Politics,* Reading: Addison-Wesley.

Watson, Adam, (1982), *Diplomacy. The Dialogue between States,* London: Methuen.

Watson, Adam, (1992), *The Evolution of International Society,* London: Routledge.

Watson, Patrick (1995), "CARICOM and the Global Integration Movement: Retrospect and Prospect". *Revue d'Économie Régionale et Urbaine,* no. 2.

Weiss, Thomas G., David P. Forsythe & Rogert A. Coate (eds.), (1994), *The United Nations and Changing World Politics,* Boulder, CO: Westview Press.

Westing, Arthur (ed.), (1989), *Comprehensive Security for the Baltic. An Environmental Approach,* London, SAGE/PRIO/UNEP.

Wiberg, Håkan, (1986), 'The Nordic Countries: A Special Kind of System', *Current Research in Peace and Violence,* Tampere: TAPRI, no. 1-2/1986.

World Bank, (1997), *World Development Report,* New York: Oxford University Press.

Wriggins, Howard (ed.), (1992), *Dynamics of Regional Politics. Four Systems on the Indian Ocean Rim,* New York: Columbia University Press.

Wriggins, W.H. et al. (1992), *The Dynamics of Regional Politics: Four Systems on the Indian Ocean Rim,* New York Columbia University Press.

Zoppo, Ciro Elliott (ed.), (1992), *Nordic Security at the Turn of the Twenty-First Century,* Westport, Connecticut: Greenwood Press.

Index